EASY CYCLING

IN BRITAIN

5,000 MILES OF ROUTES

WITH THE WIND BEHIND YOU

BY
MICHAEL Z BROOKE
and
RICHARD N HUTCHINS

The first book of British cycle routes which
takes account of wind direction throughout

This revised version of Quiet Wind Assisted Cycle Routes (© R N Hutchins 1992) is published in 1995 by Brooke Books 21 Barnfield Urmston Manchester M41 9EW

Typeset by Aitch Em Wordservice.
Printed in England by The Bath Press.

A catalogue record for this book is available from the British Library.

ISBN 1 899465 00 6

ACKNOWLEDGEMENTS

Main acknowledgements should go to Richard Hutchins and his team of cyclists who prepared the routes used here.

The production of this book has been managed by Brooke Books very expert production director, Martin Marix Evans (of Book Packaging and Marketing, 3 Murswell Lane, Silverstone, Towcester, Northamptonshire, NN12 8UT). The text has been rekeyed several times by my indefatigable PA, Liz Hickson. She has prepared the equivalent of two books a year over the last 15 years.

Wishing you happy days of good cycling, I offer you this book.

Michael Z Brooke
21 Barnfield
Urmston
Manchester M41 9EW
Tel: 0161-746 8140
Fax: 0161-746 8132

CONTENTS

EASY CYCLING IN BRITAIN

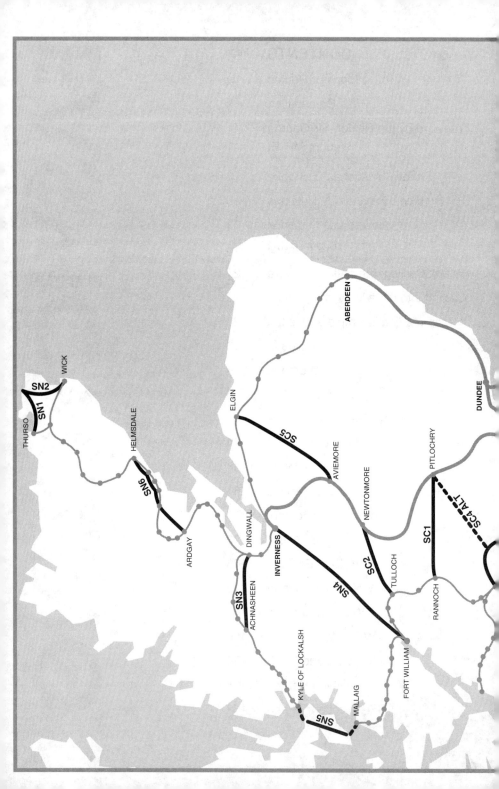

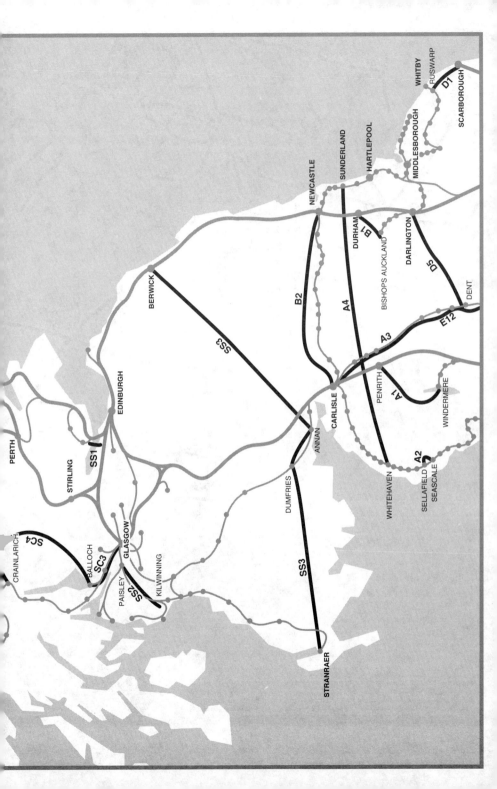

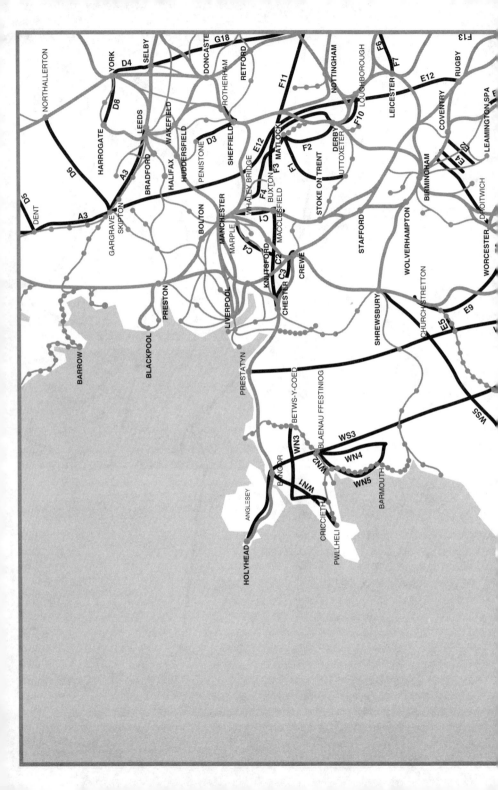

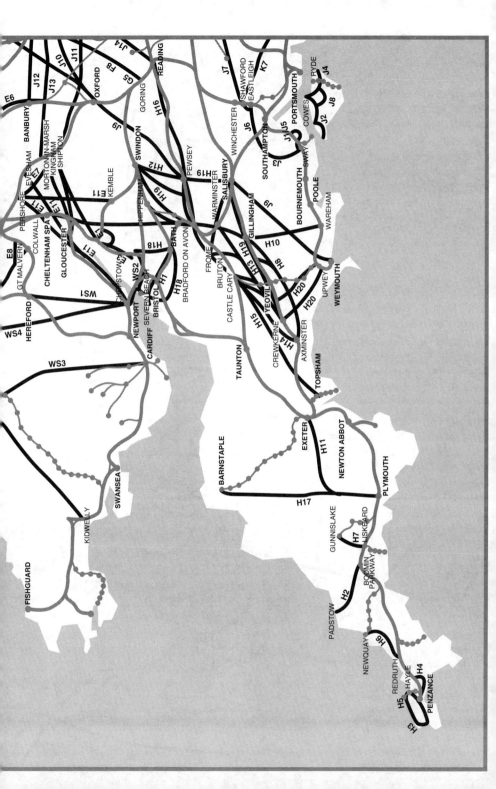

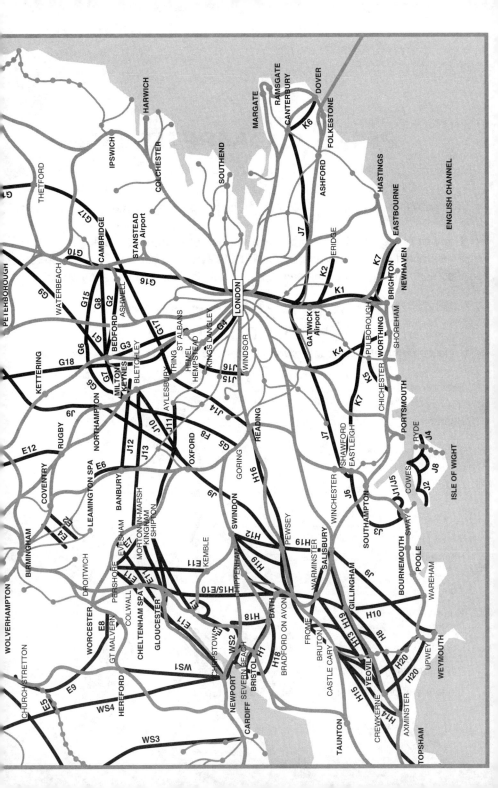

PRIZE COMPETITION

The publisher is offering a £100 prize for the first person to complete all the routes.

Copy or photocopy the form below and post to: Michael Z Brooke, 21 Barnfield, Urmston, Manchester M41 9EW. Even if you do not think you are first, send the form in all the same; I may well find some consolation prizes.

FORM OF APPLICATION FOR
PRIZE COMPETITION
(to be completed for each route. No need to cut up the book — photocopy.)

First name: ....

Surname: ....

Address: ....

....

....

Phone no: ....

Age: ....

Number
of route: ....

When ridden: ....
(give start and finish if more than one day)

Signature of proprietor or warden at overnight stop:

....

FOREWORD BY
THE RT HON
SIR GEORGE YOUNG, MP, Bt

I am pleased to commend this unpretentious but fact-filled book of cycle routes in various parts of the country. I understand that most of the routes are the same as those in a small booklet entitled 'Quiet 'Wind Assisted' Cycle Routes Between BR Stations' which I had occasion to recommend at the International Velocity Conference in Nottingham in 1983. This book is a greatly simplified version of that one.

I am particularly pleased to see that the routes still start and finish at train stations providing off-peak customers for the railways. I am also pleased to learn that this new edition will take readers through London on traffic-free routes, so long as they have permits to ride on canal towpaths.

The routes take you the easy way with the prevailing wind behind you, normally on quiet roads or tracks.

This book stands apart from the rapidly expanding list of books on cycling which are mainly designed for hobbyists.

I hope you will enjoy the rides this book outlines.

PREFACE BY
MICHAEL Z BROOKE

I am very proud to be entrusted with the task of producing a new version of the famous publication about 'Quiet Wind Assisted Cycle Routes'. I hope Richard Hutchins' many fans will accept the publication in its new dress.

I am sure you experienced cyclists will accept that a change of presentation was needed to reach out to the masses of new cyclists just coming onto the roads, but if you have any comments to make please do not hesitate to let me know. All offers of advice (however negative) and assistance are warmly welcomed. Phone 0161-746 8140. Those accepted will be incorporated in the next edition.

As I write I picture three kinds of cyclist.

* Those who do not set out to break records but rather to explore the countryside and all it has to offer.

* Elderly cyclists, wishing to continue with an exhilarating hobby to improve their health and to lengthen their lives but who are now doomed to cycle alone because they cannot keep up with younger companions.

* Young families indulging in the cycling holiday of the future. On some of the routes there are warnings like 'unsuitable for young families'. These warnings picture two children in specially fitted seats on a parent's bike. Once the children have their own bikes, they may join in the 'unsuitable' bits, carefully supervised of course. They can be left to struggle uphill but watch them carefully on the downhill stretches; many years ago a school friend of mine was killed when he lost control of his bike on a steep downhill road.

There are over five thousand miles of routes in this book. All start from train stations. Of course your ability to pursue these routes depends upon the stations remaining open. At the time of going to press, we have heard no rumours of closures among those recommended but always check. Your local telephone directory is likely to have a train enquiry number (at present, 1995, under *British Rail*). In many parts of the country, buses now carry bicycles. You can obtain a list from the Cyclists' Touring Club (CTC) if you are a member. I need hardly say that it is essential to be a member since the subscription includes third party insurance and you cannot afford to be without that these days. Allowing for the third party insurance, the membership costs very little (the address is: Cyclists' Touring Club, Cotterell House, 69 Meadrow, Godalming, Surrey, GU7 3HS.

While on the subject of things not to be without, let me recommend the Environmental Travel Association. The Association, which is sponsored by the World Wide Fund for Nature, provides a rescue service for cyclists. I know the old sweats carry every necessary spare and tool and know how to use them but, if you are like me and you can do nothing when a pedal drops off, you may be in for a long walk to the nearest cycle repairer; membership of the ETA will shorten that walk to the nearest phone box from which you can phone for help from a free-phone number. You can also use the ETA for rescuing your car, if you are old-fashioned enough still to run one; the Association is not expensive and it is as efficient as any other car rescue organization.

You will have noticed that this book does not contain tips on cycle maintenance, although many readers will have picked these up for themselves. They may still reach an age when their fingers are not nimble enough even to mend a puncture. For all cyclists, regular servicing at a cycle repair shop is recommended. This avoids awkward moments when the gear will not change or the brakes slip as a result of amateur dabbling.

Your pleasure and your safety depend on skilled servicing which usually costs little.

Some of the routes are too long for one day — they may take several days and those with young families are advised to book places to stay in advance. These can usually be found in the *Youth Hostel Handbook*, the *Ramblers' Yearbook*, the *CTC Handbook* or *Staying off the Beaten Track* by Elizabeth Gundrey (published by Arrow Books).

The word 'easy' is used because most of the routes travel from west to east, so the prevailing wind is behind you. Wind direction is the most important single characteristic of this book. The Cyclists' Touring Club assured the original editor (Richard Hutchins) that this was the first collection of British cycling routes that takes account of wind direction throughout. Of course wind direction can change; in particular strong, gusty winds keep veering — so be cautious when gales are forecast. Some of the routes are hilly and should not be attempted by young families (these are usually noted in the route descriptions).

CYCLING ON CANAL TOWPATHS

Safest of all routes for **you**, because there is no other traffic, is the canal towpath but remember that there will always be deep water on one side of you, so take precautions in wet or icy weather. Remember also that you may well be a danger to other towpath users so **watch out** for anglers and pedestrians.

After long negotiations between representatives of the Cyclists' Tourist Club (CTC) and British Waterways Board (BWB), it is now possible for you to use canal towpaths **with a permit**, so **please do not forget to obtain a permit**. Local permits are issued free and a Waterways Code for Cycling is also supplied. A national cycling pack — giving permission to cycle over most of the canal towpaths — costs £5 and can be obtained from: British Waterways Customer Services Department, Willow Grange, Church Road, Watford WD1 3QA. Permits, both national and local, come subject to a prohibition of cycling on certain towpaths. These are being clearly signed.

Remember these routes are intended for the peaceful enjoyment of the country-side including its natural history and its buildings. Do not commit yourself to timings that are too tight and do remember to take lights to avoid a panic on winter afternoons.

Finally, remember also that cyclists are great people. Many keep riding for charity. I trust they will continue to do so and not be put off by the hype for the national lottery which is doing harm to charities as well as some good.

PREFACE BY
RICHARD N HUTCHINS

Founder of the series entitled
Quiet Wind Assisted Cycle Routes
and co-author of this book

The aim of this book is to encourage the quiet enjoyment of Britain's wonderful countryside with an Ordnance Survey (OS) map and a bicycle. It is based on a small booklet published in February 1992 which met with an unexpectedly good response, calling for two reprints. It also brought a lot of interesting letters from cyclists. In the past three years, enthusiastic cyclists, members of The Cyclists' Touring Club and The Moulton Bicycle Club, helped me to increase the number of routes to 150, covering a total of more than 7,000 miles and including some exciting and more strenuous routes. These include The Wales Trail from Cardiff to Holyhead, The Scottish Border Cycleway (Stranraer to Berwick) and the Leeds, Settle Carlisle ride where the route goes alongside the railway line and which is the best way to see the striking railway architecture of Queen Victoria's favourite route to Scotland.

THE LAST THREE YEARS HAVE BEEN
GREAT YEARS FOR THE BICYCLE

In many ways 1992 was an especially great year. In February of that year the Cyclex Exhibition took over the Grand Hall at Olympia. Visitors could ride Sir Clive Sinclair's electric `Zike' along the gallery, while on the ground floor Dr Alex Moulton unveiled his All Purpose Bicycle (human powered).

Then in March 1992 came a major landmark in the history of post-war cycling, when The British Medical Association published a report entitled *Cycling Towards Health and Safety*, declaring that 'cycling is one of the simplest and most effective ways of getting and keeping fit, and riding to school or work means exercise can form part of the daily routine. Cycling should be promoted for both utilitarian and recreational purposes by local authorities, stressing its strong health, economic and environmental advantages.' Since then the BMA, with the CTC and the Bicycle Association, have circulated to Doctors' surgeries a leaflet entitled *Bike for Your Life*.

THE BEST CITIES AND TOWNS FOR CYCLING

In March 1992 also *The New Cyclist* magazine reported on the best and the good cities and towns in England and Wales. Excluding London Boroughs, the best were York, Cambridge, Peterborough, Oxford, Nottingham, Preston and Reading. The good were Stevenage, Harlow, Leicester, Lowestoft, Exeter and Bromley. For Scotland my selection is Edinburgh, Glasgow and Livingston New Town. Most of the places named are visited by routes in this booklet.

SUSTRANS

SUSTRANS (see below) is building safe routes through city and town centres. Many of their routes are included in this book.

AN OLYMPIC GOLD FOR CYCLING

July 1992 brought the most momentous cycling event of the year when, at the Barcelona Olympics, Chris Boardman won the Gold Medal for Cycling, riding a cycle designed by Mike Burrows and developed by Lotus Engineering with 'wind assisted' features. Later the Director General of the CBI was seen astride the cycle at Harrogate, and the year ended with further publicity when the MBE was awarded to Chris Boardman, and his cycle occupied pride of place at the Science Museum.

CYCLISTS INVITED TO WESTMINSTER

In October 1992 a Cabinet Minister hosted a Reception at Westminster for **SUSTRANS** (Sustainable Transport — the Bristol-based Railway Path and Cycleway Construction Charity). Cyclists mingled with members of the House of Commons informal All Party Friends of Cycling Committee. The Westminster event was reviewed in *The New Cyclist* magazine by Richard Ballantyne, no less, the 'patriarch' of English-speaking cyclists.

Velocity — Nottingham, September 1993. The Seventh International Cycling Conference (and the second held in Britain) had two government ministers at the opening who told of great changes in the policy for cycling. Delegates saw Nottingham's network of cycling routes and toured the Raleigh factory. On a personal note, my booklet on Quiet Cycling Routes was commended by one of the ministers, Sir George Young (The Cycling Baronet). Also attending the Conference were the AA who presented their report *Cycling Motorists, How to Encourage Them*, showing that of their seven million members, some 1.7 million use a bicycle.

Department of Health and Cycling. Another government department, the Department of Health, has shown signs of encouraging cycling on health grounds. This follows the publication of the BMA's publication *Cycling Towards Health and Safety* in March 1992. In the Department of Health's 1994 leaflet *Health of the Nation* (issued free at most chemists) Dr Kenneth Calman, the Chief Medical Officer, advised:

'Take the stairs instead of the lift or escalator. Exercise — cycle, jog, swim or dance'; followed by 17 other suggestions.

When I sent my original booklet to Dr Calman, his secretary wrote to say the chief medical officer had found it very interesting and had passed it on to his colleagues. The then minister of health, Mrs Virginia Bottomley and her husband, have been pictured in the press on many occasions as cyclists, usually on a tandem.

THE TOUR DE FRANCE ON ENGLISH PUBLIC ROADS

In June 1994 the Tour de France held their race on public roads in Britain for the first time (this needed an Act of Parliament). There was a warm welcome in Kent, Sussex and Hampshire for the vast cavalcade and the riders. A huge crowd of cyclists assembled at Ditchling Beacon (Route K1) and the Police Chief thanked them for their good behaviour.

ORDNANCE SURVEY AND OTHER MAPS

Among several encouraging changes on the home front, two relate to maps, the essential tool of the touring and leisure cyclist. The Ordnance Survey announced that in future they are going to show cycleways on the Landranger sheets, a course long advocated by SUSTRANS and others. This process will take years. Now that the Ordnance Survey are going to show cycleways, it is more important than ever that cyclists should make sure that they have the most up-to-date edition of the map. The easiest way to check an edition date is to contact your local library, or contact the Ordnance Survey Record Map Library on 01703 792264 at Southampton.

THE FORESTRY COMMISSION

To the relief of many, the government announced in 1994 that it was not proceeding with the wholesale sell off of the nation's forests. The following is the text of a notice I inserted in an earlier publication:

'**Cycling in the forest** Escape from the hustle and bustle of the highways and discover the pleasures of cycling through a rich mix of woodlands and forests — there are routes to suit most ages and abilities and they can be found throughout the country. Enjoy yourself in the forest, but for your safety and that of other forest visitors, cycle with care, courtesy and commonsense.'
Forest Enterprise (part of the Forestry Commission)**.**

A BED FOR THE NIGHT

The Youth Hostels Association continues to adapt to meet public demand at both ends of the 'comfort' scale. There is more family accommodation than ever in the form of family annexes, family rooms and family dormitories. The demand for modern facilities is reflected in the log book of a remote Welsh mountain hostel — 'the best shower I never had'. At the other extreme, to meet the continuing demand for 'simple' accommodation the 1995 YHA Handbook lists 25 camping barns in North Yorkshire, North Pennines, Forest of Bowland, Exmoor, Dartmoor and Tarka Country. No less than 136 of the 240 YHA Hostels in England and Wales are linked to the 150 quiet cycle routes in this book, with a further 19 youth hostels in Scotland.

NEW GOVERNMENT POLICY ON CYCLING, BRISTOL JUNE 1994

As foreshadowed at the Velocity Cycling Conference in September 1993, the government issued a Blueprint for Cycling Policy at the launch of Green Transport Week at Bristol in June 1994. The spokesman was Robert Key, then minister for Roads and Traffic. The press release for the new policy runs to 13 pages and only the headings can be given here: Cycling is an important form of transport. Government committed to **sustainable** development. 40% of trips of three miles or less are currently made by car. Notable level of cycling in some areas. Substantial demand for cycling. A change of perception is needed. Consider cycling at the outset. Parking. Role of Employers. Part of cycling in composite journeys. Local Authority Powers. Sustainable development. March 1994 planning guidance. Trunk roads. No national or local targets for cycling use to be prescribed — left to local decision. Highway Authority's transport policies and programme now expected to include cycling schemes. Health-definable benefit. Technical advice on cycling and traffic calming —

now over 40 leaflets. Cycle parking and postcoding. 'Park and Bike' and 'Bike and Ride' schemes. Composite trips. Cycles on trains. Notes for bidders for rail franchises. Role of employers — parking, showering and changing. CTC's Cycle Friendly Employer Awardincluding English Heritage, Department of Environment and Transport Department. Attitude to cycling changing. Recreational cycle paths. Local authorities need to examine good examples. Responsible behaviour. Code of conduct. Road safety — helmets — encouraged but no compulsion. Be seen. *Drive Safe Cycle Safe*' (a leaflet published by the AA and the CTC). Praise for National Bike Week and London to Brighton. The Tour de France.

NEW POLICIES BY THE DEPARTMENT OF TRANSPORT

'Cycling is a popular, sensible means of personal transport and a healthy leisure activity. The government wishes to help change perceptions so that proper account is taken of cycling. We intend to work with other organizations to create the conditions in which more people will choose to cycle.'

The Department of Transport wrote to me on 13 May 1994: 'We wish you continued success with the current and future editions of *Quiet Wind Assisted Cycle Routes* .... It is an excellent publication that every touring/leisure cyclist should consider buying.

'Cycling is a popular, sensible means of personal transport and a healthy leisure activity. The government wishes to help change perceptions so that proper account is taken of cycling. We intend to work with other organizations to create the conditions in which more people will choose to cycle.'

SUSTRANS (SUSTAINABLE TRANSPORT)

SUSTRANS have already built many hundreds of miles of traffic free routes for cyclists and are now planning a nationwide network of 5,000 miles. The two most outstanding routes are now complete (although partly following public roads). One is the sea to sea ('C2C') from Whitehaven to Sunderland and the other is the 1,000 mile route from Inverness to Dover including safe and quiet routes through the town centres on the way (see also 'Cycling, the national picture').

MY FAREWELL

After fifteen years on this project, my main regret is that I hurried too much when cycling the routes, and did not take time to savour more of the local colour of Britain's countryside and the local brew. In retrospect Smiles are more important than Miles, or, as W H Davies put it:

A Poor Life this, if
    Full of care,
        We have no time to
            Stand and Stare

For my last word, let me quote *The Times*, which, in recent years when Simon Jenkins was Editor, has been enthusiastic about maps and geography: 'Whole generations that have grown up thinking that holidays are things packaged and spent abroad are starting to discover an unknown country called Britain, and the unfamiliar pleasures of exploring it at will.' (1 August 1992).

MAPS SHOWING ALL RIGHTS OF WAY

This is the only country in the world where you can go into the local book shop/ stationer (6,000 outlets) and buy a map showing the legally defined Rights of Way. The use of the routes in this booklet demands the reading of such maps. So there should be little excuse for unintentional trespass.

THE ORIGINS OF THE EARLIER VERSIONS

In November 1980 British Rail began their November concessions for Senior Citizens with a dramatic gesture of a One Pound Fare between any two stations — Penzance to Thurso. A letter in *The Times* in December of that year from the late Professor Rée of Edinburgh summed up the thanks of many thousands of Senior Citizens. At that time also British Rail had a benevolent attitude to the carriage of non-folding bicycles by train.

Although a regular cyclist since 1924, the writer had never before taken his cycle by train. The chance to 'let the train take the strain' of the journey against the wind was too good to miss, for the wind is the cyclist's greatest enemy. These beginnings led to the compilation of the original series of *Quiet Wind Assisted Cycle Routes between BR Stations*. The November fare concessions were contin- ued by BR to November 1990 with an annual increase in fares, but then ceased in that form. The Novembers of the 1980s were remarkably mild, with the trees in their autumn glory, and Scotland was free of flies and there was very little rain. In the event, this wind assisted cycling has been continued throughout the seasons.

Although the routes were prepared with Senior Citizens in mind, the large response to a letter in *The Times* in March 1990 about an early (small) edition of the series showed that families with young children were also interested in the quiet ways; accordingly the second edition took account of them. The needs of other leisure cyclists have been incorporated into this book.

One change in mid-stream was needed when British Rail introduced new rolling stock with limited space for luggage. It became increasingly difficult to travel with a non-folding bicycle, and the cyclist lost the essential freedom of being able to travel without booking. So after exhaustive tests on six different folding bicycles the preference is for the Moulton AM7 at the top end of the market, and the Dawes Kingpin among the conventional folders. Others have not had difficulties with bikes on trains and other folding bikes have been developed, especially the Brompton.

Since those days, successive publications have used the routes which have increased from 1,500 to 7,000 miles mainly owing to help from readers of *The Times* and of *The Moultoneer*. The aim in this book has been to increase the coverage to about four routes in each tourist authority area, so that there will be a quiet route within reach of most people as an introduction. Feedback on the existing routes is always welcome.

Senior Citizens, like everyone else, are frequently urged to keep exercising their minds as well as their muscles. This book does just that; mental effort is needed in map reading and map reference skills, as well as the physical effort of cycling. If you are willing to share the secret of your favourite quiet route there is little danger that the route will get spoiled by over use.

SAFETY

Without being alarmist, it must be admitted that today cycling on many roads is hazardous and unpleasant. The vast increase in the volume of car and lorry traffic since 1945 is obvious to all road users, and the predictions for the future are frightening.

For the most part the roads are not adequate to cope with all the road users. The modern Mountain Bike — almost half of present sales — has handlebars 21 inches wide; add to this a 'spacer' (advised by RoSPA) and add also some room to allow the cyclist to divert round a perilous manhole cover, and you have a width of carriageway space which few motor drivers allow or recognize. Whatever the type of cycle, a busy road is a hazardous place for it and its rider. Small wonder, therefore, that you see law-abiding old ladies with skirt guards and cane baskets on their cycles taking to the pavements for self-preservation, as well as children over the age of 11 (the RoSPA age for proficiency testing).

In contrast to this picture there is a much brighter side. The admirable *RoSPA Bicycle Owners' Handbook* (obtainable from local authority road safety officers) gives wise advice on all aspects of cycling safety and takes a balanced view of the dangers involved. These routes, concentrating as they do on good off-road routes for cyclists, make a small contribution to safety.

Richard N Hutchins

DISCLAIMER

While every care has been taken in preparing this book, the Authors and Publisher can accept no responsibility for any loss or damage suffered by any person as a result of its use.

HOW TO USE THIS BOOK

There are 5,000 miles of routes in this book, something for almost every part of mainland Britain.

The routes are arranged by Tourist Board Region (see 'THE REGIONS') which start with northern England (A for Cumbria) and work south, followed by Scotland and Wales. The routes are shown on the map.

To choose a route, look for the region of your choice and then the map. Read through the route and note the station from which you start. To find out about the trains, either study the system timetable (which is supposed to continue after privatization; the timetable numbers in the book are for the **summer 1995** system timetable) or phone your local train enquiry office.

Each route with its title and a list of items is set out as follows.

Route no. and brief description, including note on difficulty.

County.

Quietness:
***	on principle free of motor traffic.
**	minor roads (quiet but beware of weekends especially in the holiday season.
*	busier minor roads.

All categories **may** include short lengths of much busier roads (usually short enough to walk with young children). The star rating is subjective and may not apply on summer weekends.

Mileage:
　　　　　Distance from start to finish of recommended route. Some routes may be too long, if so find somewhere to stay, either from the Youth Hostel Handbook or by phoning the Tourist Information Centre.

Direction:

The main direction of the route.

Train stations:

The names of the stations at the beginning and end of the route and the number in the **current** British Rail timetable.

Maps: The numbers of the maps in the Ordnance Survey Landranger Series (1:50,000) required for the route.

Weather forecast:

A phone number for the local weather forecast. These numbers have been checked and did not change in April 1995.

Tourist information office with phone no:

These numbers have been rechecked and updated.

Publications on area:

A brief list; other leaflets can be obtained at the tourist information centre. Brief notes on the route including places of interest.

Accommodation:

Under this heading is listed the names of Youth Hostels on the route. Remember that most hostels are not open all through the week and may have limited opening days during the winter. Very few are open every day of the year (only Cambridge and London), Oxford is only closed for the first 12 days of January. Even if open, they may be fully booked so take the Accommodation Guide (free to members) or phone the national office (01727 855215). For other accommodation, call the nearest Tourist Information Centre. At many of the centres, incidentally, you can now join the Youth Hostels Association. You do not have to be a 'youth' to stay at the hostels; they now have family rooms and car parking facilities, but not yet mixed dormitories.

Places of interest:

This gives National Trust houses and some places of interest. More complete details can be obtained from the local Tourist Information Centre.

Route:

Details are given in brief since it is assumed that you will be carrying the relevant OS map. Note that directions are abbreviated (see below). The words '**critical point**' are used where there may be difficulty in finding the route. Check that you are not going astray. Many of the routes have instructions to go in a certain direction; it may there fore be useful to carry a compass although a signpost will help in most cases.

Related routes:

The numbers of other routes that can easily be undertaken at the same time.

Date route last reconnoitred and by whom:

The date when the survey was carried out and the name (or initials) of person surveying the route.

The following abbreviations are used:

B and B	=	Bed and Breakfast Accommodation
YH	=	Youth Hostel
GR	=	Grid Reference (see 'Map reading is simple and is fun')
OS	=	Ordnance Survey
CTC	=	Cyclists' Touring Club

Otherwise we try to avoid abbreviations; they easily lead to confusion.

THE WIND

The main enemy of the cyclist is wind. A long hill usually goes down eventually (although it may not seem like it) but a strong head wind goes on forever.

This book claims to take the wind into account on all the routes. For that reason none of the routes are circular and most run from west to east, the direction of the prevailing wind. **But the wind can change**, so a phone number for a local weather forecast is given for each route. Experience shows that whatever happens about the rest of the forecasts, the wind direction is almost always correct. This phone call enables you to change direction if the wind is going to be against you. If you sketch out the route on the Ordnance Survey map it is easy to reverse your direction. Remember that a strong gusty wind changes direction frequently although remaining mostly in one direction.

HOW TO TRAVEL

The best method is by train and this is not nearly as difficult as is often supposed. Michael Brooke has **never** had any difficulty in getting his bike onto a train — the biggest difficulty he ever had was carrying a fully-loaded bike over a footbridge, (a couple of burly railway-men carried it over for him) but he is always careful to follow the simple rules listed in the most recent leaflet on the subject issued by Regional Railways.

Richard Hutchins, on the other hand, recommends a folding bike. If you want to feel safe, unworried about whether you will really be able to return home, this is far the best option. Two manufacturers are producing folding bikes: Brompton and Moulton. The Moulton is the more famous name but is also the more expensive and the heavier. The Brompton comes in four versions — lightweight 3 speed or 5 speed and Touring 3 speed or 5 speed. An optional extra is a bag for carrying the bike; with this essential extra, the bike can be carried on any train or bus as ordinary passenger's luggage but of course you'll have to devise a way of carrying your other luggage as well. Expect to pay about £500. A point to remember is that many cycle shops do not stock folding bikes, so always insist on seeing one before you buy and make sure it is really suitable for you. In particular check that you can take the bike to pieces (fold it) and put it together again without resorting to a psychiatrist. For further information on folding bikes contact: David Henshaw, The Folding Society, 19 West Park, Castle Cary BA7 7DB.

If you must, you can take the bike on the back of a car always remembering that you need a number plate fitted with rear lights and indicators to fix onto the bike. Cycle shops stock very convenient hooks for fixing the bike to the car; this is much easier than a roof rack.

Increasingly it is possible to take bicycles on buses where folding bikes can always be taken. What follows is an evolving list of coach and bus services around Britain which will carry cycles. These details have been compiled by the CTC (Cyclists' Touring Club), Britain's largest national cycling organization, and are reproduced with their permission. The details are believed to be correct at the time of publication, but will no doubt change over time. Please confirm all details with your chosen coach or bus operator before travel.

The CTC works on behalf of all cyclists — whatever their age, interest or ability — and offers a wide range of information and services to help cyclists. For details, contact the CTC at: 69 Meadrow, Godalming, Surrey GU7 3HS. Tel: 01483-417217 Fax: 01483 426994.

(1)   National Express Coaches As of December 1 1992 a 'bagged standard folding cycle' will be carried on their services subject to their normal terms and conditions of carriage, subject to space being available.

(2)   Yeomans Canyon Travel Ltd, 21 Three Elms Trading Estate, Hereford HR4 9PU, Tel: 01432-356201 carry cycles on the following services:

(a)   'The Kilvert Connection' twice a day service in each direction between Hereford, Brewardine, Hay-on-Wye and Brecon. Every Sunday and Bank Holiday Monday only. Up to four cycles in the boot, 50p per cycle.

(b)   Hereford, Ross-on-Wye, Gloucester, Cheltenham, Circencester to London Victoria. One service per day in each direction, throughout the year. Up to two cycles may be carried at off peak times (Sunday, Monday, Tuesday, Wednesday) by prior arrangement only. Cyclists are asked to turn handlebars through 90° and remove front wheel if possible.

(3)   The Ridgeway Explorer, Regis Coaches, Tel: 01367-718929, Wiltshire Bus Line, Tel: 01345-090899 or write to Jos Joslin, Ridgeway Officer, Countryside Service, Dept Leisure & Arts, Holton, Oxford OX33 1QQ. Summer Sundays and Bank Holidays only (April-October). Connects with trains at Reading, Swindon and Goring stations, this service runs four times a day and carries a limited number of cycles either in the boot or inside lockers. It runs along the foot of the Ridgeway via Wantage and Streatley. Stops on request.

(4)   Northumbria Motor Services Ltd, Gallowgate Coach Station, Newcastle-upon-Tyne NE1 4SX, Tel: 0191-232 4211.

On the 501, 505, 515 and 525 services which operate throughout the year between Newcastle, Morpeth, Alnwick, Berwick-upon-Tweed and villages in between, cycles are carried in the boot for 50p irrespective of distance. Up to eight cycles may be carried at any one time. No prebooking is needed. Unfortunately, tandems and trikes are not carried.

The service has been introduced as a result of requests from individual cyclists. If it is successful, there are plans to extend it. For further details, contact Stephen Noble, Operations Manager, at above address.

(5)   Mainline Group Ltd, Sheffield Area Office, Greenland Road Garage, Sheffield S9 5HD, Tel: 01142-567000. Services 501/502 between Meadowhall-City Centre and Jordanthorpe/Batemoor areas will carry up to two cycles, for 30p single and 50p return. Trial service from July 1994 onwards.

(6)   Southend Transport Ltd, (R G Jervis, Traffic Manager) 87 London Road, Southend-on-Sea, Essex SS1 1PP, Tel: 01702-434444. If spacepermits and the owner accepts liability for damage to the vehicle or other passenger's luggage, bikes can be carried for £1 each on the 'X' group of coaches between Southend and Heathrow Airport, via London (West End & City).

(7)   Oxford Tube (390 bus) and Thames Transit, Tel: 01865-772250. Two frequent services between Oxford and London. The first service (Oxford Tube) calls at Abingdon, Wallingford, Henley, Maidenhead, Heathrow Airport, Hammersmith, Olympia, Kensington, Victoria Station and places between. The Thames Transit is a faster service between Oxford and London. Both services carry bikes, in the boot, free of charge if space is available (approximately three bikes maximum). Cyclists are asked to remove panniers etc., and load the bikes themselves. Just turn up and board, no advanced booking system. Any problems, contact: John Rogers, Publicity, Tel: 01865-727000.

(8)   North Western Buses, Runcorn, Merseyside, Tel: 01928-572774, (Alan Booth). Between April and October on the first Sunday each month, up to 20 bikes (including tandems, trikes etc.), may be carried in the specially converted 'bike bus'. Destinations are flexible, within a 50 mile radius of Runcorn. (Groups of 16 or more cyclists may book the bus out on other Sundays too).

(9)   Town and Village Link, Tel: John Ruiz 016973-42820. A minibus service in Cumbria linking villages between Carlisle, Workington and Cockermouth (on the edge of the Lake District). Up to four bikes are carried, free of charge if space is available.

(10) Postbus Services For England and Wales contact: Public Relations Department, Royal Mail, 130 Old Street, London EC1V 9PQ.

(11) The 'Slow Coach', Providence Cottage, 71 Bradenstoke, Wiltshire SN15 4EL, Tel: 01249-891959. Folded cycles and cycles with front wheel removed, may be carried on the 'Slow Coach' if booked in advance. Travel between the following Youth Hostels: Bath, Stratford, Lakes, Edinburgh, York, Cambridge, London, Windsor. Tickets are valid without time limit and are transferable. The service is now covering the west country.

(12) W. MacDonald & Co., Tel: 01851-82367 (11am-4pm Monday-Friday). Travel between Stornoway, Ullapool, Inverness, bikes may be booked in advance and are carried free of charge.

(13) The Bike Bus Company, Harry Henniker, 4 Barclay Terrace, Edinburgh EH10 4HP, Tel: 0131-229 6274. Minibus and special cycle trailer travel to a variety of within Scotland.

(14) Haggis Backpackers Transport, 7/9 Blackfriar's Street, Edinburgh EB1 1NB, Tel: 0131-557 9393. Minibuses leave from Glasgow and Edinburgh six times a week travelling via some 30 hostels in the Highlands. Maximum of approximately four bikes (space allowing) are carried free of charge on the roofrack.

(15) The 'Go Blue Banana' minibus, Tel: 0131-228 2281. Travels between over 20 Scottish Youth Hostels, completing a regular circuit every two days, (April to September). Book cycles and seats in advance.

(16) European Bike Express, Bolero International Holidays, 31 Baker Street, Middlesbrough, Cleveland T51 2LF, Tel: 01642-251440 (day), 750077 (evenings). A cooperative venture between CTC and Bolero.

Between June and September, a luxury coach (with restaurant and lounge), and specially designed cycle trailer travels to France, Spain and Italy. A maximum of 26 bikes can be carried, including tandems and tricycles etc. by special arrangement. The coach picks up at many points in Britain (between Middlesbrough in north east England and Dover). Only £125 return 1994.

When the trailer is not being used, Bolero have expressed an interest in making the trailer available for events/tours. So if you are looking to transport a large **group of cyclists**, Bolero may be able to help.

... if all else fails ... travel **without** your bicycle, using **Parcelforce** Tel: 0800-224466. Send your bike (or tandem) between any main Post Office in Britain and also to addresses in Europe. Competitive prices, e.g. less than £10 Great Britain (takes up to one week) approximately £30 France, (six working days). NB: Registering a bike back from Europe must be done through the European country's own system. For a higher fee, quicker delivery is possible both in Great Britain and Europe. Parcelforce also offer a 'door to door' collection and delivery service. Tel: 0800-884422 for details. NB: Tandems — Parcelforce carry goods with a maximum length of 1.5 metres, so wheel/ mudguard removal may be necessary.

Further information (also courtesy CTC), the bendibuses in Sheffield will now take bikes.

CYCLING —
THE NATIONAL PICTURE

The last 20 years have seen a transformation of the cycling scene in this country. On the debit side the vast increase in motor traffic has made cycling on all trunk roads, A roads and many B roads an unpleasant experience. A letter in *The Times* in March 1990 on quiet cycle rides between British Rail stations brought no less than 109 replies to the author; the dominant themes were gratitude for quiet routes and fear of motor traffic. About half the replies were from senior citizens and half from families with young children.

There is, however, a much brighter side of the picture under various headings.

THE COUNTRYSIDE ACT 1968

This Act made cycling on bridleways legal, and the CTC has since valiantly tried to record rideable bridleways county by county: they welcome more help.

TRAILWAYS

Many disused railways have been converted for use by walkers and cyclists, usually with the aid of a grant from the Countryside Commission. Some of these trailways (most of them over five miles in length) are to be found in this book, including those made by SUSTRANS (Sustainable Transport) Railway Path Project of Bristol, Glasgow and elsewhere. See 'SUSTRANS'.

LONG DISTANCE PATHS (NATIONAL TRAILS)

Of the Long Distance Paths (National Trails) promoted and financed by the Countryside Commission, many of the recent ones are of bridleway status and thus open to cyclists; such are the South Downs Way, the Swan's Way, the western part of the Wessex Ridgeway, the Three Shires Way and most of the Peddars Way; all except the first are described in this book. The Swan's Way and the Three Shires Way are classed as local rather than National Trails.

CANAL TOWPATHS

It is now possible to cycle on about half the canal towpaths owned by British Waterways **so long as you have a permit**. For your local areas these permits are issued free; a national permit costs £5. These permits are issued on condition that you show respect to other canal users and to your own safety. If too many fishermen are upset or too many cyclists drowned they may be withdrawn, so beware. Most towpaths are ideal for cycling; although some are rough and potholed, they are all free of other traffic.

For permits phone British Waterways customer services division on 01923 226422.

SUSTRANS

Efficient new paths for cyclists and pedestrians have been built by SUSTRANS — 'sustainable transport' — which has an ambitious plan for covering the country. Some of SUSTRANS' routes are included (with its permission) in this book. For further details of the routes, as well as about how to support the organization, write to:

SUSTRANS
The Railway Path and Cycle Route Construction Charity
35 King Street
Bristol
BS1 4DZ
(Tel: 0117-928893, Fax: 0177-9294173)

SUSTRANS is also mentioned in Richard Hutchins' preface.

LOCAL AUTHORITIES

With the encouragement of the Department of Transport and the Countryside Commission, many county and district councils are producing guides to cycling routes in their areas — usually circular routes. Cumbria set the fashion in 1980, with a second edition in 1990. Also many towns are constructing special cycle ways, mostly for journeys to work and school. For comprehensive schemes Stevenage New Town was the pioneer in the 1950s, and Milton Keynes New City, with their well known 'Redways' and their lesser known (but more enjoyable) 'leisure routes', is the leader in the field today. York and Cambridge have been named recently as cycle-friendly cities.

THE FORESTS OF THE FORESTRY COMMISSION

The Forests of the Forestry Commission are a recent source of good quiet cycle routes; forests such as the New Forest (new in 1066!) whose virtues are extolled under Area J (Southern) are just as enjoyable on a shopper cycle. Founded in 1919, the Forestry Commission was given strong financial support when Hugh Dalton was Chancellor in the government of the late 1940s. Only now are the full benefits of this action being enjoyed. Over the past twenty years the Commission has promoted recreation in a big way. As an example the following are extracts from a brochure of the South of Scotland Conservancy on cycling in the Forests of South West Scotland.

'Over 200 miles of waymarked routes have been created in these forests with a wide range of lengths and grades to suit all abilities .... The waymarked routes offer the best opportunities for cycling in the forest. However, cyclists are welcome to cycle on all forest roads in the Forestry Commission woodlands of South West Scotland unless advised otherwise.' This is said to have been largely the work of one retired forester-cyclist, John Taylor.

What more could you want? As one journalist put it: 'Don't be too hard on the softwoods; they can be very pleasant too.'

The Forestry Commission now has a Forest Enterprise section in each district dealing with the recreational side of their activities — some 28 districts in England and Wales, and 29 in Scotland. The headquarters of the Commission is 231 Corstorphine Road, Edinburgh EH12 7AT.

DEPARTMENT OF TRANSPORT

Some of the ever changing Ministers for Transport and Roads have been seen on bicycles in recent years, notably the present Secretary of State (summer 1995), Sir George Young, who has written the foreword to this book. In the 1980s the Department organized regional conferences with local authorities, and county surveyors were seen riding some selected routes. A lot of existing trunk roads have been provided with cycleways. The steady progress of by-passing towns has made the old routes quite a pleasure to ride — for example, Brackley and the morecontroversial Okehampton; the latter is included in the Barnstaple to Plymouth route, which must be theflagship of the SUSTRANS routes in the West Country. One former minister emphasized that: 'both cyclists and motorists have an equal right to usethe highway'.

THE NETWORK OF MINOR ROADS

This book concentrates on quiet routes off tarmac roads where possible, but does not ignore the wonderful network of quiet minor roads (yellow or white on OS maps). It is hoped that once having discovered or re-discovered the joys of cycling you will extend your exploration on your own and let us know your favourite routes, both tarmac and on rough tracks.

CHARITY CYCLE RIDES

One significant feature of the past two decades has been the phenomenal growth of cycling for charity. The London to Brighton cycle 'fun run' was founded in 1974 by Robert Stredder with thirty cyclists taking part. In 1990 £1.3m was raised for charity and 30,000 'enrolled' cyclists took part together with many 'gatecrashers' (for no one can stop them using the public highway). Bike Events, the organizers, are now reducing the pressure by running similar rides from Manchester to Blackpool, Birmingham to Oxford, and London to Cambridge.

Among other notable charity rides are the sponsored cycle rides of the Historic Churches Trusts which started in Suffolk in 1982; nowadays 28 Counties take part and a total of £7,398,000 has been raised over the years. Route G3 is based on the St Alban's 'Cycle Round the SEE' of 1989, visiting 27 churches in 58 miles. The Historic Churches Trusts' rides are on the second Saturday in September each year.

THE ROYAL COMMISSION ON ENVIRONMENTAL POLLUTION

This powerful Commission reported early in 1995 and listed measures needed to reduce atmospheric pollution and noise to the levels proposed by the World Health Organization by the year 2005.

A main recommendation was to increase cycle use to 10% of all urban journeys by 2005. This compares with 2.5% now. In view of the number of short journeys taken by car, this should not be too difficult if people can be persuaded that the cycle is a feasible means of transport.

Another target is to reduce deaths among cyclists from 4.1 per 100 million kilometres cycled to two per 100 million kilometres cycled by the same date. This is a tougher objective than it looks, it amounts to halving the proportion of deaths at a time when the number of cyclists is expected to increase steeply.

DR BIKE CLINICS

Among the enterprises undertaken by some local cycling groups are the Dr Bike Clinics to help cyclists to look after their bikes.

FURTHER READING

If you want more books on cycling, why not start with the following?

Evans, Jeremy, *50 Mountain Bike Rides* (Crowood).

Field, Patrick, *Breathing Spaces, Bike rides within easy reach of London* (Two Heads Publishing).

For many further details you can obtain *A Bibliography of Cycling Books* by Edward Williams, Secretary of the National Cycle Archive, 18 Brookside Avenue, King's Heath, Birmingham B13 0TJ (tel: 0121-444 6426).

CYCLING INTO THE TWENTY-FIRST CENTURY

The campaign for cycling is rapidly becoming unstoppable. Better to say **campaigns** at a time when cyclists are bombarded by organizations standing up for their rights and competing for their attention.

CYCLE FOR YOUR LIFE

Heaven knows there are plenty of rights to stand up for at a time when cyclists are being crowded off highways to which they have as much right as any other citizen. Don't forget that and, above all, do not accept remarks from gullible and arrogant motorists — brain-washed by the roads lobby — that they have special rights because they pay road tax and petrol duty. They do not imagine they own the pub because they pay beer duty, do they? A landmark in the gathering revival of cycling has been the announcement that it is good for your heart — irresistible in a health conscious epoch. The all too real chance of death by accident, we were told, is negligible beside the certainty of avoiding death by heart failure or stroke as a result of the extra fitness that cycling brings.

The so-called 'feel good' factor should be added to the medical benefits of cycling. After a lapse of some years, the present writer came back to cycling during a rail strike when he borrowed his son's bike. In spite of some panics on the way, he arrived at his office feeling so much more fresh and fit for work than usual that he cycled ever after. Strikes apart, he knew that he could return by train if the weather grew too rough later in the day.

To add to the benefits of the bike is the curse of the car. Most of us are motorists at some time and it is one of the extraordinary facts of modern life that we ordinary citizens who would not think of throwing dirt into other people's faces or making rude noises at them do both every time we take a car out. Every extra cycle ride takes a nuisance off the road. Add to this the lung damage that the car causes for the motorist even more than for the rest of the community.

WHAT CAN BE DONE FOR THE CYCLIST?

Make no mistake about it, many things have already been done, so many that veteran cyclists feel pampered when they discover facilities that would have been unthinkable a few years ago. They are easily satisfied and become complacent in the face of those who demand more, but the demand for more will continue and shape road policies into the next century. Most of the following measures are already in evidence in some places and need to be intensified or brought about everywhere.

(1) A ban on private cars in city centres, with exceptions for the disabled of course. City centres are ideal places for cycling or walking. Distances are usually short and it is easy to dash for cover in the event of a storm.

Getting into the city may be more of a problem. Some cities, like Manchester and Liverpool, allow cycles free on local trains; even so there may be difficulties and cyclists should surely be expected to show consideration by travelling outside peak hours. In rural areas buses are increasingly taking bicycles and this should be extended to urban buses along with light rapid transport systems more thoughtfully designed than at present with cycle and luggage carrying facilities.

(2) Improved security for cycle parking. Already there are experiments with secure cycle lockers in some places and these should be extended to all car parks.

(3) Cycle lanes along major routes together with subways under roundabouts. This arrangement already exists on the six-lane highway into Kuala Lumpur (Malaysia) from the south. Unfortunately in that case small motorbikes are also allowed to use the cycle tracks, otherwise the combination of cycle lane and subways appears ideal.

(4) Traffic lights at cycle crossings as at present exist for pedestrians; too few already exist.

(5) Lockers so that cyclists can change their clothes. Employers should be encouraged to provide these.

A substantial report for cycling professionals has been published by Brooke Publications at £25. This report has been written by Rosemary Sharples who has a higher degree in transport policy and leads a local campaign (Sprocket) in Manchester.

MAP READING IS
SIMPLE AND IS FUN

This book takes you into map reading — grid references are used for finding where you are. These look complicated, but find them once and they are simple for ever after.

For cycling you will normally use the Ordnance Survey Landranger Series (1:50,000) which is about one and a quarter miles to the inch — a larger scale and you cycle off the map too quickly, smaller and important landmarks are missing. The grid system is explained on every map. It consists of six numbers.

To find a place — labelled GR in the routes here — you look along the top of the map until you find the first two numbers, the third number will be a judgment about the space (in tenths) between the nearest number and the one to the right. You then look down the side of the map which provides the fourth and fifth numbers while the sixth is an estimate of the distance (in tenths) to the right of the number. You then look for a point where lines from the numbers cross. Thus if you are looking at the Weston-super-Mare and Bridgwater area map (OS 182) and have a reference reading 322470, you look down from 32 (but slightly to the right and across from 47); you will then find Highbridge station without any difficulty.

Some of the references are four numbers only (omitting the third number in each dirction).

To the average adult, map reading is a pain; but future generations should know more about it since it features in the national curriculum. If still puzzled, why not check whether the curriculum works by asking the nearest 16-year old. For the 1993 version, the map references were checked by two Bedford sixth formers (Lisa Thorogood and James Ross) on an A level geography course.

AREA A

Cumbria

- **The ENGLISH LAKE DISTRICT —** a CIRCUIT of ULLSWATER (easy gradients) and KIRK STONE PASS (tough)
- **COUNTY:** CUMBRIA
- **QUIETNESS:** *
- **MILEAGE:** 47
- **DIRECTION:** north to south
- **TRAIN STATIONS and TIMETABLES:** PENRITH to WINDERMERE, 65
- **MAP(S):** OS 90, (96), (97)
- **WEATHER FORECAST:** 0891-500419
- **TOURIST INFORMATION OFFICE:** PENRITH 01768-67466
- **PUBLICATIONS:** Consult Tourist Information
- **ACCOMMODATION:** YH at ULLSWATER (PATTERDALE) and WINDERMERE
- **PLACES OF INTEREST:** Consult Tourist Information
- **ROUTE :** road and track

A. Penrith
Generally south west through REDHILLS to A592, (quiet and pleasant outside holiday season) mostly on west of Ullswater to PATTERDALE YH. Miles: 15

B. Circuit of Ullswater (feasible only by pedal cycle)
Between the minor roads at ROOKING **GR 4016** and SANDWICK (GR 4219) keep to old PONY TRACK mostly near lakeside: some pushing. MARTINDALE (GR 4319) remote church still in use: minor road to POOLEY BRIDGE and A592 back to PATTERDALE YH. Miles: 20

C. Diversion up Birkett Fell (formerly 'Nameless' Fell)
Leave A592 opposite AIRA POINT **GR 3919**. A5091 DOCKRAY: minor road to DOWTHWAITEHEAD **GR 371208** leave cycle. One and a half to two hours up to Fell (named after a great champion of National Parks) and

back. Good map and compass essential. Six miles cycle to and from A592.

D. Patterdale to Windermere
A592 over KIRKSTONE PASS 454 metres (1500 feet), some pushing but worth it for views and the descent to TROUTBECK and WINDERMERE. Miles: 12. This section is not too busy even in the holiday season but is **hilly** and is **not** recommended for young families.

- **RECONNOITRED:** November 1984, RNH

- **BRITISH NUCLEAR FUELS plc, SELLAFIELD (WINDSCALE) to SEASCALE**
- **COUNTY:** CUMBRIA
- **QUIETNESS:** **
- **MILEAGE:** 4.1
- **DIRECTION:** north to south
- **TRAIN STATIONS and TIMETABLES:** SELLAFIELD **GR NK0203**. SEASCALE **GR NK0401**, 65, 113, 110. By train from London (EUSTON) to CARLISLE, then SELLAFIELD (3 miles to Exhibition). Return via SEASCALE, BARROW and LANCASTER
- **MAP:** OS 89
- **WEATHER FORECAST:** 0891-500419
- **TOURIST INFORMATION OFFICE:** BARROW 01229-870156
- **ACCOMMODATION:** Consult Tourist Information
- **PLACES OF INTEREST:** Consult Tourist Information
- **ROUTE:** road

Whether you are for or against, see and judge for yourself (so far as you can). Exhibition Centre at **GR 033049** south of YOTTENFEWS on OS 89. No charge. Open 10-4 daily in summer, but only Saturdays and Sundays October to Easter. For conducted tours book well ahead. BNF Sellafield, Seascale, Cumbria, CA20 1PG, tel: 01940-27735. Find time to visit the Lake District National Park only two miles away; in any case do not miss the seaside route between Sellafield and Seascale stations: part of the CUMBRIA CYCLE CIRCUIT. **Note**: diversion at mouth of river Calder *GR 025027*, famous for natterjack toads.

• **RECONNOITRED:** November 1986

A3

• **LEEDS to SETTLE to CARLISLE**
Queen Victoria's favourite railroad to Scotland
• **COUNTY:** CUMBRIA, YORKSHIRE
• **QUIETNESS:** **
• **MILEAGE:** Total 130, to Skipton 27, to Ribblehead 57, to Appleby 94, to Carlisle 130
• **DIRECTION:** south east-north west
• **TRAIN STATIONS and TIMETABLES:** LEEDS *GR SE2933*, CARLISLE *GR NY4055* with 21 intermediate stations. 36, 9
• **MAP(S):** OS 104, 103, 98, 91, 86, 85
• **WEATHER FORECAST:** 0891-500417
• **TOURIST INFORMATION OFFICE:** LEEDS 0113-2478301, SKIPTON 01756-792809, SETTLE 01729-825192, HORTON IN RIBBLESDALE 017296-333, APPLEBY 017683-51177, CARLISLE 01228-512444
• **PUBLICATIONS:** OS Nicholsons *Waterways North* 5th Edn 1991; some booklets recommended under 'route'; *Settle-Carlisle Country*, Speakman/Morrison 1990
• **ACCOMMODATION:** YHs STAINFORTH, DENT DALE, KIRBY STEPHEN, DUFTON, CARLISLE
• **PLACES OF INTEREST:**
See recommended publications and consult Tourist Information
• **ROUTE:** road and track

Part 1: Leeds to Skipton by Canal Towpath, OS 104 (27 miles)
No detailed route description is needed for a canal towpath, only an occasional location

pinpointed with a Grid Reference to enable you to get back to the busy world if need be. From LEEDS CITY station *GR SE2933* make for LEEDS Canal Basin via 'Arches Arcade' and Granary Walk. Strongly recommended is *Discovering the Leeds to Liverpool Canal*, (Freethy & Woods), a detailed towpath guide to the canal (1991). Towpath on north (right) bank, part of Museum of Leeds Trail (leaflet). Near ARMLEY MILLS (at GR 2734) is a museum and two railway bridges (take the second) go to B6157 *GR 258356* divert for KIRKSTALL and Abbey — museum and station — then go to APPERLEY BRIDGE *GR 1938* and SHIPLEY *GR 1537*, station, and on to SALTAIRE *GR 1338* (Model Village built by Sir Titus Salt); go to DOWLEY GAP bridge *GR 1138*, Fisherman Pub. Cross to south side for BINGLEY *GR 1039* and station. Towpath remains on south (left) of canal to SKIPTON within reach of stations at CROSSFLATTS *GR 1040* and KEIGHLEY *GR 0641*. After FARNHILL *GR 0047*, now on OS 103 enter SKIPTON, station at *GR SD9851*. 27 miles. **Note**: If towpath unsuitable (due to weather or because you do not have a permit), start the exploration of this route at GARGRAVE station *GR SD9353*.

Part 2: From Skipton *GR 9951* to Ribblehead *GR SD7579*, OS 103 (30 miles)
From the pleasant town of SKIPTON with pedestrianized centre and helpful Tourist Information, make for towpath of Leeds-Liverpool canal taking to the south bank **(care with young children)** just north of station at *GR 9851* go north west to GARGRAVE *GR 9353*. This avoids the busy A65. Join the PENNINE WAY at its crossing of the canal uphill (some pushing) and go to BELL BUSK *GR 9056*, then minor road OTTERBURN *GR 8857* south west over railway go to HELLIFIELD *GR 8556* and A65, half a mile to GALLABER *GR 8456* go east of BENDGATE *GR 8457*. West to cross river RIBBLE and again west to WIGGLESWORTH *GR 8157*; north to RATHMELL (now OS 98; minor road to GIGGLESWICK and SETTLE *GR 8163* over A65, minor road to LITTLE STAIN-FORTH *GR 8167* (YH over river RIBBLE). To reduce ride on A65 take quieter **(hilly)** minor road SWARTH MOOR *GR 8068* north east to HELWITH bridge *GR 8189*. North on B6479 to HORTON IN RIBBLESDALE *GR 8072*.

Part 3: Ribblehead to Appleby, OS 98 & 91 (37 miles)
Leave HORTON by B6479 north west to RIBBLEHEAD *GR 7679* and north east on B6255 to road junction at *GR 795836*, a **critical point**, go west and north west by minor road — Dales Way — under railway (another fine viaduct) STONEHOUSES *GR 7784*: YH DENT DALE and B and B. COWGILL *GR 7587* go up by minor road past DENT station and onto remote minor road go to GARSDALE HEAD *GR 7892*. A684 one mile go north north west, then B6259 following the railway to LITTLE ING *GR 7899* (now on OS 91). Easy route: Continue B6259 to KIRBY STEPHEN, where there is a youth hostel and B and B, minor road north west to SOULBY *GR 7410*. Quieter **hilly** route: (easiest with mountain bike) Cross River EDEN *GR 7802*. PENDRAGON Castle is nearby, go to unfenced track north and north west: CROOP House *GR 7704* under railway twice to WAITBY *GR 7508* north to join easier route at SOULBY. Both routes: nine miles north west quiet minor road to B6260 BURRELLS *GR 6818* north to APPLEBY (Tourist Information and ample B and B).
Part 4: Appleby *GR NY6820* to Carlisle *GR NY4055*, OS 91,86, 85 (36 miles)
Leave APPLEBY by B6542. Pick up minor road north of school *GR 680212* to DUFTON YH *GR 6825* go to KNOCK *GR 6727* then to MILBURN *GR 6529*, BLENCARN *GR 6331*, then go to KIRKLAND *GR 6432*, go to SKIRWITH *GR 6132*, a **critical point**. Here go north west A686, then minor road to HUNSONBY *GR 5835* to crossroads near MARIAN LODGE *GR 573366*. Minor road GLASSONBY *GR 5738* north west by another minor road (ignore one mile of OS 90, now OS 86) KIRKOSWALD *GR 5541* north north west through BARUCH Cottages *GR 5444* and west to cross river EDEN and under railway at ARMATHWAITE *GR 5046*. Keep north close to railway for nine miles to B6263 north east to WETHERAL *GR 4654*. Now on OS 85 minor road to SCOTBY *GR 4455* over M6 BOTCHERBY *GR 4155* for quiet cycle route Botcherby Avenue pushing over footbridge at *GR 415554* to hospital and town centre of CARLISLE.

Some words of wisdom from the field: best stretch the Eden Valley. High sections would be uncomfortable in rain and dangerous in mist. Pay attention to weather forecasts. It is quite easy to miss turnings. The publications are very useful and worth reading before setting off, even if you have to leave them at home. This rail line saved from the brink of closure — please use it even though the railway architecture is best seen from a cycle.

- **RECONNOITRED:** RNH, BK, K and D Lofthouse of Scholes

A4

- **C2C SEA to SEA CYCLEWAY — Whitehaven and Workington to Sunderland and Newcastle**
- **COUNTIES:** Cumbria, Northumberland, Durham, Tyne & Wear
- **QUIETNESS:** ** mainly minor roads, several Trailways
- **MILEAGE:** 140 approx.
- **DIRECTION:** west to east
- **TRAIN STATIONS AND TIMETABLES:** (selected): Workington (OS 89, *GR NX9928*) and Whitehaven (OS 89, *GR NX9718*) 218, Penrith (OS 90, *GR NY5129*) 65, Langwathby (OS 91, *GR NY5733*) 36, Chester-le-Street (OS 88, *GR 2751*) 26, Sunderland (OS 88, *GR NZ3956*) 43, Newcastle (OS 88, *GR NZ2463*) 26, 39, 51
- **MAP(S):** OS 89 (1994), 90 (1994), [91 (1990) 3.107 miles only], [86 (1991) 6.214 miles only], 87 (1992), 88 (1994)
- **WEATHER FORECAST:** 0891-500 + west 419, east 418
- **TOURIST INFORMATION OFFICES:** (selected) Workington 01900-602923, Whitehaven 01946-695678, Keswick 017687-72645, Penrith 0176867-466, Alston 01434-381696, Sunderland 0191-565 0960/0565, Newcastle 0191-261-0691
- **PUBLICATIONS:** SUSTRANS leaflet (1995 revision £3.00) *Sea to Sea Cycle Route — Whitehaven and Workington to Sunderland and Newcastle*. From SUSTRANS, Rockwood House, Barn Hill, Stanley, Co Durham DH9 8AN. Tel/Fax 01207-281259. Also from there *The Celestial Railroad. A novel by John Dowie & Other Sculptures.*

- **ACCOMMODATION:** YHs at Cockermouth OS 89 *GR 118291* (a 17c Watermill), Ennerdale OS 89 *GR 142141* (dramatic situation), Keswick OS 86/90 *GR 267235* (ex Hotel riverside), Alston OS 86/87 *GR 717461* (purpose built YH), [Ninebanks OS 86/87 *GR 771514* (traditional simple YH)], Edmundbyers OS 87 *GR 017500* (17c Inn), Newcastle OS 88 *GR 257656* (ex Hotel near city centre, good cycling track network.) [Brackets indicate YH near, not on the official route.]
- **PLACES OF INTEREST:** See SUSTRANS leaflet and consult Tourist Information Offices. Promises to be a very popular route. Article in *The Times* 18 October 1994 gave rise to over 500 requests for leaflet to SUSTRANS at Stanley in four days.
- **ROUTE:**

Part 1: Workington/Whitehaven to Keswick YH, OS 89 (25 miles) Choice (A): From Workington station or sea front *GR NX9928* to north crossing river Derwent *GR 0029* joining Trailway to Seaton *GR 0130* to minor road east Great Broughton *GR 0731* to minor road Cockermouth *GR 1230* YH at *GR 117298* (17c Watermill). Leave town by minor road from road junction *GR 127298* (critical point) to over A66 south east and east Wythop Mill *GR 1829* to east south east road junction north west of Wythop Hall *GR 199288* (critical point) to north east and east to track and minor road beside Bassenthwaite lake to south on west of A66 to Thornthwaite *GR 2225* to south east Braithwaite *GR 2323*.
Choice (B): From Whitehaven harbour or station *GR 9717* signed route through housing estate to join former railway line Mirehouse *GR 9815* to south east below A5595 *GR 9914* to north east Cleator Moor *GR 0115*, over A5086 winding to Rowrah (*GR 0518* (end of Trailway) to A5086 briefly to road junction *GR 062185* (critical point) to minor road south east and east Kirkland *GR 0718*. (For Ennerdale YH take minor road south east Croasdale *GR 0917* to south east to track on north east of Ennerdale Water to YH, dramatic situation *GR 143141*).
MAIN ROUTE: from Kirkland *GR 0718* to east and north (National Park Boundary) Lamplugh *GR 0820* to north east and south east Waterend to road junction *GR 127216* (critical point) to north crossroads *GR 115255* (critical point), to east Low Lorton *GR 1525* to over B5289 (now OS 90 but 8.924 miles overlap) to minor road to junction with B5292 *GR 1825* to B5292 east and south east Braithwaite *GR 2323* to join Choice (A) (Workington Route).
BOTH ROUTES: From Braithwaite *GR 2323* south over B2592 to south east over Newlands Beck *GR 2322* to minor road north east Ullock to south east and north east Derwent Bank *GR 2523* to minor road north east Keswick *GR 2623*, YH *GR 267235* - former hotel on river Greta. YH since 1933.
Part 2: Keswick YH to Alston YH OS 89, 90(91), (86) (43 miles)
Choice (A) as far as Greystoke *GR 4430*, avoiding crossing of A66 by Old Coach Road — surface variable. Leave Keswick by A5271 east to road junction *GR 280237* (critical point) to minor road past Goosewell farm *GR 2923* (now OS 90 — eight and a third miles overlap) to winding minor roads over Naddle Beck to road junction *GR 304239* (critical point) to south east minor road crossing John's Beck and B5322 *GR 3123* to Old Coach Road all way to crossroads High Row *GR 3821* to north and north west over Dacre Beck to Hutton John to under A66 east of Penruddock *GR 4427* to north to B5288 to north Greystoke *GR 4430*.
Choice (B) with crossing of A66. Leave Keswick by Trailway east of YH *GR 2723* to Threlkeld *GR 3225* crossing A66 (care) for Guard House *GR 3325* to over Mossdale Beck to Wallthwaite *GR 3526* to east minor road Troutbeck *GR 3827* crossing A66 (care) to minor road north east and north to road junction south of Berrier *GR 404289* (critical point) to east and north east Greystoke *GR 4430*.
BOTH ROUTES: From Greystoke to north east Little Blencow *GR 4532* to north east and south east Newton Reigny *GR 4731* to over M6 to Penrith *GR 5130*. Leave town by minor road north of Museum and Tourist Information *GR 5130* to north east and east minor road to join A686 briefly east of Roundthorn *GR 5430* taking minor road at *GR 550311* (critical point) to north east Edenhall *GR 5632* to north rejoin A686 crossing river Eden to Langwathby *GR 5633* (station on Settle-Carlisle Line, see Route A3). [Dufton YH lies 14 miles to south east *GR 6825* see Route A3 for quiet approach.] To north under railway Little Salkeld

GR 5636 (now OS 91 for three and three quarter miles only) to north east minor road crossing minor road east of Maughanby Farm *GR 5837* to road junction *GR 588384* **(critical point)** to north crossing Hazelrigg Beck *GR 5839* (now OS 86 — six and a quarter miles only) to north east Mooredge *GR 5941* winding past Huddlesceuch Hall *GR 6042* to Raven Bridge east Haresceugh *GR 6043* to east south east Selah *GR 6142* to south east by bridleway route to Hartside Cross *GR 6441* (viewpoint) to A686 north east (now OS 87 — eleven miles overlap) to minor road *GR 6943* **(critical point)** to Leadgate *GR 7043* to minor road Scalebank *GR 7144* to Alston YH at *GR 717461* (purpose built YH on Pennine Way).

Part 3: Alston YH Edmundbyers YH, OS 87 (33 miles)

From Alston YH retrace route to Leadgate *GR 7043* to south east minor road over Burn to Garrigill *GR 7441* crossing river South Tyne by ford or bridge to Dodbury Crossing B6277 to north east Nenthead *GR 7843* up via Whitehall to Coalcleugh *GR 8045* to east north east over Swinehope Moor *GR 8246* swinging round south east minor road Allenheads *GR 8645* to minor road south east to road junction Lintzgarth *GR 9243*.

Choice (A): To Blanchland *GR 9650* and Edmundbyers YH *GR 0150* to minor road north east Hunstanworth Moor *GR 9346* to Townfield *GR 9548* to south Ramshaw *GR 9547* to north east and north Baybridge to Blanchland to B6306 north east and south east above Derwent reservoir *GR 0152* to Edmundbyers YH (17c Inn).

Part 4: Edmundbyers YH to Newcastle YH with alternative to Sunderland, OS 87, 88 (88 miles — Newcastle 25, Sunderland 33)

Choice (A): For direct route from Edmundbyers YH to rejoin Sea to Sea at Waskerley Way make for road junction south of Burnhope Burn *GR 014496* **(critical point)** to minor road north east Muggleswick *GR 0450* to south east winding road to junction near Healeyfield *GR 0648* (now OS 88) to minor road south east to join Waskerley Way south west of Rowley *GR 0545*.

Choice (B): If not stopping overnight at Edmundbyers. From Lintzgarth *GR 9242* to Rookhope and up incline of dismantled railway ruins *GR 9444* to north east rough track to join Waskerley Way *GR 0545* to north east (now

OS 88). You need to take the alternative signed route on certain grouse shooting days. Both routes converge here. Current OS sheet 88 (1994) shows Consett and Sunderland Cycle Route as well as Waskerley Way and Derwent Walk. Hence this description gives only brief details. Both the route to Sunderland and that to Newcastle keep to the Waskerley Way as far as Consett *GR 0951* then —

Choice (A): To Sunderland along the Sculpture Trail. The Trail keeps south east of A692 to Templetown *GR 1050* to Leadgate *GR 1251* to Annfield Plain *GR 1751* to Stanley *GR 1953*. (Here divert north by minor road on west of A6076 for Causey Arch oldest railway bridge *GR 1955*). Beamish Open Air Museum lies to north *GR 2154*. Trail to north edge Chester-le-Street *GR 2652* (station) to Washington New Town and old village *GR 3156*. (The Hall (National Trust) well worth a visit) to the James Steel Park to crossing river Wear Cox Green *GR 3255* over golf course, under A19 to Pallion *GR 3757* to Bishopwearmouth *GR 3856l*.

Choice of routes to sea. Choice (A): To north east crossing river Wear *GR 3957* to north east along A183 to north pier and lighthouse *GR 4158*.

Choice (B) to the sea: From Bishopwearmouth *GR 3856* to near ski slope *GR 3754* to south east to sea at Ryhope *GR 4152*.

Choice (C): From Consett *GR 0951* to Newcastle YH via Derwent Walk (open to cyclists): Leave Waskerley Way at *GR 0949* to crossing A692 to north crossing A691 Blackhill *GR 1051* to north Shotley Bridge *GR 1052* to Hamsterley *GR 1156* to Rowlands Gill *GR 1658* to Derwent Walk Country Park *GR 1860* to below maze of trunk roads crossing river Tyne *GR 1963* to Scotswood *GR 206636* **(critical point)** to east to city centre. River Tyne cycle route project is completed in part. **Great care** in city centre. YH is north east in Jesmond Street *GR 257656*. Newcastle has made much progress on cycleway network and is good centre for unspoilt coast and plenty of National Trust and English Heritage properties, especially Roman.

- **RECONNOITRED:** SUSTRANS creation opened 1994. This description by RNH with permission of SUSTRANS and great help on the maps by David Gray, project man-ager of the Route, Stanley, Co Durham. Bed and breakfast guide now available from SUSTRANS.

Northumbria

Cleveland, Durham, Northumberland, Tyne Wear

B1

- One of the five excellent Trailways in the MOORLANDS WEST of DURHAM
- **COUNTY:** DURHAM
- **QUIETNESS:** ***
- **MILEAGE:** BISHOP AUCKLAND-BRANDON route 13 miles
- **DIRECTION:** south west to north east
- **TRAIN STATIONS and TIMETABLES:** BISHOP AUCKLAND to DURHAM, 26, 41
- **MAP(S):** OS 93, 92, 88
- **WEATHER FORECAST:** 0891-500418
- **TOURIST INFORMATION OFFICE:** (ALL YEAR) DURHAM 0191-3843720
- **PUBLICATIONS:** DURHAM Tourist Information leaflets
- **ACCOMMODATION:** DURHAM YH Summer holidays only. For B and B consult Tourist Information.
- **PLACES OF INTEREST:** Consult Tourist Information
- **ROUTE:** rough lanes

BISHOP AUCKLAND station north to Trail at pub *GR 206300*. Trail proper ends at junction with other Trails at *GR 254416*. Continue by road to NEVILLE'S CROSS and cul de sac at *GR 264421* to city centre and DURHAM station.
- **RELATED ROUTES:** Derwent 10.5 miles; WASKERLEY 6.5 miles; LANCHESTER 12 miles; DEERNESS 7 miles look equally inviting. Cyclists really welcomed on these trails.
- **RECONNOITRED:** November 1988, RNH

B2(A3)

- CARLISLE to NEWCASTLE, close to Hadrian's Wall with a stopping train in attendance

- **COUNTY:** CUMBRIA, TYNE AND WEAR, NORTHUMBERLAND
- **QUIETNESS:** *
- **MILEAGE:** 51 to WYLAM; 60 to NEWCASTLE
- **DIRECTION:** west to east
- **TRAIN STATIONS and TIMETABLES:** CARLISLE *GR NY4055*; NEWCASTLE *GR NZ2463* with no less than 14 intermediate stations. 65, 48, 26.
- **MAP(S):** OS 85, 86, 87, 88
- **WEATHER FORECAST:** 0891-500419/418
- **TOURIST INFORMATION OFFICE:** CARLISLE 01228-512444, HEXHAM 01434-605225, NEWCASTLE 0191-2610610
- **PUBLICATIONS:** Numerous classic works on Hadrian's Wall including: HMSO, Birley, Collingwood. Also Tourist Information Special 2″ OS map.
- **ACCOMMODATION:** YHs at CARLISLE *GR 385569*, GREENHEAD *GR 659655*, ONCE BREWED *GR 752668*, ACOMB *GR 934666*, NEWCASTLE *GR 257656*
- **PLACES OF INTEREST and NOTE:** If a busy season for the B6318, some of it can be avoided by using the good stopping train which is in attendance (16 stations in all). Journey can be broken at will.
- **ROUTE:** road

From CARLISLE Station make for school north of station *GR 4056* and walk over river footbridge at *GR 410564*, then to RICKERBY *GR 4157* over M6 quiet road to LINSTOCK *GR 4358*. Minor road to B6234, but if dry PARK BROOM and riverside to join B6264 at phone box at *GR 448595*. (Now OS 86) south east by minor road go to NEWBY EAST *GR 4758*. North east by minor road to rejoin B6264 to BRAMPTON. A69 for about 300 yards, then minor road LANERCOST *GR 5563*. By minor road alongside Roman Wall, with rich harvest of turrets and B6318 to

GILSLAND *GR 6366* and GREENHEAD *GR 6665*. YH (now OS 87 11 miles overlap). Uncoloured track *GR 6766* will give quiet access to Wall before rejoining B6318 at *GR 7065*. ONCE BREWED YH at *GR 752668*. The B6318 generally quiet but alternative for busy days is via CHESTERHOLM *GR 7766* and minor road to NEWBROUGH *GR 8767*; then B6319 to WALWICK *GR 9070* and CHESTERS FORT and MUSEUM *GR 9170*. B6318 go to BRUNTON Turret *GR 9269*. On by B6318 to HARLOW HILL *GR 0768* [Now OS 88]. Suggest leave B6318 at road junction *GR 104676* and south on minor road go to WYLAM ON THE TYNE (station). Take 'Cycle Route' east along TYNE RIVERSIDE COUNTRY PARK to NEWBURN *GR 1665*. As a rail traveller don't miss George Stephenson's Cottage (National Trust) at *GR 126651*. On to NEWCASTLE itself.

• **RECONNOITRED:** 1980, RNH

AREA C

North West

Cheshire, Greater Manchester, Lancashire, Merseyside

C1

- **MIDDLEWOOD TRAIL and LYME PARK**
- **COUNTY:** CHESHIRE
- **QUIETNESS:** ***
- **MILEAGE:** 12
- **DIRECTION:** south to north
- **TRAIN STATIONS and TIMETABLES:** MACCLESFIELD *GR ST9273* — MIDDLEWOOD — MARPLE, 79, 81, 90
- **MAP(S):** OS 118, 109
- **WEATHER FORECAST:** 0891-500416
- **TOURIST INFORMATION OFFICE:** MACCLESFIELD TOWN HALL, 01625-504114
- **PUBLICATIONS:** Cycle Pack
- **ACCOMMODATION:** BUXTON YH and Consult Tourist Information
- **PLACES OF INTEREST:** LYME PARK (National Trust)
- **ROUTE:** rough tracks

From Macclesfield station, north to official start of Trail (October 1985) GRIMSHAW LANE *GR 929774* via busy A523 and B5090; (avoid by starting in old station yard *GR 917742*). Trail proper is segregated for walkers, cyclists and horses with a lot of Trail furniture which means some dismounting for cyclists. Diversions: (1) to LYME PARK (1,300 acre deer park, open all year (National Trust) or (2) at Middlewood station to Buxton for other Trailways.
• **RELATED ROUTES:** F3 and F4

C2

- **CHESTER to KNUTSFORD and PRESTBURY (extension to MACCLESFIELD) Cheshire Cycleway**
- **COUNTY:** CHESHIRE
- **QUIETNESS:** **
- **MILEAGE:** 29 to KNUTSFORD, 40 to PRESTBURY, 45 to MACCLESFIELD
- **DIRECTION:** south west to north east
- **TRAIN STATIONS and TIMETABLES:** CHESTER, KNUTSFORD, MACCLESFIELD, 80, 98
- **MAP(S):** OS 117, 118
- **WEATHER FORECAST:** 0891-500416
- **TOURIST INFORMATION OFFICE:** CHESTER 01244-313126 (answering machine at some times of year), MACCLESFIELD 01625-504114
- **PUBLICATIONS:** *Cheshire Cycleway*
- **ACCOMMODATION:** YH at CHESTER *GR SJ3965* and Consult Tourist Information
- **PLACES OF INTEREST:** NETHER ALDERLEY MILL *GR 844763* (this old mill is now owned by the National Trust). TATTON PARK north of KNUTSFORD *GR 745815* also owned by the National Trust.
- **ROUTE:** road

CHESTER station at *GR SJ4167*. Follow minor roads through HOOLE *GR 4267* and over A56 and railway to NEWTON *GR 4268* then north east under A41 and M53 to HOOLE BANK *GR 4369* but short length of A56 necessary to cross river GOWY at *GR 4471* go east to MOULDSWORTH *GR 5171* (motor museum) and go to DELAMERE FOREST (Cycle Routes) *GR 5471*, HATCHMERE and NORLEY *GR 5772*, then go to RULOE *GR 5872*. North to ACTON BRIDGE station *GR 5975* [now OS 118]. North and east over TRENT and MERSEY Canal to LITTLE LEIGH. North east over A533 go to COMBERBACH *GR 6477*. East over A559 GREAT BUDWORTH *GR 6677* to BATE HEATH *GR 6879* cross over M6 near TABLEY HILL *GR 7379*, south east to KNUTSFORD station. **Extension to PRESTBURY:** Exit KNUTSFORD via A537 south east to OLLERTON *GR 7776* go east to MARY DENDY HOSPITAL *GR 8177* and NETHER

ALDERLEY *GR 8476* (National Trust); go south east to VARDENTOWN *GR 8675* and north east over B5087 to PRESTBURY (station) *GR 9077*. **Extension to MACCLESFIELD:** If and when the MIDDLEWOOD TRAILWAY is extended to that town; via A538, B5090 to join TRAILWAY at *GR 927764*.

* **RELATED ROUTES:** C3 and C4 — route is signposted in direction of ride.
* **RECONNOITRED:** April 1990, RNH

C3

* **CHESTER to CREWE by CHESHIRE CYCLEWAY**
* **COUNTY:** CHESHIRE
* **QUIETNESS:** **
* **MILEAGE:** 50+
* **DIRECTION:** south east then north east
* **TRAIN STATIONS and TIMETABLES:** CHESTER *GR SJ4167*, CREWE *GR SJ7154*, 65, 83
* **MAP(S):** OS 117, 118
* **WEATHER FORECAST:** 0891-500416
* **TOURIST INFORMATION OFFICE:** CHESTER 01244-313126, CREWE 01270-537730 (answering machine at some times of the year).
* **PUBLICATIONS:** *Cheshire Cycleway*
* **ACCOMMODATION:** Consult Tourist Information
* **PLACES OF INTEREST:** See *Cheshire Cycleway*
* **ROUTE:** road

CHESTER station at *GR SJ4167*. Join canal towpath in City Road (150 yards from station) go to CHRISTLETON *GR 4465* to join **Cheshire Cycleway** proper, but in anti-clockwise direction (contrary to the signposting throughout) at crossroads *GR 453652* go south east by BROWN HEATH ROAD and south west over canal to WAVERTON; then south east to recross canal at *GR 4861* go to HUXLEY *GR 5061* go south east and south to cross canal at the SHADY OAK *GR 5360*; over railway keeping east of Castle to BEESTON *GR 5458* south to PECKFORTON go south west to join A534 **(care)** at BULKLEY *GR 531545* go to A534 left and immediately right to GALLANTRY BANK *GR 514537* go south

west BICKERTON *GR 5052* to cross A41 at *GR 4851* go west to TILSTON *GR 4551* — CARDEN ARMS — (here circular extension north west to STRETTON *GR 4452* WORKING MILL and PICNIC SITE. LOWER CARDEN south to CARDEN ARMS again). Then south east by Roman Road to MALPAS *GR 4847*. East to cross A41 at NO MANS HEATH *GR 5147* north north east to cross A49 near BICKLEY MOSS *GR 5448* go south south west over canal to MARBURY *GR 5645*; north and east GAUNTONS BANK *GR 5647* to WRENBURY [now OS 118] *GR 6047* station; generally east and south east crossing A530 at ASTON *GR 6146*. Minor roads via KINGSWOODGREEN Farm *GR 6244* to join A525 at *GR 644431* for AUDLEM *GR 6643* (canal shop). North east over A529 **(care)** HANKELOW *GR 6745*, HATHERTON *GR 6947*, WYBUNBURY *GR 6949* then north east on B5071; SHAVINGTON *GR 6951* to CREWE station. If this B road is busy, try longer alternative by minor road from WYBUNBURY through HOUGH *GR 7151* and WESTON *GR 7252*.

* **RELATED ROUTES:** C2 and C4
* **RECONNOITRED:** April 1990, RNH

C4

* **KNUTSFORD to TIMPERLEY (Greater Manchester).** This is a marvellous route ridden by the author several times. It is quiet and mostly off-road except for a brief busy stretch in the middle (see below), it passes two National Trust houses.
* **COUNTY:** CHESHIRE
* **QUIETNESS:** ***
* **MILEAGE:** 20+
* **DIRECTION:** south west to north east
* **TRAIN STATIONS AND TIMETABLES:** KNUTSFORD, ALTRINCHAM (at Altrincham you can only take your bike on the trains **not** the trams), 84
* **MAP(S):** OS 118 and 109
* **TOURIST INFORMATION OFFICE:** Try CHESTER 01244-351609 or MANCHESTER 0161-234 3157
* **PUBLICATIONS:** KNUTSFORD is much written about, visit a bookshop while you are there. A much-quoted nineteenth century novel about the town is *Cranford* by Mrs Gaskell.

- **ACCOMMODATION:** MANCHESTER YH, Potato Wharf, Castlefield, bookings to central reservations 0171-248 6547. Plenty of attractive bed and breakfasts on the way.
- **PLACES OF INTEREST:** The route starts through the grounds of Tatton Hall (National Trust). Visit the lake, the Japanese garden, the orangery and the house (summer only, you can cycle round the grounds at any time). Dunham Massey, also National Trust and also a deer park. Visit the house and garden in the summer, but keep away at weekends; refreshments at both houses.
- **ROUTE:** road and track

From KNUTSFORD Station turn left and left again and enter Tatton Park at end of town, visit places of interest mentioned above, and note the lake, the wildlife and the other items of interest as you pass through. Move on to map 109. Leave Tatton Park by ROSTHERNE exit, cross road straight ahead and sharp left in ROSTHERNE village (view of Rostherne Mere) and continue to traffic lights on A556. Straight across and forward along minor road to T-junction turn right (B5159), follow this road over the motorway and on under canal aqueduct to edge of Lymm. Follow busy A6144 for a short distance until fork right, when main road turns left, onto minor road to DUNHAM (B5160). Follow this road as it twists and turns until it passes under canal after which turn right into Dunham Massey Park. Chain bike beside carpark attendant's hut and walk to house, garden and cafe.
- **RECONNOITRED:** 1990-1995, MZD

AREA D

Yorkshire and Humberside

- **SCARBOROUGH to WHITBY, Trailway**
- **COUNTY:** NORTH YORKSHIRE
- **QUIETNESS:** ***
- **MILEAGE:** 22
- **DIRECTION:** north to south
- **TRAIN STATIONS and TIMETABLES:** RUSWARP *GR 8909*, Malton or SCARBOROUGH *GR TA0388*, 26, 39, 42
- **MAP(S):** OS 95, 101
- **WEATHER FORECAST:** 0891-500418
- **TOURIST INFORMATION OFFICE:** WHITBY 01947-602674 or SCARBOROUGH 01723-373333
- **PUBLICATIONS:** Excellent publications from either Tourist Information Centre
- **ACCOMMODATION:** BOGGLEHOLE YH *GR NZ9504*, WHITBY *GR NZ9011*, SCARBOROUGH
- **PLACES OF INTEREST:** For a feast of railwaymania de-train at MALTON station *GR 7871*; cycle nine miles (dead flat) to PICKERING. Steam train to GROSMONT (Summer). Then train to RUSWARP station for route below.
- **ROUTE:** track and road

RUSWARP station at *GR 891092* minor road NE to S end of viaduct at *GR 896095*. Trailway continuous with minor diversions for tunnels to outskirts of SCARBOROUGH *GR 016908* (SCALBY; estate roads). Then roads or push along footpath.
- **RELATED ROUTES:** F12
- **RECONNOITRED:** Summer 1988, RNH

- **QUIETNESS:** **
- **MILEAGE:** 6 or 15
- **DIRECTION:** north to south
- **TRAIN STATIONS and TIMETABLES:** HESSLE *GR 0225*, 29, 39
- **MAP(S):** OS 106, 112
- **WEATHER FORECAST:** 0891-500413
- **TOURIST INFORMATION OFFICE:** HULL 01482-223559
- **PUBLICATIONS:** Tourist Information Hull issues generous cycle route information for all of HUMBERSIDE
- **ACCOMMODATION:** Consult Tourist Information
- **PLACES OF INTEREST:** Consult Tourist Information
- **ROUTE:** road

From HESSLE STATION *GR 0225*. Alternative approaches from road junction *GR 025255*: (1) left to Country Park (with beached Ferry Steamer and other attractions) and then footpath (steps) to Bridge, or (2) right by road to *GR 023257* for official cycle access. Joint cycle and footpath on both sides of bridge. Wind little problem as roadway gives protection. Return to Hessle by upstream sides of bridge or continue by minor roads via VIKING WAY *GR 0019* and back road to WORLABY *GR 0113* and ELSHAM station *GR 0110* if time permits.
- **RELATED ROUTES:** F12 and FORTH BRIDGE route SS1 and SEVERN BRIDGE route WS3
- **RECONNOITRED:** November 1986

- **The HUMBER BRIDGE**
- **COUNTY:** HUMBERSIDE

- **PENISTONE to SHEFFIELD and ROTHERHAM — RIVER VALLEY, FOREST and CANAL**
- **COUNTY:** WEST and SOUTH YORKS

- **QUIETNESS:** *
- **MILEAGE:** 16 to SHEFFIELD, 25 to ROTHERHAM
- **DIRECTION:** north west to south east
- **TRAIN STATIONS and TIMETABLES:** PENISTONE **GR SE2503**, ROTHERHAM **GR SK4192**, 53, 34, 29 (an exception, this route is easiest from north west to south east)
- **MAP(S):** OS 110, 111
- **WEATHER FORECAST:** 0891-500417
- **TOURIST INFORMATION OFFICE:** SHEFFIELD 0114-2734671, ROTHERHAM 01709-382121
- **ROUTE:** track and road

PENISTONE station SE on B6462 (busy at times). THURGOLAND 2801: diversion South of HUTHWAITE HALL. Cross river Don twice by minor roads to WHARNECLIFFE FOREST track at **GR 299993**. OUGHTIBRIDGE, at bridge, ash path on riverside BEELEY WOOD to Sheffield. **Care** through city (A6 GIBRALTAR ST bus and cycle lane) to vast roundabout at **GR 360871** where towpath of canal signposted (small): follow this quiet canal (with some minor diversions) to ROTHERHAM station. Remember to obtain permit.
- **RECONNOITRED:** November 1985, RNH

D4

- **SELBY to YORK, Trailway**
- **COUNTY:** NORTH YORKSHIRE
- **QUIETNESS:** ***
- **MILEAGE:** 15
- **DIRECTION:** south to north
- **TRAIN STATIONS and TIMETABLES:** SELBY **GR SE6132** TO YORK, 26
- **MAP:** OS 105
- **WEATHER FORECAST:** 0891-500417
- **TOURIST INFORMATION OFFICE:** SELBY 01757-703263, YORK 01904-621756 and at station
- **PUBLICATIONS:** Leaflet Tourist Information
- **ACCOMMODATION:** YH (Rowntree House **GR SE5852**, excellent
- **PLACES OF INTEREST and NOTES:** SUSTRANS, Railway Path Project, has converted a dull straight railway track in dead flat featureless country into a

pleasurable cycle ride — the only one so far found with mile posts to inform you of progress. YORK, spoilt for choice: MINSTER (restored after fire), YORK Railway Museum, walk around the walls, Yorvic (Viking reconstruction)
- **ROUTE:** tracks mainly offroad

North west of station cross river Ouse. Either walk along riverside path to TURNHEAD Farm **GR 6335** or old A19 (now bypassed) through BARLBY to join Trailway at **GR 6336** through RICALL and onwards for 5 miles to river Ouse again at **GR 5946**. Alternative: (1) Official route through BISHOPTHORPE (new housing) and across KNAVESMIRE Racecourse **GR 5949** to YORK or (2) walk along permissive path on west of river diverting around the Palace **GR 5947** to EBOR WAY to YORK.
- **RELATED ROUTES:** D1 using MALTON alternative
- **RECONNOITRED:** December 1988, RNH

D5

- **YORKSHIRE DALES NATIONAL PARK — DENT to DARLINGTON**
- **COUNTY:** NORTH YORKSHIRE
- **QUIETNESS:** **
- **MILEAGE:** 48
- **DIRECTION:** south west to north east
- **TRAIN STATIONS and TIMETABLES:** DENT **GR SD7687** to DARLINGTON **GR NZ1429**, 26, 36
- **MAP(S):** OS 98, (99), (92), 93
- **WEATHER FORECAST:** 0891-500417
- **TOURIST INFORMATION OFFICE:** SKIPTON 01756-792809, DARLINGTON 01325-382698
- **PUBLICATIONS:** Leaflets Tourist Information and National Park Authority
- **ACCOMMODATION:** YH at DENTDALE, HAWES and GRINTON, Accommodation Guide from National Park Authority 01756-752748
- **PLACES OF INTEREST and NOTES:** From DENTDALE to ASKRIGG route coincides with YORKSHIRE DALES CYCLEWAY 1987. Leaflet from Tourist Information or National Park Authority.
- **ROUTE:** roads, **warning**: hilly, not suitable for young families

From DENT station steep descent to minor road south south east past Sportsmans Inn (B and B) and YH under DENT HEAD VIADUCT to join B6255 north east over moors towards HAWES: take minor road *GR 8489* via THORNEY MIRE to A684 to HAWES: cross river URE after Museum to T-junction where east to ASKRIGG. Here depart from Yorkshire Dales Cycleway to NEWBIGGIN *GR 9591*. Make sure you get junction at *GR 953920* (unsigned): delightful quiet, lonely road up (544 metres) and down to GRINTON (YH) keeping south of river SWALE. Then B6270 and A6108 to RICHMOND and SKEEBY (B and B). After Skeeby at *GR 046033* go south east and north east over A1(T) **(danger)** *GR 217034* to MOULTON *GR 2303* north to MIDDLETON TYAS, BARTON, STAPLETON *GR 2612*. In Darlington keep south of PARK at *GR 2813* and take quiet road just west of railway to station.

- **RELATED ROUTES:** D6 NORTHALERTON TO SKIPTON. See also *Mountain Bikeways in Mid Wharfedale and Craven* by J Keavey 1988, from Tourist Information Centre
- **RECONNOITRED:** November 1989, RNH

D6

- **YORKSHIRE DALES — NORTHALLERTON to GARGRAVE and SKIPTON**
- **COUNTY:** NORTH YORKSHIRE
- **QUIETNESS:** **
- **MILEAGE:** 56
- **DIRECTION:** north east to south west
- **TRAIN STATIONS and TIMETABLES:** NORTHALLERTON *GR SE3693*, GARGRAVE *GR SD9353*, SKIPTON *GR SD9851*, 26, 36
- **MAP(S):** OS 99, 98, 103
- **WEATHER FORECAST:** 0891-500417
- **TOURIST INFORMATION OFFICE:** DARLINGTON 01325-382698, SKIPTON 01756-792809
- **PUBLICATIONS:** Leaflet on Yorks Dales Cycleway Tourist Information and National Park Authority
- **ACCOMMODATION:** YH at KETTLEWELL. LINTON GRASSINGTON *GR SD9962*. B and B list Tourist Information and

National Park Authority.
- **PLACES OF INTEREST and NOTES:** Literature from Tourist Information, but the route is all that is needed
- **ROUTE:** road

This route uses minor crossings of the rivers SWALE, URE, COVER and WHARFE to give glimpses of the Yorkshire Dales. From Northallerton station go north west by minor road under the goods line at *GR 357936* to YAFFORTH then south and south west (100 yards muddy) to THRINTOFT *GR3293* north west to GREAT LANGTON *GR 2996* for bridge over SWALE, to KIRKBY FLEETHAM, THE FENCOTES crosses A1(T) **(danger)** at *GR 2693*. South west to WASTE WOOD *GR 2391*. South east to cross NEWTON BECK at CRAKEHALL *GR 2490* pushing south west to level crossing *GR 238893*. South west and west to COCKED HAT *GR 1988*. South to cross river URE *GR 1986*, through JERVAULX PARK (bridleway) Abbey open to the public. One mile on A6108 **(careful)**. South on minor road at EAST WITTON (a peach of a village with a post office stores) past BRAITHWAITE HALL (National Trust working farmhouse) *GR 117857*. Over river COVER at COVERHAM: minor road to CARLTON *GR 0684*. (Now OS 98). HORSEHOUSE (B and B) WOODALE (B and B) over the top (half mile). **Danger** steep descent to KETTLEWELL. Walk the PARK RASH section *GR 9774* to enjoy the view. KETTLEWELL *GR 9772*. Excellent YH. Keep east of river WHARFE through CONISTONE *GR 9867* — both DALES WAY and CYCLEWAY — crossing river Wharfe at GRASSINGTON *GR 9963*. Keep south by minor road to BOW Bridge and south east at junction *GR 998631* go south east on B6160 to branch right to THORPE *GR 0161* then minor road to THREAPLAND *GR 9860*. This avoids the slimy lime on the B6265 and follows Dales Cycleway. CRACOE *GR 9760*, minor road to HETTON and GARGRAVE. If Gargrave station not open, divert at *GR 936552* to A65(T) to SKIPTON. To avoid this use towpath of LEEDS and LIVERPOOL Canal if you have permit.
- **RELATED ROUTES:** D5
- **RECONNOITRED:** December 1989, RNH

D7(F12)

- **LINCOLN to BRIDLINGTON.**
  The HUMBER Bridge linking the
  WOLDS of LINCOLNSHIRE and
  HUMBERSIDE with the HORNSEA
  RAIL TRAIL
- **COUNTY:** LINCOLNSHIRE and
  HUMBERSIDE
- **QUIETNESS:** **
- **MILEAGE:** 83 (two or three days)
- **DIRECTION:** south to north
- **TRAIN STATIONS and TIMETABLES:**
  LINCOLN **GR SK9771**. BRIDLINGTON
  GR TA1768. Intermediate stations HULL
  and Others: 19, 30, 28, 29, 38.
- **MAP(S):** OS 121, 112, 107, 101
- **WEATHER FORECAST:** 0891-500413
- **TOURIST INFORMATION OFFICE:**
  LINCOLN 01522-529828, HULL
  01482-223559, BRIDLINGTON
  01262-673474
- **PUBLICATIONS:** Admirable cycling
  package from Hull Leisure Services
- **ACCOMMODATION:** KIRTON LINSEY Ellis
  GR 9398; BARTON upon HUMBER (two)
- **PLACES OF INTEREST and NOTES:** This
  is a ridge route with wide grass verges
- **ROUTE:** road

LINCOLN station **GR SK9771**. Try to make
time to see both the Cathedral and the
NATIONAL CYCLES MUSEUM up two flights
(BRAYFORD POOL) well signed from station.
Leave LINCOLN by B1398 (BURTON RD),
few villages (the A15 ERMINE ST to the east
hopefully takes the bulk of the traffic (OS 112
starts just before junction to FILLINGHAM
GR 9586). Only town on B1398 is KIRTON IN
LINDSEY **GR 9398** (refreshments, cycle
shop and B and B) go to on B1398 (quarry
areas well screened). Leave B1398 at
MANTON WARREN **GR 9405** minor road go
to SCAWBY **GR 9605**. Problem of finding
quiet crossing of NEW RIVER ANCHOLME.
Options: **Either** (1) busy A roads through
BRIGGS **GR 0007**, (2) good quiet route
needing permission of BROUGHTON Farms
Ltd. B12077 BROUGHTON VALE **GR 9607** to
BROUGHTON and WRESSLE **GR 9709** over
river at BRIDGE Farm **GR 9810**. Private farm
roads via BROUGHTON CARRS **GR 9910** to
new bridge over M180 at **GR 0109** to

WRAWBY **GR 0209**, or (3) **(not reconnoitred)**
north from BROUGHTON by B1207 to
APPLEBY **GR 9514** north north east with
some walking to cross river at **GR 972164**.
SAXBY ALL SAINTS, then minor road to join
(1) and (2) at **GR 994175**.
Resuming from WRAWBY north east to
ELSHAM station and HALL COUNTRY PARK
(Winter Sundays only). Then B1207 WORLABY
('Wishing Well' Pub serves coffee mid-afternoon
cheerfully) go to minor road walk to spot height
87 metres **GR 021144** then north north west
by fine ridge or drove road all the way (no
villages) to join VIKING WAY at **GR 989193**
(critical point); follow pleasant descent, minor
road north east over A15 to BARTON UPON
HUMBER. B and B 15 BOWMANDALE **GR
028217** and Manor. From BARTON UPON
HUMBER station **GR TA0222** go north by
Brown Road and west by minor road to special
cycle access to HUMBER bridge **GR 025228**
(west side). (Now OS 107). At north end leave
via car park and tourist information centre and
go under A15 east on busy A1105, mostly dual
carriageway with ample footways. One stretch
of cycleway at **GR 0726**; make for pleasant
pedestrianized city centre **GR 095287**.
Leave by GEORGE ST and NORTH Bridge
GR 103293, then north (LIME ST) to
CHAMBERLAIN ROAD and make sure you
pick up HORNSEA RAIL TRAIL at **GR 109306**
(many good Cycleways in HULL). Good
tarmac surface in HULL CITY ends at
HOLDERNESS DRAIN **GR 1234**. Then
adequate gravel or cinder surface all the way
through quiet farming countryside (only pubs
noticed at NEW ELERBY **GR 1639** and
between the HATFIELDS at **GR 1843**). TRAIL
ends at edge of HORNSEA at housing
GR 190464. Relatively quiet seaside town.
Good refreshments at 'ODD SPOT' overlooking sea at **GR 210478**. Then minor road
nearest sea north north east for bridleway,
west at **GR 202496 (critical point)**. North
north west on B1242 SKIPSEA **GR 1755**
(garage/shop). At LISSETT **GR 1458** join A165
north (now OS 101). Some stretches of this
busier road have tarmac footways (remnants
of old meandering road?) if your tyres will take
them. BRIDLINGTON and station at **GR 1768**.
- **RELATED ROUTES:** F9, F11, D1
- **RECONNOITRED:** November 1990, RNH.
  Dry after 24 hours rain; HORNSEA RAIL
  TRAIL best with mountain bike.

D8

- **HARROGATE to YORK including Battlefield of MARSTON MOOR**
- **COUNTY:** YORKSHIRE
- **QUIETNESS:** **
- **MILEAGE:** 23.5
- **DIRECTION:** west north west to east south east
- **TRAIN STATIONS and TIMETABLES:** HARROGATE *GR SE3055*, YORK *GR SE5961* and 5 intermediate stations, 35, 9
- **MAP(S):** OS 104, 105
- **WEATHER FORECAST:** 0891-500417
- **TOURIST INFORMATION OFFICE:** HARROGATE near Pump Room *GR 299556*, 0423-525666 **(very helpful)**
- **PUBLICATIONS:**
- **ACCOMMODATION:** Consult Tourist Information, YORK
- **PLACES OF INTEREST and NOTES:** Harrogate Gardens; YORK - spoilt for choice, handful of Museums
- **ROUTE:** road

From HARROGATE station *GR OS104* SE3055 go east to THE STRAYS two hundred acres. East on A59 after Hospital trace route south east through Woodlands Estate to join minor road at *GR 352553* **(critical point)** go past Ron Kitchen cycle shop to CALCUTT (walk on pavement) cross B6163 at *GR 350560* **(critical point)** and pick up and walk footpath on right bank of river NIDD for a little over a mile to next bridge on B6164 at *GR 363562* (pleasant detour there and back over river NIDD at *GR 368559* to GOLDSBOROUGH *GR 3856*), south east for three miles to minor road at *GR 3952* (now OS 105) go over A1 *GR 4052* to COWTHORDE *GR 4252*, TOCKWITH *GR 4652*, past MARSTON MOOR BATTLE OBELISK (1644) *GR 490521* go south east to B1224, go north east and east over YORK bypass *GR 5551* (walk over roundabout) enter YORK; after first roundabout take minor road at junction *GR 577514* **(critical point)** signed YORK CITY CYCLE ROUTE to CITY CENTRE. For YH make for road junction A59 *GR 581522*.

- **RELATED ROUTES:** D4
- **RECONNOITRED:** June 1992, RNH with advice from locals at Tockwith

AREA E

Heart of England

Gloucestershire, Hereford and Worcester, Shropshire, Staffordshire, Warwickshire and West Midlands

E1

- **STROUD VALLEYS PEDESTRIAN/ CYCLE TRAIL**
- **COUNTY:** GLOUCESTERSHIRE
- **QUIETNESS:** ***
- **MILEAGE:** 12
- **DIRECTION:** north west to south east
- **TRAIN STATIONS and TIMETABLES:** STONEHOUSE *GR ST8005*, STROUD *GR 8505*, 125, 126
- **MAP:** OS 162
- **WEATHER FORECAST:** 0891-500405
- **TOURIST INFORMATION OFFICE:** STROUD 01453-765768
- **PUBLICATIONS:** Leaflet and good Stroud guide with five local circular routes from Tourist Information STROUD
- **ACCOMMODATION:** YH SLIMBRIDGE *(GR SO7304)*
- **ROUTE:** track

STONEHOUSE station *GR 8005* to start of Trail at SHIP INN *GR 807047* for six miles to NAILSWORTH *GR 8499*. Return on Trail to former railway junction at DUDBRIDGE *GR 835045* where take trail to STROUD station.
- **RELATED ROUTES:** SLIMBRIDGE, starting from STONEHOUSE station, E3
- **RECONNOITRED:** November 1985, RNH

E2

- **WEST MIDLANDS COMMUTER LAND (1)**
- **COUNTY:** WEST MIDLANDS
- **QUIETNESS:** **
- **MILEAGE:** 16
- **DIRECTION:** south west to north east
- **TRAIN STATIONS and TIMETABLES:** LAPWORTH *GR SP1871*, TILE HILL *GR SP2777*, 68, 71

- **MAP(S):** OS 139, 140
- **WEATHER FORECAST:** 0891-500411
- **TOURIST INFORMATION OFFICE:** COVENTRY 01203-832303
- **PUBLICATIONS:** See under route E4
- **PLACES OF INTEREST and NOTES:** PACKWOOD (see text)
- **ROUTE:** road

LAPWORTH station *GR 1871*. North: diversion to BADDESLEY CLINTON moated manor house 14th century, *GR 199722*, National Trust — no winter opening. To crossroads *GR 1872*. North to *GR 185725* avenue (some stiles) to PACKWOOD HOUSE, National Trust: yew garden (Sermon on the Mount) (closed winter), minor road north west DARLEY GREEN. East to Towpath of canal at *GR 194743*. North to A4023: minor road past ELVERS Green Farm to BARSTON *GR 2078*, WOOTTON GREEN. BERKSWELL *GR 2479* (Now OS 140), REEVES GREEN. TILE HILL station.
- **RELATED ROUTES:** E4, E10
- **RECONNOITRED:** RNH

E3

- **SLIMBRIDGE WILDFOWL and WETLANDS TRUST**
- **COUNTY:** AVON
- **QUIETNESS:** **
- **MILEAGE:** 18
- **DIRECTION:** Varies
- **TRAIN STATIONS and TIMETABLES:** STONEHOUSE *GR 8005*, 127.
- **MAP:** OS 162
- **WEATHER FORECAST:** 0891-500405
- **TOURIST INFORMATION OFFICE:** STROUD 01453-765768
- **PUBLICATIONS:** Slimbridge Guide
- **ACCOMMODATION:** YH SLIMBRIDGE *GR 730043*

- **PLACES OF INTEREST and NOTES:**
November is one of the best months to visit
- **ROUTE:** road

Minor roads LEONARD STANLEY, FROCESTER, CAMBRIDGE, SHEPHERDS PATCH to SLIMBRIDGE WILDFOWL and WETLANDS TRUST *GR 7204*. Return same route or vary slightly.
- **RELATED ROUTES:** E1
- **RECONNOITRED:** November 1981, RNH

E4

- **WEST MIDLANDS COMMUTER LAND (2)**
- **COUNTY:** WEST MIDLANDS
- **QUIETNESS:** **
- **MILEAGE:** 20
- **DIRECTION:** east and north west
- **TRAIN STATIONS and TIMETABLES:** DORRIDGE *GR SP1674*, BERKSWELL *GR SP2477*, 68, 71
- **MAP(S):** OS 139, 140 (151)
- **WEATHER FORECAST:** 0891-500411
- **TOURIST INFORMATION OFFICE:** KENILWORTH 01926-52595
- **PUBLICATIONS:** *The West Midlands Bicycle Rides*
- **PLACES OF INTEREST and NOTES:** KENILWORTH CASTLE — one of the finest and most extensive in Britain
- **ROUTE:** road

DORRIDGE station south east minor road DARLEY GREEN *GR 1874*. PACKWOOD HOUSE and avenue east to *GR 185725* — a few stiles. BADDESLEY CLINTON. House and Church *GR 203714*: minor road south and east to Five Ways: BEAUSALE. ROUNDSHILL farm *GR 266700* swing south east and north east to minor road (cycle path) and estate roads KENILWORTH CASTLE *GR 2772* (English Heritage) B4103 A452 (¹/₃ mile): minor road *GR 2774* BURTON GREEN and north west (cycle path) to WINDMILL at *GR 248760* and BERKSWELL station at *GR 244776*.
- **RELATED ROUTES:** E2, E10
- **RECONNOITRED:** 1980s, RNH

E5

- **THE WELSH BORDERS, KNIGHTON to BUCKNELL**
- **COUNTY:** SHROPSHIRE
- **QUIETNESS:** *
- **MILEAGE:** 7-8 or 4-4 and a half
- **DIRECTION:** west to east (mainly)
- **TRAIN STATIONS and TIMETABLES:** KNIGHTON, BUCKNELL, 129
- **MAP:** OS 148
- **WEATHER FORECAST:** 0891-500491
- **TOURIST INFORMATION OFFICE:** 0547-528753
- **ACCOMMODATION:** KNIGHTON YH, 'temporarily closed' 1995
- **PLACES OF INTEREST AND NOTES:** A charming view of the border country, including two historic towns and the Hindwell Brook. Trotting races at KNIGHTON always held on the Football Association Cup Final Day.
- **ROUTE:** road

Leave KNIGHTON *GR 2872* by the A488 then, either: (1) stay on the A488, a quiet A road, to a village with the unlikely name of NEW INVENTION. Watch your brakes on the descent and turn right for the meandering valley road to BUCKNELL. This route is a hilly seven to eight miles.
(2) The alternative route follows the river valley and national boundary through 4 to 4¹/₂ miles to BUCKNELL railway station — the trains are not frequent so check beforehand. May is the best month for flowers in the bluebell woods.
- **RECONNOITRED:** 1994, Mike Flamank

E6

- **LEAMINGTON SPA to KING'S SUTTON**
- **COUNTY:** WARWICKSHIRE, NORTHAMPTONSHIRE
- **QUIETNESS:** **
- **MILEAGE:** 31
- **DIRECTION:** north west to south east
- **TRAIN STATIONS and TIMETABLES:** LEAMINGTON SPA, KING'S SUTTON, 116
- **MAP(S):** OS 151, 152
- **WEATHER FORECAST:** 0891-500411
- **TOURIST INFORMATION OFFICE:** BANBURY 01295-259855, LEAMINGTON

SPA 01926-311470
- **ACCOMMODATION:** BADBY YH five and a half miles to east of route *GR 5658*
- **PLACES OF INTEREST and NOTES:** Consult Tourist Information
- **ROUTE:** road

ROYAL LEAMINGTON SPA *GR SP3165* east by A425 **(careful)** to RADFORD SEMELE: Minor road at *GR 344646* OFFCHURCH crossroads *GR 3765* south west to SOUTHAM *GR 4161* south east (WELSH ROAD) to MARSTON DOLES south at junction *GR 469583* then south south east to BODDINGTONS *GR 4853* and *4852*, to ASTON le WALLS *GR 4950* over A631 to TRAFFORD bridge *GR 5147* (Now OS 152), CULWORTH *GR 5446* south for less than half a mile on B4525. Road junction *GR 547452* south to east of MARSTON ST LAWRENCE to FARTHINGHOE *GR 5339* (Now OS 151); south west and south CHARLTON *GR 5236* and west to KING'S SUTTON station SP 4936.
- **RELATED ROUTES:** E5
- **RECONNOITRED:** February 1990, RNH

- **KINGHAM to PERSHORE**

E7

- **COUNTY:** OXFORDSHIRE, HEREFORD and WORCESTER
- **QUIETNESS:** **
- **MILEAGE:** 33
- **DIRECTION:** south east to north west
- **TRAIN STATIONS and TIMETABLES:** KINGHAM *GR SP2522*, PERSHORE *GR SO9548*, 126
- **MAP(S):** OS 163, 150
- **WEATHER FORECAST:** 0891-500405
- **TOURIST INFORMATION OFFICE:** STOW ON THE WOLD 01451-31082
- **PUBLICATIONS:** Consult Tourist Information
- **ACCOMMODATION:** YH at STOW ON THE WOLD and CLEEVE HILL *GR 983267*
- **PLACES OF INTEREST:** Consult Tourist Information
- **ROUTE:** road

From KINGHAM station south west and north west BLEDINGTON *GR 2422* to B4450 STOW

ON THE WOLD YH at *GR 193258* go west B4068 LOWER SWELL *GR 1725*. East north east quiet ridge route CHALK HILL *GR 1226* GUITING POWER *GR 0924* (now OS 150), then north east to INCHCOMBE *GR 0228* and north west to GRETTON *GR 0030*, ALDERTON *GR 0033*. BECKFORD *GR 9735*, north east ASHTON UNDER HILL *GR 9938* weave to ELMLEY CASTLE *GR 9841* north west LITTLE COMBERTON *GR 9643* PERSHORE station at north *GR 9548*.
- **RELATED ROUTES:** G7
- **RECONNOITRED:** 1980s, E and JB

E8

- **GREAT MALVERN to LEOMINSTER**
- **COUNTY:** HEREFORD and WORCESTER
- **QUIETNESS:** **
- **MILEAGE:** 28
- **DIRECTION:** south east to north west
- **TRAIN STATIONS and TIMETABLES:** GREAT MALVERN (or COLWALL), LEOMINSTER, 126, 131
- **MAP(S):** OS 150, 149
- **TOURIST INFORMATION OFFICE:** MALVERN 01684-892289, LEOMINSTER 01568-616460
- **ACCOMMODATION:** YH MALVERN HILLS *GR 774449*
- **PLACES OF INTEREST:** Consult Tourist Information
- **ROUTE:** road

From GREAT MALVERN station *GR SO783456* or MALVERN HILLS YH at *GR 774499* COLWALL station *GR 7542*, west to COLWALL (now OS 149) and CODDINGTON *GR 7142*, BOSBURY *GR 6943* and CATLEY SOUTHFIELD *GR 6843* go north west B4214 over A4103 go to BISHOPS FROME *GR 6648*; west RED WYCHEND *GR 6247* and north to LITTLE COWARNE *GR 6051*, PENCOMBE *GR 5952*, north west to RISBURY *GR 5455*, STOKE PRIOR *GR 5256* and LEOMINSTER station.
- **RELATED ROUTES:**
- **RECONNOITRED:** 1980s, E and JB

E9

- **LEOMINSTER to CHURCH STRETTON**
- **COUNTY:** HEREFORD and WORCESTER, SHROPSHIRE
- **QUIETNESS:** **
- **MILEAGE:** 41 (allow time to explore LONG MYND - **hilly**)
- **DIRECTION:** south to north
- **TRAIN STATIONS and TIMETABLES:** LEOMINSTER *GR SO5058*, CHURCH STRETTON *GR SO4593*, 129, 131
- **MAP:** OS 137
- **WEATHER FORECAST:** 0891-500410
- **TOURIST INFORMATION OFFICE:** LEOMINSTER 01568-616460, CHURCH STRETTON 01694-723133 (Summer)
- **PUBLICATIONS:**
- **ACCOMMODATION:** YH at BRIDGES *GR 3996*
- **PLACES OF INTEREST:** Consult Tourist Information
- **ROUTE:** road

LEOMINSTER station west and north on B4361; at road junction *GR 492604* north west to EYTON *GR 4761* and ASTON, LUCTON *GR 4364*, MORTIMER'S CROSS *GR 4263*. North on A4110 — surprisingly quiet —(Now OS 137). WIGMORE *GR 4169* then north east to LEINTHALL STARKES *GR 4369* and north BURRINGTON crossroads junction *GR 436720*. West and north west to LEINTWARDINE *GR 4074* (good Church and teashop), now B4385 but north west minor road at *GR 404744* over river CLUN to 'BEDSTONE', north east on B4367 HOPTON HEATH station *GR 3877* to B4385 PURSLOW *GR 3680* and KEMPTON, LYDBURY NORTH *GR 3586*, then north west to BISHOP'S CASTLE *GR 3288* and north east to B4383 MORE *GR 3491*, LINLEY NORBURY *GR 3692*, WENTNOR *GR 3892*, north BRIDGES YH at *GR 394964* to RATLINGHOPE *GR 4096*; then south east over LONG MYND (unfenced roads) to CHURCH STRETTON station *GR 456936*.

- **RELATED ROUTES:** E8
- **RECONNOITRED:** 1980s, E and JB. Allow extra time to explore the tracks on the LONG MYND at the end.

E10

- **TOPSHAM (EXETER) to CHELTENHAM.** See Route H15 for details

E11

- **GLOUCESTERSHIRE COUNTY CYCLEWAYS divided into six 'wind assisted' routes between stations**
- **COUNTY:** GLOUCESTERSHIRE, HEREFORD and WORCESTER
- **QUIETNESS:** **
- **MILEAGE:** Total 310 miles in six routes
- **DIRECTION:** Various, see below
- **TRAIN STATIONS and TIMETABLES:** CHEPSTOW, LYDNEY, GLOUCESTER, CHELTENHAM, PERSHORE, EVESHAM, MORETON IN MARSH, KINGHAM, SHIPTON, KEMBLE, STROUD, STONEHOUSE, as detailed below. 7, 126, 127.
- **MAP(S):** OS 150, 151, 162, 163
- **WEATHER FORECAST:** 0891-500405
- **TOURIST INFORMATION OFFICES:** CHELTENHAM 01242-522878, CIRENCESTER 01285-654180, GLOUCESTER 01452-421188, PAINSWICK 01452-813552, ROSS ON WYE 01989-62768, STOW ON THE WOLD 01451-31082, STROUD 01453-765768, TEWKESBURY 01684-295027
- **PUBLICATIONS:** *Cycle Touring routes in Gloucestershire*, County Council, six excellent sheets of mainly circular routes, the basis of these six routes, 2nd Edn 1992 with good accommodation list, published by the County Council
- **ACCOMMODATION:** YHs at CLEEVE HILL, STOW ON THE WOLD, DUNTISBOURNE ABBOTS, SLIMBRIDGE, ST BRIAVELS, MONMOUTH, WELSH BICKNOR and see above
- **PLACES OF INTEREST and NOTES:** Numerous — see text and consult Tourist Information. All six routes are on roads.
- **ROUTE:** roads. Six options (A to F).

E11A: CHEPSTOW to PERSHORE via St Briavels, Coleford, The Bicknors, Mitcheldean, Newent, Upleadon, Tewkesbury, Bredon, Comberton. Direction south west to north east, OS 162 (59 miles).

From CHEPSTOW station *GR ST5393* go north by bridge over river WYE *GR 5394* then A48 to B4228 and eight miles to ST BRIAVELS *GR 5504* (YH), minor road north west to MORK *GR 5505* and north east to STOWE and north at *GR 564066* **(critical point)** to join B4231, north west CLEARWELL and SLING *GR 5708*, then north through COLEFORD *GR 5710* and north to B4228 ENGLISH BICKNOR, WELSH BICKNOR *GR 5817*, south east and east minor road through JOY'S GREEN *GR 6016*, RUARDEAN *GR 6117*, east to DRYBROOK *GR 6417*, north east to MITCHELDEAN *GR 6618* and north on B4224 but soon minor road at *GR 665192* **(critical point)**, north over A40 **(care)** to join B4222 *GR 6723*, then north east to B4221 NEWENT *GR 7226*, north east and east LITTLEFORD *GR 7327* UPLEADON *GR 7527*, BRIDGE STREET *GR 7827* over A417 to B4211 (now OS 150) to A438 *GR 8433* east TEWKESBURY *GR 8932*, leave by B4080 under M5 BREDON, continue along B4080 north to road junction *GR 926405* **(critical point)** minor road east and north east to the COMBERTONS and north west to PERSHORE and station at *GR SO9548*.

E11B: LYDNEY to EVESHAM via The Soudleys, Cinderford, Tibberton, Hartpury, Apperley, Gotherington, Beckford, Elmley Castle, Evesham. Direction south west to north east, OS 162, 150 (54 miles).

LYDNEY station *GR SO6301* north and north east to minor road *GR 636033*, then north west and north past viewpoint through ALLASTON *GR 6304* to YORKLEY *GR 6306*, east and south east VINEY HILL *GR 6506*; then north on minor road over B4431 to join B4227, follow to road junction in UPPER SOUDLEY *GR 657105* **(critical point)**, then minor road north to LITTLEDEAN *GR 6713*; near CINDERFORD to A4151 and minor road to junction south of FLAXLEY ABBEY *GR 693150* **(critical point)** for many miles north east to BOSELEY COURT and NORTHWOOD GREEN *GR 7116*, then north to UPPERLEY and HUNTLEY *GR 7219* and north east to TIBBERTON *GR 7621*, B4215 for minor road HIGHLEADON *GR 7723*, north east to HARTPURY *GR 7925* and over A417 to ASHLEWORTH *GR 8125*.

Via STONEBOW Farm and east of HASFIELD *GR 8227* to B4213 and cross river SEVERN by HAW bridge *GR 8427* — now OS 150 —

north east to APPERLEY B4213 to A38 **(care)** and south and east to RUDGEWAY Farm *GR 905281* **(critical point)**, over M5 three times in *GR 9128* and *9129* TREDINGTON and BOZARD'S Farm *GR 9330* to GOTHERINGTON *GR 9629* and east to road junction *GR 982300* **(critical point)**, north through DIXTON and ALSTONE to the WASHBOURNES *GR 9933* and *9834* and north west over A435 **(care)** BECKFORD *GR 9735*, north east ASHTON under HILL *GR 9937* through KERSOE to ELMLEY CASTLE *GR 9841* then east and north by minor road to A44 *GR 0143* **(care)** for EVESHAM and station at *GR SP0344*.

E11C: CHEPSTOW to SHIPTON via Severn Bridge, Berkeley, Cam, Westonbirt, Tetbury, Kemble, Cherington, Tarlton, Cotswold Water Park, Ampney Crucis, Coln St Aldwyns, Burford, Swinbrook. Direction west to east, OS 162, 163 (79 miles).

Part 1: Chepstow to Kemble
From CHEPSTOW station *GR ST5392*, south by path close to railway to BULWARK *GR 5392* (see Welsh route WS2 for detail) to join service road of M4 at *GR 537916* over SEVERN bridge on north side. After AUST Service Station (cafe) east on B4461 ELBERTON *GR 6088* following minor road to LITTLETON on SEVERN *GR 5989*, then OLDBURY ON SEVERN *GR 6192*, north east to HILL *GR 6495*, HAM, BERKELEY *GR 6899* (famous Castle) and east to B4066 and minor road cross A38 **(care)** south east by minor road over railway *GR 7197* over M5 CROSSWAYS *GR 7197*, then minor road north east to STINCHCOMBE *GR 7298*, B4060 to CAM *GR 7599*, south east by minor road ULEY *GR 7998*, cross B4066 at *GR 785979* **(critical point)** minor road south east over B4058 to A4135 for about a mile to minor road, south west on A46 *GR 8293* **(care)** to LEIGHTERTON *GR 8291*, then minor road east and north east four miles, WESTONBIRT ARBORETUM, south at *GR 8489* to TETBURY *GR 8893* (now OS 163). Leave by B4067 over A433 minor road, north to CHERINGTON *GR 9098*, north east and east TARLTON *GR 9599* and south east over A433 and under railway KEMBLE station *GR 9896*.

Part 2: Kemble to Shipton via Cotswold Water Park and Burford
Leave KEMBLE and follow south east minor road to SOMERFORD KEYNES *GR 0295*

(COTSWOLD WATER PARK), leave by minor road north near UPPER SIDDINGTON *GR 0299* to CIRENCESTER *GR SP 0201*. Leave town by A417 east AMPNEY CRUCIS *GR 066017* **(critical point)**. Instead of by-passing Cirencester: divert east to EASTLEACH TURVILLE *GR 1905*. If by-passing CIRENCESTER take minor road north east over A419 at *GR 0300* and minor road to PRESTON and west of HARNHILL to rejoin route at *GR 066017* follow north north east to AKEMAN ST (Roman Road) at *GR 0703* **(critical point)** then north east and diversion through QUENINGTON *GR 1404* and COLN ST ALDWYNS *GR 1405* to leave it at *GR 193068* **(critical point)**, north east on minor road WESTWELL *GR 2210* to BURFORD *GR 2512* and minor road south of river WINDRUSH to SWINBROOK *GR 2812* and north by minor road to SHIPTON UNDER WYCHWOOD station at *GR SP2818*.

E11D: KEMBLE to PERSHORE via Sapperton, Cowley, Badgeworth, Tewkesbury, Twyning, Defford. Direction south to north, OS 163, 150 (46 miles).

Part 1: Kemble to Tewkesbury, 33 miles From KEMBLE station *GR ST 9897* — near source of the Thames — north west under railway to TARLTON *GR 9599* near Canal Tunnel to crossroads *GR 9200* and north east over A419 to SAPPERTON *GR 9403*; resume minor road to crossroads PARK CORNER *GR 9604* then north leaving DUNISBOURNE ABBOTS YH less than a mile east to WINSTONE *GR 9509*, then north over A417 ERMIN WAY and COWLEY *GR 9614*, north west by minor roads COTSWOLD WAY, SHURDINGTON *GR 9218* over A46 **(care)** BADGEWORTH *GR 9019*; north over railway and under A40 to BAMFURLONG *GR 9021* and west over M5 then north to STAVERTON BRIDGE and STAVERTON *GR 8923* to BODDINGTON *GR 8925* over A4019 north east to HARDWICKE *GR 9027* and outskirts of STOKE ORCHARD *GR 9128* (now OS 150). North west over M5 TREDINGTON *GR 9029*; over M5 yet again twice near FIDDINGTON *GR 9230*; north west via WALTON CARDIFF *GR 9032* to TEWKESBURY.

Part 2: Tewkesbury to Pershore, 13 miles Leave TEWKESBURY north by A38 **(care)**. Soon SHUTHONGER *GR 8835*, minor road north east to TWYNING *GR 9037*, north over M50 and M5 to LOWER STRENSHAM *GR 9040*, north east A4104 *GR 9142* and north east minor road over railway to DEFFORD *GR 9143*, then north minor road to RAMSDEN *GR 9246* and east to PERSHORE *GR 9446* and station *GR SP9548*.

E11E: GLOUCESTER to KINGHAM via Cheltenham, Syreford, Brockhampton, Hawling, Naunton, The Slaughters, Wyck Rissington, Bledington. Direction west to east, OS 162, 163 (35 miles).

GLOUCESTER station *GR SO8318* (foot-bridge over both railway and A38 in Grid Sq 8417); east from station to cross railway and A38 to pick up minor road *GR 855184*, south east to road junction *GR 875172* **(critical point)**, then north east under A417 to CHURCHDOWN (now OS 163) at *GR 890200* **(critical point)** over M5 to BADGEWORTH *GR 9019* and north east to UPPER HATHERLEY *GR 9120*. Either visit town centre or follow minor roads to CHARLTON KINGS *GR 9721* then north east HAM steep hill **(walk)** to east WHITTINGTON *GR 0121* and SYREFORD *GR 0220*, north to SEVENHAMPTON *GR 0321* and BROCKHAMPTON *GR 0322*, north east and east to HAWLINGS *GR 0623*, HAWLING LODGE and east NAUNTON *GR 1123*; south east over B4068 and east to the SLAUGHTERS *GR 1523 and GR 1622*, over A429 *GR 1722* then south east WYCK RISSINGTON *GR 1921* — wall maze in Church — then south east on minor road to WYKE BEACON *GR 2020* and north over A424 and minor road north east to ICOMB *GR 2122*, minor road to B4450 and BLEDINGTON *GR 2422* and KINGHAM station *GR SP2522*.

E11F: SHIPTON to GLOUCESTER via Taynton, Windrush, Northleach, Chedworth Roman Villa, Withington, Cowley, Brimpsfield, Cranham, Upton St Leonards. Direction east to west, OS 163, 162 (36 miles).

SHIPTON station *GR SP2818* then west MILTON UNDER WYCHWOOD and south west TAYNTON *GR 2313*, west to GREAT BARRINGTON WINDRUSH *GR 1912*, north west to SHERBORNE, west to FARMINGTON *GR 1315* and south west to NORTHLEACH *GR 1114*; south west over A429 west to YANWORTH *GR 0713*, CHEDWORTH ROMAN VILLA *GR 056134* (National Trust, **don't miss**); north west to CASSEY COMPTON *GR 0415*, WITHINGTON

GR 0215, west to UPPER COBERLEY
GR 9715 and south west over A435
COWLEY *GR 9614*, south west over A417
BRIMPSFIELD *GR 9312*, west CLIMPERWELL
Farm *GR 9112* over B4070 CRANHAM
GR 8912 (now OS 162); west over A46 **(care)**
and north west to UPTON ST LEONARDS
GR 8614, over M5 *GR 861152* **(critical point)**
trace quiet route through WHEATRIDGE
GR 8515, SAINTBRIDGE
GR 8416 to footbridge over A38 *GR 846172*
(critical point) trace footpath crossing two
railways and to GLOUCESTER station
GR SO8318.
- **RELATED ROUTES:** WS1 and others
- **RECONNOITRED:** RHN

E12

- **THE NORTHERN STAR
  CYCLEWAY — RUGBY to CARLISLE**
- **COUNTIES:** WARWICKSHIRE,
  LEICESTERSHIRE, DERBYSHIRE,
  SOUTH YORKSHIRE, NORTH
  LANCASHIRE, LANCASHIRE, CUMBRIA
- **QUIETNESS:** ** mainly minor roads
- **MILEAGE:** 280 approximately; allow for
  deviations to B & B
- **DIRECTION:** mainly south east to
  north west
- **TRAIN STATIONS AND TIMETABLES:**
  (selected) RUGBY (OS 140, *GR SP5175*),
  MARKET BOSWORTH (OS 140, *GR
  SK3903*), BURTON ON TRENT (OS 128,
  GR SK2423), HOPE (OS 110, *GR
  SK1883*), HEBDEN BRIDGE (OS 107, *GR
  SD9926*), KIRKBY STEPHEN (OS 91, *GR
  NY7606*), CARLISLE (OS 85, *GR NY4055*).
  For RUGBY 65, 68, for CARLISLE 65 (36
  to SETTLE etc.)
- **MAP(S):** OS 140(1992), 128(1991),
  119(1989), 110(1993), 103(1991),
  104(1990), 98(1989), 91(1990), 90(1988),
  86(1991), 85(1992)
- **WEATHER FORECAST:** 0891-5004 11
  (WARWICKSHIRE), 12 (DERBYSHIRE),
  17 (SOUTH and NORTH YORKSHIRE),
  19 (CUMBRIA)
- **TOURIST INFORMATION OFFICE:**
  RUGBY 01788-71813, ASHBOURNE
  01335-43666, HOLMFIRTH 01484-687603,
  HEBDEN BRIDGE 01422- 843831,

APPLEBY 017683-51177, CARLISLE
01228-512444
- **PUBLICATIONS:** *New Riders of the Open
  Road, Guide to Northern Star Cycleway*
  £2.40 inc. P&P. from: Phil Horsley, New
  Riders of the Open Road Guides, Lauriston
  Hall, Castle Douglas, Kirkcudbrightshire,
  Scotland DG7 2NB. As a general rule you
  only need the route description and the
  OS Landranger map to follow the ride.
  However, in this, and the two other *New
  Riders of the Open Road* routes you need
  Phil Horsley's Guides for the full enjoyment
  of the routes. The first of his routes, *The
  Scottish Border Cycleway* (Stranraer to
  Berwick — 210 miles), appears as route
  SS3 where it is described as the 'handiest
  and most informative guide to a long cycle
  route that I have found in sixty years of
  adult cycling'; all three guides are two
  colour illustrated 16 page booklets showing
  Tourist Information, shops, cafes, cycle
  shops, gradient diagram and much else
  besides. The second route is the *North
  Sea Cycleway* (Berwick to Hull — 300
  miles). For all three send £4.55 (inc. P & P)
  to the address given above.
- **PLACES OF INTEREST:** Plenty in Phil
  Horsley's guide
- **ROUTE: Much of the route is hilly, some
  steep. It is unsuitable for young families
  and should be undertaken by adult
  riders only with provision for overnight
  stops.**

**Part 1 - Rugby to Market Bosworth, OS 140
(30 miles)**
From RUGBY station *GR 5175* take minor
roads and A426/A407 under railway and over
river Avon to the B4112. North west to road
junction *GR 484774* **(critical point)**, then
minor road west to LITTLE LAWFORD
GR 4677 **(critical point).** North over railway
and Oxford canal to EASENHALL *GR 4679*,
go north north east over M6 then the B4112
to PAILTON *GR 4781*. West on the A427 to
crossroads *GR4582* **(critical point)** to
MONKS KIRBY *GR 4683*, go north over
B445 and north east, minor road over A5 to
CLAYBROOKE PARVA and MAGNA *GR 4988*.
West on B577 at road junction *GR 490887*
(critical point) then minor road north east
FROLESWORTH *GR 5090*, north west over
FOSS WAY Roman Road to B4114 and minor

road to SAPCOTE *GR 4993*. Minor road to STONEY STANTON *GR 4894*, go north west B581 over M69 and railway to ELMESTHORPE *GR 4696* the B581 to BARWELL *GR 4496* and crossroads *GR 4396*, minor road to STOKE GOLDING *GR 4097*. North north west to DADLINGTON *GR 4098*, north north east over ASHBY DE LA ZOUCHE canal (Battle of Bosworth Country Park GR 3900) then north east to MARKET BOSWORTH *GR 4003*, the Battlefield Line Steam Railway.

Part 2 — Market Bosworth to Tutbury via Walton on Trent, OS 140, 128 (30 miles)

Leave MARKET BOSWORTH west by B585 road junction *GR 388033 (critical point)*, minor road over canal twice, go north west to CONGERSTONE *GR 3605* go to West Bilstone then to TWYCROSS *GR 3304*. West and south west to ORTON ON THE HILL *GR 3003*, north west to AUSTREY *GR 2906*, go under M42 NO MAN'S HEATH *GR 2808* (now OS 128, just over a mile overlap). Over A453 minor road north west to CLIFTON CAMPVILLE *GR 2510*, go north over river Mease to LULLINGTON *GR 2513* then minor road to COTTON IN THE ELMS *GR 2415*. North west to WALTON ON TRENT *GR 2118*, go west over river Trent and the A38 BARTON UNDER NEEDWOOD B5016. Minor road north north east, Church, *GR 187186 (critical point)* to TATENHILL *GR 2021*, go north over B5017 to ANSLOW *GR 2125*. North north west to BUSHTON then to TUTBURY *GR 2028* old market town; tannery; cut glass etc.

Part 3 — Tutbury to Hartington or Ashbourne, OS 128, 119 (28 miles)

Leave TUTBURY *GR SK2028* via A50 north over river Dove to cross railway to HATTON *GR 2129*, go west on minor road to SCROPTON *GR 1930*. North over A50 to CHURCH BROUGHTON *GR 2033* on minor road north to ALKMONTON *GR 1838* (now OS 119). North on minor road to YEAVELEY *GR 1840*, north on minor road to WYASTON *GR 1842*, minor road north to ASHBOURNE *GR 1846*. Leave ASHBOURNE on minor road north north west to MAPPLETON on start of TISSINGTON TRAIL *GR 177468* car park etc. Follow TISSINGTON TRAIL (the first post WW2 Trailway) for 10 miles north to HEATHCOTE *GR 1459* then east to HARTINGTON YH *GR 131603*. The TISSINGTON TRAIL is best followed if you

wish to stay at HARTINGTON HALL YH *GR 131603*. (Here tree planted by Richard Schirmann, Founder of YH Movement in 1910), or at ILAM HALL (National Trust stately mansion) *GR 131506* approached by THORPE *GR 1550*, ILAM *GR 1350*. (For DOVE and MANIFOLD VALLEYS). An alternative route via CARSINGTON WATER and the HIGH PEAK TRAIL is described below.

Part 4 — Hartington *GR 1360* to Castleton, or Ashbourne to Castleton, OS 119, 110 (30 miles)

From HARTINGTON *GR 1360* rejoin TISSINGTON TRAIL north to Trail junction, PARSLEY HAY *GR 1463*, then leave Trail to continue main route on minor road to MONYASH *GR 1566*. Alternative route from ASHBOURNE *GR 1846* on B5035 to KNIVETON *GR 2150* go north east to *GR 234525 (critical point)*. Minor road north to BRASSINGTON *GR 2354*, north to LONGCLIFFE *GR 2255* to join the HIGH PEAK TRAIL (main route) at PARSLEY HAY *GR 1463* to main route over A515, minor road north to MONYASH *GR 1566*. Minor road north to TADDINGTON *GR 1471* then over A6 north west to B6049 north north east to MILLER'S DALE *GR 1473*. (RAVENSTOR YH at *GR 152732*, large country house — David Bellamy's first botany lesson). North on B6040 to TIDESWELL *GR 1575* to B6049 north east at LANE HEAD *GR 159764 (critical point)*, take minor road north to LITTLE HUCKLOW *GR 1678* (now OS 110). North and north west to CASTLETON YH *GR 150828*. Castle, caves etc.

Part 5 — Castleton to Langsett via Ladybower, OS 110 (19 + 13 mile circuit of Derwent Valley Reservoir)

Leave CASTLETON *GR 1582* go east by A625 if quiet; otherwise retrace to *GR 157824 (critical point)* and back road to HOPE *GR 1883*, A625 east briefly over bridge to minor road at *GR 176834 (critical point)* then cross railway to ASTON *GR 1883*, go east to THORNHILL *GR 1983*. North on minor road to YORKSHIRE BRIDGE *GR 197849* to LADYBOWER reservoir *GR 1986*. If time permits enjoy the 13 mile circuit of the Derwent Valley reservoir from the ASHOPTON viaduct *GR 1986*. North on west bank to KING'S TREE *GR 1694* retrace to FAIRHOLMES *GR 173895*, Tourist Information etc. **(critical point)** take east bank south to A57 at

Heart of England E12

GR 1986. Continue A57 north east road junction at GR 225876 (critical point), north on minor road to STRINES public house GR 2290 and minor road on edge of moors all the way past BROOMHEAD HALL GR 2496 to LANGSETT YH at GR 211005. Simple purpose-built; non-resident warden; self cooking. Peak Park Tourist Information nearby.

Part 6 — Langsett to Mankinholes (Todmorden), OS 110, 104, 103 (37 miles)
Leave LANGSETT GR 2100 by A616 crossing A628 at FLOUCH INN GR 1901 go north to crossroads GR 195035 (critical point) north west and north on B6106 to HOLMFIRTH 'Last of the Summer Wine' country, crossing river Holme at GR 1408. Go north west to UPPERTHONG GR 1308 on minor road, north west B6107 GR 1109 to MELTHAM GR 0910 to B6107, north west to crossroads GR 078123 (critical point). Take the B6109 north to SLAITHWAITE GR 0813 (station go west over river Colne, under the railway and minor road to BRADSHAW GR 0514, go north east to WORTS HILL GR 0615, go over A640 on minor road north to CAMPHILL GR 0516. Cycle clockwise round SCAMMONDEN WATER GR 0415 to DEAN HEAD GR 0415 then take tiny road below M62 GR 049168 (critical point) to KRUMLIN GR 0518. Go north west on minor road over B6114 to RIPPONDEN crossing river Ryburn at GR 040197 (now OS 104 briefly). Minor road round to LIGHTHAZELS GR 0220, LUMB GR 0221, HUBBERTON GREEN GR 0322 then north west all the way to MYTHOLMROYD GR 0126 (station). Over river Calder to towpath of Rochdale canal then north west GR 0026, now OS 103. Canal towpath or A646 to HEBDEN BRIDGE GR 9927. South west on towpath of Rochdale canal (restored section four miles towards TODMORDEN) to bridge GR 960247 (critical point). Minor road south to MANKINHOLES YH. Ancient manor house near Pennine Way (canal trips and paragliding) over 40 years a YH GR 960235.

Part 7 — Mankinholes YH (Todmorden, GR SD9623 to Earby (north west at Colne) OS 103 (25 miles)
Retrace route to HEBDEN BRIDGE GR 9927 and leave town by minor road passing museum GR 986280 to SLACK GR 9728 then to HARDCASTLE CRAGGS GR 9630. Go north and north west past Pack Horse

public house GR 9531, north west on minor road north of WIDDOP reservoir to THURSDEN GR 9034. Go north between COLDWELL reservoirs GR 9036 and north west to crossroads at Clarion House GR 8937. North east to TRAWDEN GR 9138 then the B6250 and over A6068 GR 9040 on minor road to BLUE BELL GR 9041. West on minor road A56 and north between reservoirs, FOULBRIDGE GR 8842, go north Hey Road junction GR 882447 (critical point). Minor road north east over B6383 SALTERFORTH GR 8945 and minor road north east EARBY YH at GR 915468. A memorial YH with waterfall etc.

Part 8 — Earby YH (Nr Colne) to Dent Dale YH (Cowgill) GR 7785 via Giggleswick, Settle and Ribblehead, OS 103, 98 (35 miles)
From YH at EARBY GR 9146 retrace south west to SALTERFORTH GR 8945 B6383. North west B6383 to BARNOLDSWICK GR 8746, north and north west B6251 to BRACEWELL GR 8648. North west over A59 and STOCK BECK to HORTON GR 8550 then west and north west to NEWSHOLME GR 8451. South west A682 on minor road and north west over river Ribble to PAYTHORNE GR 8251 Buck Inn. North west on minor road all way to join B6478 and north east to WIGGLESWORTH GR 8056 on minor road north north west to RATHMELL GR 8059, now OS 98. Minor road north on west of river Ribble under railway to north GIGGLESWICK GR 8063. (Divert over river to SETTLE and museum of Craven Life etc). Resuming west of river Ribble over A65 to Stack House GR 8165 then to LITTLE STAINFORTH GR 8167 go east over railway. STAINFORTH YH at GR 821668, Victorian listed building, excellent high and low level cycling. Go north preferably east of river on minor road to HELWITH BRIDGE GR 8169. B6479 north to HORTON IN RIBBLESDALE GR 8072 and north west B6479 to RIBBLEHEAD GR 7779, go north north east B6255 to NEWBY HEAD MOSS to road junction at GR 79836 (critical point). Here divert by minor road under railway to DENTDALE YH at GR 773850 or Sportsman's Inn GR 767863 both recommended.

Part 9 — Dentdale (Cowgill) to Dufton YH via Kirby Stephen YH, OS 98, 91 (31 miles)
Choice A: Retrace to NEWBY HEAD MOSS GR 7983, go north east B6255 over top and

down the WIDDALE to HAWES. YH at
GR 867897 (purpose built YH).
Choice B: To avoid the A684 (HAWES to
Moorcock Inn) from YH DENTDALE or Inn go
to COWGILL **GR 7587**, up **very steep hill**
past DENT station now open again but marked
closed on recent OS maps. Go over the top of
GARSDALE COMMON **GR 7890** to join A884
then north west to Moorcock Inn **GR 7992**.
Both routes from Inn go north east B6250
crossing into CUMBRIA at Aisgill Moor
Cottage **GR 7796**. North on B6259 to
HAZELGILL **GR 7899**, now OS 91, to B6259
east of river Eden to NATEBY **GR 7706** to
KIRKBY STEPHEN with YH **GR 774085**
(attractive converted chapel). Leave KIRKBY
STEPHEN by minor road to SOULBY
GR 7411 and go north west on minor road to
GRASSGILL **GR 7212**. North west on minor
road over railway **GR 7015**, go north west
joining B6260 **GR 6818** and north to APPLEBY
IN WESTMORLAND **GR 6820** (station). Fine
market town. Leave by minor road under
A66 at **GR 680215** to DUFTON with YH
GR 688251 (on Pennine Way, log fire).
**Part 10 — Dufton to Carlisle via
Armathwaite, OS 91, 86, 85 (32 miles)**
Leave DUFTON **GR 6825** by minor road, north
west to KNOCK **GR 6727**. Minor road north
west and south west and north west to
MILBURN **GR 6529**. *North west to
BLENCARN (**GR 6331** and north west to
SKIRWITH **GR 6132**. North west on minor
road over A686 **GR 5834** to HUNSONBY
GR 5835 then north west to MARION LODGE
GR 5736. North east and north west to
GLASSONBY **GR 5738** then north west,
now OS 86, on minor road north to
KIRKOSWALD **GR 5541**. Minor road north
west to SPRINGFIELD **GR 5443**, minor road
north west and west to cross river Eden to
ARMATHWAITE **GR 5046**. Go under railway
on minor road north west to COTEHILL
GR 4650, north west to join B6283
CUMWHINTON **GR 4552**, now OS 85. Go
south west on B6263 to road junction
GR 448526 **(critical point)**, Lowther Arms.
Minor road north north west under railway
SCOTBY **GR 4455** to minor road under
railway and over M6 **GR 4355**. Minor road to
BOTCHERBY to cross footbridge over river
Petteril at **GR 415554** **(critical point)** for quiet
way into CARLISLE city centre. YH north west
of city **GR 386569** (up for sale, so may close

soon) on CUMBRIAN CYCLEWAY.
The Horsley *Northern Star Cycleway* has a
further recommended route from Carlisle to
Burgh on Sands and the Silvery Solway. Try
and make time for it. Full guide from New
Riders of the Open Road Guides, Laurieston
Hall, Castle Douglas, Scotland DG7 2NB.
£1.95 plus 45p P&P.
• **RECONNOITRED:** 1993, Phil Horsley;
  adapted by RNH

East Midlands
Derbyshire, Leicestershire, Lincolnshire, Northamptonshire and Nottinghamshire

F1

- **THE MANIFOLD VALLEY TRACK and HIGH PEAK TRAIL**
- **COUNTY:** STAFFFORDSHIRE, DERBYSHIRE
- **QUIETNESS:** *** between Waterhouses and Cromford; remainder **
- **MILEAGE:** 42
- **DIRECTION:** south west to north east mainly
- **TRAIN STATIONS and TIMETABLES:** UTTOXETER *GR 0952*, CROMFORD *GR   SK3057*, 54, 80
- **MAP(S):** OS 128, 119
- **WEATHER FORECAST:** 0891-500412
- **TOURIST INFORMATION OFFICE:** BAKEWELL 01629-813227
- **PUBLICATIONS:** Leaflet about High Peak Trail from Tourist Information
- **ACCOMMODATION:** HARTINGTON YH *GR SK1360*
- **PLACES OF INTEREST and NOTES:** **Hilly** between Rocester and Waterhouses. If too long start at CROMFORD station and go part way and back. Manifold Valley Track a pioneer Trailway in 1937.
- **ROUTE:** track

From Uttoxeter station *GR 0953* by bylanes or bridleways to Rocester, Alton, Farley, Threelows, Cauldon, Waterhouses. Manifold Track (est 1937), Hulme End, Hartington, Parsley Hay, High Peak Trail to CROMFORD station *GR SK3057*.
- **RELATED ROUTES:** F2, F3
- **RECONNOITRED:** 1982, RNH

F2

- **HIGH PEAK and TISSINGTON TRAILS**
- **COUNTY:** DERBYSHIRE. Peak District National Park.
- **QUIETNESS:** *** and **
- **MILEAGE:** 44
- **DIRECTION:** south to north mainly
- **TRAIN STATIONS and TIMETABLES:** CROMFORD *GR SK3059*, DERBY, 53, 54
- **MAP(S):** OS 119, 128
- **WEATHER FORECAST:** 0891-500412
- **TOURIST INFORMATION OFFICE:** MATLOCK BATH 01629-55082
- **PUBLICATIONS:** Leaflets on the 2 trails from Tourist Information
- **ACCOMMODATION:** YH MATLOCK *GR SK3060*
- **PLACES OF INTEREST and NOTES:** Tissington was the first Trailway designated after the war of 1939-1945. **Avoid** the A52 ASHBOURNE-DERBY road.
- **ROUTE:** track

From station at CROMFORD *GR SK3057* by road or Cromford Canal south to High Peak Trail *GR 315558* (up two steep inclines) 17 miles to PARSLEY HAY *GR 1463* south west on TISSINGTON TRAIL (Now OS 128) to Ashbourne *GR 1844*; lanes at *GR 184457*. Osmaston Park *GR 2042*, Shirley, Hollington, Longlane *GR 2238*, Langley Common *GR 2937*, Derby station.
- **RELATED ROUTES:** F3
- **RECONNOITRED:** 1982, RNH

F3

- **THE MONSAL TRAIL**
- **COUNTY:** DERBYSHIRE. Peak District National Park.
- **QUIETNESS:** ** **Not suitable for young families**
- **MILEAGE:** 23
- **DIRECTION:** north west to south east
- **TRAIN STATIONS and TIMETABLES:**

BUXTON *GR SK0573*, MATLOCK
GR 2960, 81, 54
- **MAP:** OS 119
- **WEATHER FORECAST:** 0891-500412
- **TOURIST INFORMATION OFFICE:**
BUXTON 01298-25106, BAKEWELL
01629-813227
- **PUBLICATIONS:** Leaflet Tourist
Information. Bakewell Youth Hostel offers
map and guidebook hire.
- **ACCOMMODATION:** Plenty of good YHs,
including BAKEWELL YH *GR SK2168*
- **PLACES OF INTEREST and NOTES:** This
is a **hilly** route unless the tunnels are
opened to cyclists. If the whole route is too
daunting until the tunnel problem is solved,
try parts of it such as MONSAL Viaduct
GR 1871 or walk the stretch between
LITTON and CRESSBROOK MILLS,
'WATER CUM JOLLY' *GR 1772*. Steam
traction is being restored to the BUXTON
end of the route but it is expected that the
Trail for walkers and cyclists will be
retained with access through tunnels as
at Bristol.
- **ROUTE:** track and road

BUXTON station: south west on A6 to first car
park *GR 104725*. Minor limestone road to
second car park; steps up to Trail. Three
tunnels shown on Peak Park Planning Board
leaflet. (1) *GR 1273* CHEE DALE: diversion
difficult for cyclists. (2) LITTON MILLS
CRESSBROOK *GR 1672*: easier diversion
but some lifting of cycle. (3) HEADSTONE
(MONSAL HEAD)
GR 1871: short steep exit to road at Head.
Footpath at *GR 187716* to rejoin Trail which
continues via BAKEWELL to COOMBS Road
Viaduct at *GR 230679*. By track and minor
road to ROWSLEY. A6 south for two miles
(care). DARLEY BRIDGE gated road to OKER
'BURMA ROAD' at *GR 287600* to riverside
path to MATLOCK station. Allow five hours
at least.
- **RELATED ROUTES:** F1, F2
- **RECONNOITRED:** RNH

F4

- **WHALEY BRIDGE to CROMFORD**
- **COUNTY:** DERBYSHIRE
- **QUIETNESS:** *** unsuitable for young

families. All beware of weather.
- **MILEAGE:** 36
- **DIRECTION:** north west to south east
- **TRAIN STATIONS and TIMETABLES:**
WHALEY BRIDGE *GR SK0181*,
CROMFORD *GR SK3057*, 54, 81
- **MAP(S):** OS 110, 119
- **WEATHER FORECAST:** 0891-500412
- **TOURIST INFORMATION OFFICE:**
BAKEWELL 01629-813227, BUXTON
01298-25106
- **PUBLICATIONS:** Leaflet from Tourist
Information
- **ACCOMMODATION:** YH BUXTON
GR SK0672 and YH MATLOCK *GR SK3060*
- **PLACES OF INTEREST:**
Acknowledgements to Railway Path Project
(Bristol), Route 8: relatively quiet extension
to Derby station on Route F10
- **ROUTE:** track and road

WHALEY BRIDGE station *GR 011814*. South
east over A6; minor road over railway to
GR 015804. South crossing A5002 to reservoirs;
east of FERNILEE; west of ERWOOD. GOYT
VALLEY Road (restricted for cars). PC
GR 017716 a little over a mile west to the CAT
and FIDDLE, claims to be the highest pub
open all year round at 1,690 feet. *GR 002718*:
retrace minor roads over AXE EDGE MOOR
and cross A53; follow National Park boundary.
DALEHEAD *GR 0469*. EARL STERNDALE
GR 0967 to *GR 108665*. Footpath to start of
HIGH PEAK TRAIL, continues car-free for
seventeen and a half miles south east to
bottom of incline at HIGH PEAK JUNCTION
GR 315560; towpath or minor road to
CROMFORD station.
- **RELATED ROUTES:** C1, F1, F2, F3
- **RECONNOITRED:** October 1984 on
icy roads

F5

- **RUTLAND WATER, Europe's
largest man-made lake**
- **COUNTY:** LEICESTERSHIRE
- **QUIETNESS:** ***
- **MILEAGE:** 25 (including the circuit of the
UPPER HAMBLETON peninsula 8 miles)
- **DIRECTION:** Mostly east
- **TRAIN STATIONS and TIMETABLES:**

East Midlands F3/5

OAKHAM *GR SK8509*, STAMFORD
GR TF0206, 18, 26, 49, 53
- **MAP:** OS 141
- **WEATHER FORECAST:** 0891-500412
- **TOURIST INFORMATION OFFICE:**
OAKHAM 01572-724329, STAMFORD
01780-55611
- **PUBLICATIONS:** Leaflet from Tourist
Information and County Council
- **ACCOMMODATION:** Consult Tourist
Information
- **PLACES OF INTEREST:** Circuit of
HAMBLETON peninsula best cycled in
close season for fishing, 16 March-16 June.
Cycle hire at north and south of reservoir.
- **ROUTE:** track and road

OAKHAM station A606 to *GR 876086*, road to
UPPER HAMBLETON; take lane at car park
GR 899077 and complete the outer circle of
the Peninsula, not forgetting the road end at
GR 926066 hugging the waterside. On return
to junction at *GR 884086* go south quietly with
permission through NATURE RESERVE to
GR 876054, main route is through EGLETON.
At MANTON regain waterside trail via
bridleway *GR 8860509*. At EDITH WESTON
follow diversion around sailing club to half
submerged CHURCH (Rutland Memorial and
water exhibition) *GR 933063*. Continue circuit
trail counter-clockwise via Tourist Information
office and cycle hire at *GR 9308* past
BARNSDALE to County Council cycle path
alongside busy A606; return to OAKHAM
station one and a half miles on town roads.
Routes to STAMFORD (1) From EDITH
WESTON *GR 9305* then minor road to
KETTON AND COLLYWESTON (two great
names in the building stone world), **great care**
for two miles on A43(T) to EASTON ON THE
HILL; then east and B1081 to STAMFORD
station ten miles or (2) From EMPINGHAM
GR 9508, TICKENCOTE, GREAT CASTERTON,
STAMFORD station eight miles.
- **RELATED ROUTES:** F6, F9
- **RECONNOITRED:** Summer 1985, RNH

F6

- **EASTERN LEICESTERSHIRE and
RUTLAND**
- **COUNTY:** LEICESTERSHIRE

- **QUIETNESS:** **
- **MILEAGE:** 15
- **DIRECTION:** east to west
- **TRAIN STATIONS and TIMETABLES:**
LEICESTER *GR SK5904*, OAKHAM
GR SK8509, 53, 18, 49
- **MAP(S):** OS 140, 141
- **WEATHER FORECAST:** 0891-500412
- **TOURIST INFORMATION OFFICE:**
LEICESTER 0116-2511300, OAKHAM
01572-724329
- **ACCOMMODATION:** Consult Tourist
Information
- **ROUTE:** road

(The Fox Cub mini-bus service No. 52 from
Humberston St will take folded wrapped cycle
in quiet times to Scraptoft de Montfort
University campus *GR 650056*). Then the
rolling hills to edge of Keyham, Hungarton,
White's Barn *GR 707074*, Lowesby, Marefield,
Owston, Knossington to OAKHAM station.
Fine view of Rutland Water from TV Mast
GR 830089.
- **RELATED ROUTES:** F5, F9
- **RECONNOITRED:** RNH

F7

- **LEICESTER CITY and the
RIVER SOAR**
- **COUNTY:** LEICESTERSHIRE
- **QUIETNESS:** ***
- **MILEAGE:** 8
- **DIRECTION:** Varied
- **TRAIN STATIONS and TIMETABLES:**
LEICESTER *GR SK5904*, 53 18
- **MAP:** OS 140 (City plan from Tourist
Information for detail)
- **WEATHER FORECAST:** 0891-500412
- **TOURIST INFORMATION OFFICE:**
LEICESTER 0116-2511300
- **PUBLICATIONS:** Three good Leicester
leaflets 1992
- **PLACES OF INTEREST:** Another exciting
route (not yet reconnoitred) Great Central
Way north towards Bradgate Country
Park, Beacon Hill *GR 5114* (Viewpoint)
to LOUGHBOROUGH station OS 129,
about 17 miles (minor roads)
- **ROUTE:** track

From Leicester station to Newarke Street subway to Newarke bridge; right to Duns Lane, Corah Street to steps of Iron Railway bridge **GR 579044**; follow Way to Wood at **GR 565996**. Return by joining at **GR 566006** the towpath of river Soar to Newarke bridge and station (Go outward on towpath route if wind against you).
- **RELATED ROUTES:** F5, F10
- **RECONNOITRED:** December 1986, RNH

F8

- **NORTHAMPTON to GORING - THE SWAN'S WAY**
- **COUNTY:** NORTHAMPTONSHIRE, BUCKINGHAMSHIRE, BERKSHIRE.
- **QUIETNESS:** **
- **MILEAGE:** 66 total. To MILTON KEYNES 17; to STONE 38; to GORING 66.
- **DIRECTION:** north east to south west
- **TRAIN STATIONS and TIMETABLES:** NORTHAMPTON **GR SP7460**, GORING and STREATLEY **GR SU6080**, 66, 68, 116
- **MAP(S):** OS 152, 165, 175
- **WEATHER FORECAST:** 0891-500406
- **TOURIST INFORMATION OFFICE:** AYLESBURY 01296-382308, MILTON KEYNES 01908-691995, WALLINGFORD 01491-35351
- **PUBLICATIONS:** *The Swan's Way* (Buckinghamshire County Council) includes list of ten B and B places
- **ACCOMMODATION:** See above and YHs at BRADWELL Village (MILTON KEYNES) and STREATLEY. Beacon Cottage on RIDGEWAY **GR 727977** was the only B and B sign noticed on the whole 66 miles, but check in the lists of the Tourist Information.
- **PLACES OF INTEREST:** See **Publications**. WADDESDON Manor (National Trust); MILTON KEYNES fine network of cycle 'REDWAYS' and leisure routes well worth exploring: leaflet available.
- **ROUTE:** track

NORTHAMPTON to GORING and STREAT-LEY ON THAMES. THE SWAN'S WAY — a 66 mile Bridle route here adapted for the pedal cyclist (symbol of SWAN'S WAY is a horse-shoe enclosing a bridled swan). This route has

been marked on OS maps since 1986 and a leaflet is published. These notes concentrate on getting to the start of the Swan's Way at SALCEY FOREST and parts where a deviation from the bridleway is advisable. You need a large scale map to enjoy the MILTON KEYNES routes.
Part 1: Northampton to Milton Keynes, OS 152 (17 miles)
From NORTHAMPTON station (or bus station) make for roundabout north west of Carlsberg brewery **GR SP752603** to join Nene Way keeping north of river until the track becomes a cycle path crossing the river at **GR 774595** and St Peter bridge and cycle route south and south west to HARDINGSTONE **GR 7657**; then south east on B526, road junction **GR 8055** to PIDDINGTON and south to SALCEY FOREST at **GR 804529** (for a really quiet route, walk the footpath from SKETTY CLOSE **GR 781583** through SAUCEBRIDGE Farm **GR 7857**). Then follow route signed 'SWAN'S WAY' south through SALCEY FOREST (sound gravel tracks) with variants as shown: **take care GR 8148** (use compass or find yourself in STOKE PARK WOOD). Under M1 at **GR 8247**, TATHALL END **GR 8246**; find your way through HANSLOPE Park with its security fences. Then some of Milton Keynes lakeland and canal to BLACK HORSE, canal bar, **GR 846424** go south west along old railway line to WINDMILL **GR 8341**, beware new roads, go to Neverton Valley and see the notorious concrete cows (eroded by age, vandals and grafitti) at A422 **GR 828399** east of railway (nearest roundabout at BANCROFT) to YH next OLD BRADWELL Church **GR 831395** (find time to see something of the new city and its 'REDWAYS' and leisure routes for cyclists).
Part 2: Milton Keynes to Stone (south west of Aylesbury), 21 miles
Retrace to ingenious path utilizing old culvert under railway at **GR 828396**, then south under A5 go to LOUGHTON under old A5 SHENLEY CHURCH END **GR 8336**. Depart from Swan's Way by roads to south of WHADDON **GR 8034**. South over A421 at **GR 806325** (overlap between OS 152 and 165), minor road to SWANBOURNE (tea) from north as on Swan's Way; go to junction **GR 7925** then west by minor road to GRANBOROUGH **GR 7625** and minor road to NORTH MARSTON **GR 7722**, west to STONEHILL Farm **GR 7522**; south

along minor roads (Roman road) and south west over A41 (Waddesdon National Trust) to junction at **GR 7515**, south east to join bridleway (north BUCKINGHAMSHIRE WAY) at **GR 760151**: **(care)** — this parkland now crops; keep to cartway (not crop route) but can divert on footpath to see stately mansion: over river THAME to STONE **GR 7812**, County Arms pub.

Part 3: Stone (Near Aylesbury) to Goring and Streatley, 28 miles
From STONE minor road to BISHOPSTONE, **GR 8010** minor road past MARSH **GR 8109**, KIMBLE WICK **GR 8007**. minor road go to OWLSWICK **GR 7906**. Minor road over A4129 (busy) under railway and on bridleway to THE FORD **GR 7703**; minor road to PITCH GREEN, BLEDLOW Church **GR 7702**; at **GR 777018** join SWAN'S WAY and RIDGEWAY: after steep stony rise going is easier for 10 miles; fewer SWAN signposts hereabouts. B and B at BEACON Cottage **GR 727977** and teas at HILL Farm **GR 723967**. You are now on OS 175. Deviate from Swan's Way at SLIDING HILL **GR 666915** and follow minor road south west signed WALLINGFORD and later GORING to cross A423 at OAKLEY WOOD **GR 6388**. Minor road go to IPSDEN **GR 6385** and gradual descent south west to GORING Station and YH at STREATLEY over the THAMES.
*   **RELATED ROUTES:** F8, G2, G5, G6, G7
*   **RECONNOITRED:** September 1990, RNH

F9

*   **OAKHAM to LINCOLN via GRANTHAM**
*   **COUNTY:** LEICESTERSHIRE, LINCOLNSHIRE
*   **QUIETNESS:** **
*   **MILEAGE:** 45, both alternatives
*   **DIRECTION:** south to north
*   **TRAIN STATIONS and TIMETABLES:** OAKHAM **GR SK8509**, LINCOLN **GR SK9770**, 49, 26, 30
*   **MAP(S):** OS 141, 130, 121
*   **WEATHER FORECAST:** 0891-500413
*   **TOURIST INFORMATION OFFICE:** OAKHAM 01572-724329, GRANTHAM 01476-66444, LINCOLN 01522-529828
*   **ACCOMMODATION:** YH at LINCOLN and

consult Tourist Information
*   **PLACES OF INTEREST:** GRANTHAM — the birthplace of Thatcher (the word 'Thatcherism' is now in dictionaries)
*   **ROUTE:** road

From OAKHAM station east and north east by minor road to LANGHAM, north east on minor road to ASHWELL **GR 8613**, north on minor road to TEIGH **GR 8616**, EDMONDTHORPE **GR 8517**, WYMONDHAM **GR 8518**; minor road go to COSTON LODGE **GR 857218**, SPROXTON **GR 8524**, SALTBY **GR 8526**. Then:
Either (1) north east **GRANTHAM** by minor road over VIKING WAY at **GR 8628** to road junction **GR 877306**. Minor road over A1 to B1174 for GRANTHAM (Isaac NEWTON Museum; Coaching Inns). Leave GRANTHAM north west on B1174 go to GREAT GONERBY **GR 8938** then by minor road **GR 8940** to MARSTON **GR 8943**, minor road to BRANDON **GR 9048** (now OS 121). STRAGGLETHORPE **GR 9152**, minor road go to BRANT BROUGHTON **GR 9154** and north on minor road on line of rivers BRANT and WITHAM to LINCOLN.
Or (2) BELVOIR CASTLE (cutting out GRANTHAM), go north west from SALTBY to CROXTON KERRIAL **GR 8329**. KNIPTON **GR 8231**, west of BELVOIR Castle **GR 8133** minor road (or walk along JUBILEE WAY) to WOOLSTHORPE **GR 8434**; cross GRANTHAM Canal **GR 8435** then north east and north SEDGEBROOK **GR 8538** to north ALLINGTON **GR 8540**, north east over A1 to MARSTON (to join main route).
*   **RELATED ROUTES:** F5, F6
*   **RECONNOITRED:** RNH

F10

*   **LOUGHBOROUGH to MATLOCK**
*   **COUNTY:** LEICESTERSHIRE, DERBYSHIRE, NOTTINGHAMSHIRE
*   **QUIETNESS:** *** and **
*   **MILEAGE:** Copt Oak YH 10; Matlock 48
*   **DIRECTION:** south to north mainly
*   **TRAIN STATIONS and TIMETABLES:** LOUGHBOROUGH **GR SK5420**, MATLOCK **GR SK2960**, 53, 57, 54
*   **MAP(S):** OS 129, 128, 119

- **WEATHER FORECAST:** 0891-500412
- **TOURIST INFORMATION OFFICE:** LOUGHBOROUGH 01509-230131, DERBY 01332-255802
- **PUBLICATIONS:** Derby Cycle Route County Council and Tourist Information, a great help for Derby section. OS/Nicholson for canals.
- **ACCOMMODATION:** YHs at COPT OAK, MATLOCK and SHINING CLIFF (closed much of the year, check before going on 01629 6503941). Consult Tourist Information.
- **PLACES OF INTEREST:** LOUGHBOROUGH — carillion, bell foundry, steam railway. MATLOCK BATH — Spa, show caves, Heights of Abraham. A complex route, especially around Derby, but probably one of the most worthwhile.
- **ROUTE:** track and road

Part 1: Loughborough to Copt Oak, 10 miles
LOUGHBOROUGH station *GR 5420* south to bridge over Soar Navigation; towpath on northside to bridge at *GR 557187*, pylons, go south west over A6 to WOODTHORPE *GR 5417*; footpath south east to B591 and up to BEACON HILL *GR 5114* (viewpoint); B591 then south on B5350 (**busy**; Motorway fever near Junction 22 of M1). When explored there was a delightfully simple YH with all essentials, lovingly kept by Warden, Pennine Way veteran, at *GR 481129*.
Part 2: Copt Oak to Derby, 18 miles
From YH, north west on B587 to crossroads *GR 4515*; north east to crossroads *GR 472168*; north east to crossroads near windmill at *GR 4618*. For Trailway buffs the old line is rideable from *GR 463186* to Blackbrook Farm only. For others, go to A512 west for three quarters of a mile, then minor road north to BELTON *GR 4420*, minor road north west past Merril Grange go to TONGE and BREEDON ON THE HILL *GR 4022* (Now OS 128). A453(T) south west for one mile to minor road at *GR 400224*; west to CALKE Park - National Trust, very popular; north to viewpoint *GR 376228* (**critical point**). Walk on Water Co Permissive Path to *GR 371229*. Then follow STAUNTON HARROLD Reservoir Road round and past sailing club to MELBOURNE *GR 3825* (hall and gardens always open, but house in August only); through town north to

TRAILWAY at *GR 390266* - fine bridge over Trent. Take towpath or minor road to river bridge on A5132 at *GR 375289*; towpath to bridge over canal *GR 371292* (critical point); North on towpath of Derby Canal; follow Railway Path Project north to DERBY CITY CENTRE (signed); below old railway at *GR 370309*; over A5132 and north through ALLENTON to cross A5111 at *GR 374328*; North over A6 and east of college to river DERWENT; follow riverside path upstream to City Centre.
Part 3: Derby to Matlock, 20 miles
North by LITTLE CHESTER *GR 3537* and through riverside meadows and B6179 to LITTLE EATON *GR 3641*. Minor road up valley to MILFORD *GR 3545*. Cross river and north on minor road by Chevinside *GR 3446* (now OS 119); minor road BELPER LANE END *GR 333494*. Minor road north through SHINING CLIFF WOODS, National Trust and YH (limited opening), to join CROMFORD CANAL towpath at WHATSTANDWELL station *GR 3354*. To CROMFORD. At CROMFORD choice of routes to MATLOCK. (1) For the weary, train. (2) A6, busy but flat. (3) Steep minor road through STARKHOLMES *GR 3058*.
- **RELATED ROUTES:** F11, F3
- **RECONNOITRED:** RNH, October 1990

F11

- **MATLOCK to NEWARK and LINCOLN**
- **COUNTY:** DERBYSHIRE, NOTTINGHAMSHIRE, LINCOLNSHIRE
- **QUIETNESS:** **
- **MILEAGE:** To NEWARK 41 miles; to LINCOLN 60 miles.
- **DIRECTION:** west to east, then south west to north east
- **TRAIN STATIONS and TIMETABLES:** MATLOCK *GR SK2960*, LINCOLN *GR TF9770*, 53, 54, 30, 19
- **MAP(S):** OS 119, 120, 121
- **WEATHER FORECAST:** 0891-500412/413
- **TOURIST INFORMATION OFFICE:** MATLOCK BATH 01629-55082, NEWARK 01636-78962, LINCOLN 01522-529828
- **ACCOMMODATION:** YHs at MATLOCK and LINCOLN and consult Tourist Information
- **ROUTE:** road

East Midlands F11

From MATLOCK station cross river DERWENT; A615 south east to **GR 303598** minor road **(very steep)**. RIBER HILL; south after 'Hall' at **GR 312588**, generally south east by minor roads to LEA **GR 3257**, PLAISTOW **GR 3456** and PLAISTOW GREEN near CRICH (Tram Museum); B5035 a third of a mile minor road to WINGFIELD PARK. **GR 3754**: under railway cross B6013 PENTRICH, under A38 at **GR 3952** to HAMMERSMITH (now OS 120), south of BUTTERLEY Reservoir **GR 4051** (relics of heavy industry and mining area for few miles although called 'GOLDEN VALLEY', a Butterley Company were the builders of St Pancras Station; private road with public path east (north of Police Headquarters) to **GR 437515**, below is a long tunnel of the Cromford Canal, south east and east to cross main railway lines and EREWASH river into NOTTS at JACKSDALE **GR 4451** (shops). South east and north west WESTWOOD **GR 4551** BAGTHORPE **GR 4751**; north and north east through SELSTON over M1 at **GR 4853**; ANNESLEY WOOD HOUSE; south on A611 and soon minor road south east at **GR 508535** to NEWSTEAD village **GR 5152**; official road to NEWSTEAD ABBEY is through Colliery **GR 519529**, but there is an unofficial approach near Pub at **GR 522527**; drive goes under surviving ornamental iron railway bridge at **GR 525527** to grounds and gardens of NEWSTEAD ABBEY (small charge to NOTTINGHAM City). Exit by drive north east to SWINECOTTE DALE to A60 at **GR 556545**, then south east along minor road to LONGDALE; lovely descent through forest to cross A614 at **GR 6052** to cross A6097, then to OXTON **GR 6351** and north east on B6386 SOUTHWELL **GR 7053** (MINSTER); leave by A612 **(care)**. (If B6386 is busy, try quiet diversion north east through HALAM **GR 6754**, **hilly**.) At EASTHORPE **GR 7053** go south east to BRINKLEY and FISKERTON station **GR 7352**, then north east ROLLESTON **GR 7452** to STAYTHORPE and AVERHAM **GR 7654** go to A617 north east and south east to NEWARK **GR 7954** station (now OS 121). For quiet exit from Newark make for bridleway **GR 810535** (critical point) under A1 to Windmill **GR 8353**; north and through CODDINGTON **GR 8354** east to new bypass roundabout **GR 845546**. Delightful minor road through STAPLEFORD WOOD to STAPLEFORD **GR 8857**; go to NORTON DISNEY and over

river WITHAM to north edge of BASSINGHAM **GR 9160**, go to AUBOURN **GR 9262**. If dry walk over river WITHAM again **GR 9363** and go north to SOUTH HYKEHAM **GR 9364**. (If wet, cross river WITHAM by road bridge **GR 9162**) and go to NORTH HYKEHAM **GR 9566** and minor roads to LINCOLN city centre and station — Cathedral, visit Cycle Museum.
* **RELATED ROUTES:** F3, F9, F10
* **RECONNOITRED:** 1990, RNH and DC

AREA G

East Anglia
Bedfordshire, Hertfordshire, Cambridgeshire, Norfolk, Suffolk, Essex

G1

- **BEDFORD to HUNTINGDON**
- **COUNTY:** BEDFORDSHIRE, CAMBRIDGESHIRE
- **QUIETNESS:** **
- **MILEAGE:** 16 to ST NEOTS, 25 to HUNTINGDON
- **DIRECTION:** south west to north east
- **TRAIN STATIONS and TIMETABLES:** BEDFORD *GR 0449*, HUNTINGDON *GR TL2371*, 52, 25
- **MAP:** OS 153
- **WEATHER FORECAST:** 0891-500407
- **TOURIST INFORMATION OFFICE:** BEDFORD 01234-215226
- **ACCOMMODATION:** Consult Tourist Information
- **ROUTE:** road

BEDFORD station south east two mini-round-abouts to PREBEND STREET County bridge *GR 046494*. South bank river Great Ouse under Town bridge; riverside parkland NEWNHAM bridge *GR 064494*. Barkers Lane GOLDINGTON, SALPH END, SEVICK END, WILDEN, DUCK'S CROSS, COLESDEN, CHAWSTON. Land Settlement Association. North end: cattle creep under A1 at *GR 165583*, east of EATON SOCON Church to ST NEOTS bridge, minor roads to B1043 to HUNTINGDON station.
- **RELATED ROUTES:** G2, G3, G15
- **RECONNOITRED:** 1985

- **TRAIN STATIONS and TIMETABLES:** BEDFORD *GR TL0449*, ASHWELL and MORDEN *GR TL2938*, 52, 25
- **MAP:** OS 153
- **WEATHER FORECAST:** 0891-500407
- **TOURIST INFORMATION OFFICE:** BEDFORD 01234-215226
- **PUBLICATIONS:** Contact Tourist Information
- **ACCOMMODATION:** Contact Tourist Information
- **PLACES OF INTEREST:** BEDFORD pleasant riverside, ICKWELL VILLAGE, SHUTTLEWORTH COLLECTION (historic aircraft), ASHWELL (source of Cam, also interesting Church)
- **ROUTE:** road

BEDFORD station follow river GREAT OUSE downstream to CARDINGTON SLUICE. *GR 078488*. CARDINGTON, COPLE, NORTHILL, ICKWELL, SHUTTLEWORTH COLLECTION (planes and cycles). *GR 1544*. Minor road to *GR 178452* south and east HOLME MILL to A6001 at *GR 187427*. North through BIGGLESWADE make for DUNTON Corner *GR 204436* through DUNTON to *GR 245454* go south south east to MOBB'S HOLE and ASHWELL. Station one and a half miles to south east.
- **RELATED ROUTES:** G1, G4, G15
- **RECONNOITRED:** 1989, RNH

G2

- **BEDFORD to ASHWELL**
- **COUNTY:** BEDFORDSHIRE, HERTFORDSHIRE
- **QUIETNESS:** **
- **MILEAGE:** 25
- **DIRECTION:** north west to south east

G3

- **ST ALBANS to BEDFORD**
- **COUNTY:** HERTFORDSHIRE and BEDFORDSHIRE
- **QUIETNESS:** **
- **MILEAGE:** 58
- **DIRECTION:** south to north
- **TRAIN STATIONS and TIMETABLES:**

ST ALBANS *GR TQ156071*, BEDFORD
GR TL042497, 52, 61
- **MAP(S):** OS 166, 153
- **WEATHER FORECAST:** 0891-500407
- **TOURIST INFORMATION OFFICE:** ST
  ALBANS 01727-864511, BEDFORD
  01234-215226
- **PUBLICATIONS:** Number of leaflets from
  Tourist Information
- **PLACES OF INTEREST:** Several places of
  interest mentioned in text of route with
  acknowledgement to St Albans Diocese.
  'Cycle Round the See' May 1989 raised
  £10,000 for Church Urban Fund, 2 of 3
  circular routes, freely adapted. If 58 miles
  is too long, this route can be divided by the
  use of the stations at LETCHWORTH
  GR 2132 or from SOUTHILL or OLD
  WARDEN to BIGGLESWADE *GR 1944*.
- **ROUTE:** road

ST ALBANS station. Assuming you want to
visit the Cathedral. North north west to Tourist
Information and south west to Cathedral at
GR 146071. Then north east to B651
SANDRIDGE *GR 1710*.
If direct from station quiet route through
FLEETVILLE and MARSHALSWICK
neighbourhoods worth exploring. Continue
B651 WHEATHAMPSTEAD *GR 1714*. North
east minor roads (very narrow) to AYOT ST
LAWRENCE *GR 1916*. Two churches (one
ruined) and SHAWS CORNER (National Trust,
closed winter), lanes and B651 to KIMPTON
GR 1718 WHITWELL *GR 1821*, ST PAULS
WALDEN *GR 1922* (Queen Mother's
birthplace), Point 105 at *GR 197238* west
and north west to PRESTON *GR 1724* north
to Gosmore *GR 1827*. East across B656
ST IPPOLLITTS *GR 1927*, south east to
REDCOATS GREEN *GR 207266*. North and
north east over railway to GREAT
WYMONDLEY *GR 2128*. WILLIAN *GR 2230*
west and north west through LETCHWORTH,
World's first Garden City, *GR 214314* to main
central boulevard to station, then north west
and west to (now OS 153) point 57. WILBURY
Farm *GR 1933*, north ARLESLEY *GR 1935*,
at CHURCH END *GR 1937* west along A507
for less than half a mile crossing railway and
north at bridleway *GR 185377* **(careful map
reading)** pleasant route past HENLOW
GRANGE, a famous beauty farm joining
A6001 near church and shortly east. CLIFTON

Church *GR 1639* west of STANFORD *GR 1641*
to SOUTHILL (church and burial place of
Admiral Byng) through woods to OLD
WARDEN *GR 1343* (picturesque estate village)
at *GR 146447* (diversion to SWISS GARDEN
and SHUTTLEWORTH plane collection), then
ICKWELL, NORTHILL *GR 1446* and west to
COPLE *GR 1048*, CARDINGTON, crossing
A603 at *GR 083486* to SLUICE and riverside
path and COUNTRY PARK at *GR 178488*.
Follow splendid riverside path through town
centre keeping north or true left bank at Town
bridge *GR 050496* and onwards to KEMPSTON
Mill *GR 024476* (a little walking). Seek out
causeway path *GR 022474* to KEMPSTON
CHURCH END *GR 0147* north west
STAGSDEN on over A428 to STEVINGTON
GR 9853.
Choice: either to BROMHAM *GR 0051* (MILL
MUSEUM) Cycleway on A428 from
BROMHAM bridge *GR 0150* to *GR 035501*.
South for quiet route to BEDFORD station
(Thameslink and 125 services) **or** OAKLEY
GR 0153 CLAPHAM *GR 0252* (Church Saxon
Tower) A6 (cycleway for part) to roundabout
GR 039508, quiet route south west to station.
Note 27 Churches in 58 miles.
- **RELATED ROUTES:** G1, G3, G15
- **RECONNOITRED:** RNH, May 1989

G4

- **KING'S LANGLEY to PADDINGTON
  (LITTLE VENICE)**
- **COUNTY:** HERTFORDSHIRE, LONDON
- **QUIETNESS:** ***
- **MILEAGE:** 33
- **DIRECTION:** north to south then west
  to east
- **TRAIN STATIONS and TIMETABLES:**
  KING'S LANGLEY *GR TQ0802* 66,
  PADDINGTON *GR TQ2681*
- **MAP(S):** OS 166, 176
- **WEATHER FORECAST:** 0891-500401
- **TOURIST INFORMATION OFFICE:** Canal
  Office LITTLE VENICE
- **PUBLICATIONS:** Nicholson/OS '*Guide to
  Waterways*' South 5th Edn 1991.
  Indispensable companion, generous scale
  2in to mile. All towpaths, bridge numbers,
  pubs, history and places of interest; leaflets
  BWB Canal Office Delamere Terrace,

London W2 6ND Tel: 0171-289-9897.
- **ACCOMMODATION:** Seven YHs in London
- **PLACES OF INTEREST:** See publications
- **ROUTE:** track

From KING'S LANGLEY Station north west by footpath south of Works at **GR 078019** to bridge number 159 for towpath on west side. Towpath is easy to follow all way to LITTLE VENICE (PADDINGTON): a few key points given in case you need to get back to the busy world. Soon quietly under M25. After going under A405 towpath goes to east side at bridge 163. Then bridge 164 at **GR 086989**. Ornamental stone bridge ordered by the Earl of Essex (Now OS 176 at RICKMANSWORTH **GR 0594**). After WATFORD industry **GR 0895**, it is virtually a lake district to UXBRIDGE and A4020 at bridge number 185 **GR 0584** (Pub). Soon after saying goodbye to the SLOUGH Arm, Grand Union turns east at Yiewsley (WEST DRAYTON STATION) bridge number 192 at **GR 0680**; on to BULL'S BRIDGE (BRITISH WATERWAYS YARD) Bridge number 21 at **GR 1079**. Go left (north east) on PADDINGTON ARM through SOUTHALL, HAYES, GREENFORD. (Black Horse Pub) **GR 1584**, route surprisingly quiet for west London, to LITTLE VENICE PADDINGTON near DELAMERE TERRACE **GR 258818**. End of towpath route. After 33 miles of car-free cycling you will probably push south west under A40 Motorway to PADDINGTON station. As with all canal towpaths, a permit is needed. You may find some prohibited stretches. Watch the notices and be prepared to divert.
- **RELATED ROUTES:** Canal from Little Venice to LIMEHOUSE Basin, not yet recconnoitred
- **RECONNOITRED:** Derby Day 1990, RNH

IMPORTANT NOTES: This route is only to be cycled if you have a permit to cycle on the towpath in which case you take the towpath 'as you find it'. There are a few unrideable sections and an occasional barrier to keep out motor cycles and such like.
Remember that canals are best cycled 16 March to 15 June, the close season for coarse fishing. For several miles at the London end, the towpath consists of concrete slabs covering cable ducting. Some have deteriorated — **take care**.

G5

- **Latter part of THE SWAN'S WAY to GORING, BRIDLE ROUTE, adapted for cyclists. See F8. [track]**

G6

- **NEW CYCLE CITY (MILTON KEYNES) to OLD CYCLE CITY (CAMBRIDGE)**
- **COUNTY:** BUCKINGHAMSHIRE, BEDFORDSHIRE, CAMBRIDGESHIRE
- **QUIETNESS:** **
- **MILEAGE:** 66
- **DIRECTION:** Mostly west to east
- **TRAIN STATIONS and TIMETABLES:** MILTON KEYNES **GR SP8438**, CAMBRIDGE **GR TL4657**, 25, 21, 65, 66
- **MAP(S):** OS 152, 153, 154
- **WEATHER FORECAST:** 0891-500407
- **TOURIST INFORMATION OFFICE:** MILTON KEYNES 01908-232585, BEDFORD 01234-215226, CAMBRIDGE 01223-322640
- **PUBLICATIONS:** Tourist Information and Bedfordshire County Council leaflet on Three Shires Way 1990 for circuit of Grafham Water and Cambridgeshire County Council leaflet on WIMPOLE WAY 2nd edn 1990
- **ACCOMMODATION:** YHs BRADWELL Village (MILTON KEYNES) and CAMBRIDGE and consult Tourist Information
- **PLACES OF INTEREST:** This is a tarmac route; if you fancy the Bridleway Route see G15 — The Three Shires Way
- **ROUTE:** road

(OS 152) After some time seeing New City, leave from station at **GR 8438** or YH at **GR 8339**. Keep to cycle leisure route east of railway to cross canal at bridge **GR 8241** to roundabout at **GR 822415** go north to HAVERSHAM **GR 8343**. Minor road north east over M1 go to GAYHURST. Church (beloved of Sir Hugh Casson and others) B526 and minor road TYRINGHAM **GR 8547** minor road go to FILGRAVE; minor road and A509 go to PETSOE END **GR 8949** minor road go to CLIFTON REYNES. Quiet crossing of river OUSE, LAVENDON MILL **GR 9052** B565 and minor road north east go to LAVENDON *GR 9153* A428 **(care)** minor road north east (now OS 153) HARROLD *GR 9556*. Country Park scene of opening THREE SHIRES WAY 7 October 1990 go to minor roads ODELL, SHARNBROOK *GR 9959*; to A6 at *GR 0060*. North west for less than one mile, minor road go north KNOTTING *GR 0063*, MELCHBOURNE *GR 0365*, east to SWINESHEAD *GR 0565* PERTENHALL minor road and B660 STONLEY *GR 1067* over A45 **(care)** north east to north circuit of GRAFHAM WATER bridleway route from *GR 122694* HIGH PARK FARM, well signposted and well worth any pushing needed. GRAFHAM *GR 1669*. Leave Reservoir by B661 BUCKDEN (divert to station at HUNTINGDON to north or ST NEOTS to south if you wish). Continue quiet roads OFFORDS *GR 2166*. GRAVELEY *GR 2464* YELLING *GR 2662*, crossing old A14 (now B1040) west of PAPWORTH EVERARD *GR 2863*. Minor roads ELSWORTH *GR 3163* 'POACHER' Pub (now OS 154). Minor road go to KNAPWELL *GR 3362* to A45 *. If you must have tarmac, brave A45 east for two miles to roundabout *GR 367597* minor road and A1303 AMERICAN CEMETERY *GR 4059* — a MUST if you have not seen it. South through COTON to join WIMPOLE WAY east over M11; hard surface all way to city centre.

- **RELATED ROUTES:** G15
- **RECONNOITRED:** October 1990, RNH

* **NOTE:** To avoid all A45 and enjoy quiet route cross at *GR 3359* south south west (signed 'BOURN') to pick up the only bridle-way going north east at *GR 329576* **(critical point** on join of maps) east to join WIMPOLE WAY proper at *GR 3558*; bridleway surface to join main route at COTON *GR 4058*.

G7

- **BEDFORD to MILTON KEYNES**
- **COUNTY:** BEDFORDSHIRE, BUCKINGHAMSHIRE
- **QUIETNESS:** **
- **MILEAGE:** 19
- **DIRECTION:** north east to south west
- **TRAIN STATIONS and TIMETABLES:** BEDFORD *GR TL0449*, MILTON KEYNES *GR SP8439*, 52, 53, 64, 65, 66

- **MAP(S):** OS 153, 152
- **WEATHER FORECAST:** 0891-500407
- **TOURIST INFORMATION OFFICE:** BEDFORD 01234-215226, MILTON KEYNES 01908-232525
- **PUBLICATIONS:** Get *Guide to Redways* in advance from Tourist Information (MILTON KEYNES) if possible
- **ACCOMMODATION:** BEDFORD Tourist Information list, BRADWELL Village (MILTON KEYNES) YH
- **PLACES OF INTEREST:** Too many to list. Consult Tourist Information.
- **ROUTE:** road (**Note**: the 'Redways' are a system of cycle paths in MILTON KEYNES)

Alternative starts: (1) After seeing something of BEDFORD (riverside and museums etc.) from Town bridge *GR TL050496* take signed riverside path on north side upstream west under County bridge to QUEEN'S bridge (handsome timber) *GR 039488*. (2) From BEDFORD station push south through car park of DIY store and push west along the metal footbridge over the railway by FORD END road to roundabout *GR 037493* go south by cycle path to join first route at QUEEN'S bridge. BOTH ROUTES continue on signed cycle paths all the way to SAXON CENTRE KEMPSTON (Sainsbury) *GR 027474* go to minor road at *GR 022473*, go to WOOTTON *GR 0045*. Minor road to CRANFIELD *GR 9542*, minor road south west to junction **(critical point)** *GR 946414* (now OS 152). Minor road east to MOULSOE *GR 9041*. **Care** over M1 Junction 14 *GR 8940*. At roundabout *GR 892404* footpath on left to join REDWAY (cycleway) system; go below A509 and go south west with WILLEN LAKE on right. At roundabout *GR 862388* go north west with shopping centre on left to second roundabout *GR 856404*. South west with LINFORD WOOD on right. At the roundabout after the Wood *GR 845397* follow Redway west north west to BRADWELL. YH is stone building next to Church.

- **RELATED ROUTES:** G15
- **RECONNOITRED:** 1979, CTC Bed/VB

G8

- **BEDFORD to CAMBRIDGE**
- **COUNTY:** BEDFORDSHIRE, CAMBRIDGESHIRE
- **QUIETNESS:** **
- **MILEAGE:** 32
- **DIRECTION:** west to east
- **TRAIN STATIONS and TIMETABLES:** BEDFORD *GR TL042495*, CAMBRIDGE *GR TL463573*, 52, 63, 21, 25
- **MAP(S):** OS 153, 154
- **WEATHER FORECAST:** 0891-500407/408
- **TOURIST INFORMATION OFFICE:** BEDFORD 01234-215266, CAMBRIDGE 01223-322640
- **ACCOMMODATION:** YH CAMBRIDGE, consult Tourist Information
- **ROUTE:** road

From BEDFORD station *GR TL042497* go south east to PREBEND St bridge (renamed County bridge afer rebuilding in 1992) to join Riverside Path *GR 046495*; follow north bank downstream to Town bridge *GR 051496* and cross to south bank go east to below A5140 *GR 064494* through Cinema complex to join old BEDFORD to CAMBRIDGE line all the way to WILLINGTON. *GR 113503* go south south east over A603 *GR1149* minor road and bridleway. South east to minor road at *GR 134477* go north and south east THORNCOTE GREEN and HATCH *GR 1547* go over B658 BEESTON and footbridge over A1 (while this book is being prepared for press, the A1 is being reconstructed to motorway standards) at *GR 170484* ('GREENSAND WAY') go to minor road over river at *GR 176483*. North SANDY station go to minor road *GR 178488* EVERTON *GR 2051*, minor road east to GAMBLINGAY *GR 2352*, take minor road to join B1046 *GR 2754* to LONGSTOWE crossing A1198 *GR 3155* go to south of BOURN (now OS 154), TOFT *GR 3656*, COMBERTON *GR 388504* go north to pick up WIMPOLE WAY bridleway *GR 388584* through COTON *GR 4058* over M11 and well marked route east to central Cambridge (Garret Hostel Lane). YH is near station on the other side of the city.

- **RELATED ROUTES:** G15
- **RECONNOITRED:** Summer 1991, RNH

NOTE ON PLEASURE CYCLING IN THE NEW CITY OF MILTON KEYNES

The layout of Milton Keynes New City (designated in 1967) does not lend itself easily to the framework of this book which uses OS Landranger Map (Sheet 152) and map references. The City had in 1993 no less than 120 miles of Redways (routes for pedestrians and cyclists) and approximately 60 miles of leisure routes in the city's parks system; both of these will increase as the City grows. There is a (1992) leaflet on the Redways and Leisure Routes and the 1992 Official City Atlas (Scale 1/10,000 — Six inches to the Mile) and shows the pattern of roads and cycle routes in the City. The following notes (vetted by Don Perkins, Planning Manager with the Development Corporation for the duration) may help you to enjoy this remarkable network — which is at times like cycling through National Trust gardens.

Rail Access
Milton Keynes Central Station *GR SP8438* and Wolverton Station *GR SP8241* are on the main line from Euston, and both have direct access to the Redways within a few yards of the station entrance. The best railway stations on the Bedford line for a start are Bow Brickhill *GR SP8934* with direct access to a Redway or Fenny Stratford *GR SP8734*, where you can join the canal tow path.

City's road numbering system
The numbering system used for the City's roads is easily understood ('V' stands for 'vertical' roads which run roughly North/South and 'H' stands for 'horizontal' which run roughly East/West. The old A5 (Watling Street) is now V4 and the A4146, running North/South is the V8 (Marlborough Street). The A422 Trunk Road becomes the H3 (Monks Way) and the A509 is the H4 (Dansteed Way).
The nearest roads to Milton Keynes Central Station are the H5 (Portway) and the H6 (Childs Way) which runs from just south east of station eastwards to run south of Willen Lake *GR SP 8739* the best meeting place for a cycling view of the New City. Generally all the EVEN numbered 'V' and 'H' roads have a

parallel Redway, so there should be no need to negotiate the innumerable roundabouts (which in the past few years have been helpfully named). So if a cyclist gets lost he can put his head above the parapet and check the name of the nearest roundabout.

What the New City has to offer the cyclist
Milton Keynes has everything ancient and modern including a Motte and Bailey at Bradwell; restored brick kilns at Great Linford; an Armada Beacon, a Totem Pole and other sculptures in Campbell Park; a turf and gravel maze; a Japanese Pagoda and miniature steam railway at Willen Lake with a full size Tree Cathedral nearby; a restored windmill and a canal aqueduct completed in 1991; a full scale model of the 'Bloomer' railway engine built by British Rail apprentices at the Wolverton works as well as the famous concrete cows (donated to the city by an American artist on returning home). The line of the Grand Union Canal within the City has been most attractively landscaped and a parallel bridleway plus leisure route has been developed into one of the City's most enjoyable leisure facilities. This is just a small sample of the goodies that can be found in the City with a little exploration on the cycleways. In short, you can cycle for three days in the New City without negotiating a roundabout or touching a classified road. Where else in Britain are there equal opportunities to ride in such a relaxed atmosphere? It is an ideal place for teaching youngsters to ride their cycles. Cycle hire is available at Willen Lake and at other centres within the City. Don Perkins is willing to give further advice on tailor-made tours and routes to individuals and parties: 203 Kimbolton Road, Bedford MK41 8AA (SAE please). Pleasant YH at BRADWELL GR 831395 one mile from central station.

G9

- TWO FENLAND BIRD SANCTUARIES (MANEA to DOWNHAM MARKET)
- **COUNTY:** CAMBRIDGESHIRE, NORFOLK
- **QUIETNESS:** **
- **MILEAGE:** 24 to MANEA, 33 to

DOWNHAM MARKET
- **DIRECTION:** south west to north east
- **TRAIN STATIONS and TIMETABLES:** HUNTINGDON **GR TL2371**, DOWNHAM MARKET **GR TF6003**, 25, 22
- **MAP(S):** OS 153, 142, 143
- **WEATHER FORECAST:** 0891-500408
- **TOURIST INFORMATION OFFICE:** HUNTINGDON 01480-425831, KINGS LYNN 01553-763044, Wisbech 01945-583263
- **ACCOMMODATION:** KINGS LYNN YH **GR TF6119**, and ask at Tourist Information
- **PLACES OF INTEREST:** Best in Winter. Follow the wind forecast — if unfavourable, consider MANEA station solely for visiting one or both of the reserves.
- **ROUTE:** road

HUNTINGDON STATION A141 north east (now OS 142) OLD HURST; SOMERSHAM; CHATERIS; HORSEWAY; MANEA (best kept village, Nature Reserve RSPB **GR 4787** and station); WELNEY; LADY FEN (Wildfowl Refuge of World Wide Trust **GR 5494**); TEN MILE BANK; HILGAY; FORDHAM; DENVER; DOWNHAM MARKET station. Towards end two miles on A10(T) unavoidable, otherwise very quiet Fenland roads.
- **RELATED ROUTES:** G1, G13, G15
- **RECONNOITRED:** June 1988, RNH

G10

- **CAMBRIDGE to WICKEN FEN (Nature Reserve)**
- **COUNTY:** CAMBRIDGESHIRE
- **QUIETNESS:** ***
- **MILEAGE:** CAMBRIDGE to WICKEN 16; WATERBEACH STATION to WICKEN 11; WICKEN to CAMBRIDGE via SWAFHAM PRIOR 20
- **DIRECTION:** Mainly south west to north east
- **TRAIN STATIONS and TIMETABLES:** CAMBRIDGE, WATERBEACH **GR TL5065**, 22
- **MAP:** OS 154
- **WEATHER FORECAST:** 0891-500408
- **TOURIST INFORMATION OFFICE:** CAMBRIDGE 01223-322640
- **PUBLICATIONS:** *There and back*, 12 Circular Routes

- **ACCOMMODATION:** YH at CAMBRIDGE *GR 460575*
- **PLACES OF INTEREST:** Spoilt for choice
- **ROUTE:** road and trail

CAMBRIDGE station. Make for towpath (called 'HALING WAY') on south side of river CAM at *GR 449594*. Cross to north bank at *GR 467597*; continue on Haling Way over 5 miles on firm gravel to CLAYHITHE *GR 5064*. Through WATERBEACH to minor road north north east at *GR 507657*. Take northernmost minor track south south west to Cam-side footpath at *GR 533697* for 1 mile of 'push and lift' north to farm track at *GR 536714*. DIMMOCK'S COTE. East on A1123 to WICKEN FEN *GR 563704*. 600 acre wetland reserve National Trust. Return: retrace north west on A1123 one and half miles; minor road to UPWARE *GR 5370*. 'RIVER BANK' *GR 5368*, HIGHBRIDGE farm *GR 5465*. SWAFFHAMS (PRIOR and BULBECK) B1102 STOW CUM QUY; over A45(T); minor road by BLACK House *GR 497597* to Cam-side path and through city to CAMBRIDGE station. The mileage (31) can be cut by seven if WATERBEACH station used as start, but you miss the HALING WAY of river CAM. If the 'push and lift' south of DIMMOCK'S COTE *GR 5372* is too daunting (allow one hour for it) try CAMBRIDGE to WICKEN and back by the return (east of river Cam) route (34 miles). Cambridge makes widespread provision for cyclists. Cycle hire GEOFFS next to YH at *GR 460575*.

- **RELATED ROUTES:** G15
- **RECONNOITRED:** Summer 1985, RNH

G11

- **THE NORFOLK BROADS** (ACLE to CROMER)
- **COUNTY:** NORFOLK
- **QUIETNESS:** **
- **MILEAGE:** ACLE TO GUNTON 22 miles or CROMER 28 miles
- **DIRECTION:** south east to north west
- **TRAIN STATIONS and TIMETABLES:** ACLE *GR TG3910*, GUNTON *GR TG2535*, CROMER *GR TG2141*, NORTH WALSHAM 11, 16, 17
- **MAP(S):** OS 134, 133
- **WEATHER FORECAST:** 0891-500408

- **TOURIST INFORMATION OFFICE:** RANWORTH 01603 270453 (answering machine in December 1994), CROMER 01263-512497
- **PUBLICATIONS:** Leaflets Tourist Information or County Council
- **ACCOMMODATION:** Consult Tourist Information
- **PLACES OF INTEREST:** THE BROADS
- **ROUTE:** road

From ACLE station *GR 3910*. North and north west B1140; SOUTH WALSHAM, RANWORTH BROAD *GR 359146* (Nature Trail and other interests), WOODBASTWICK, WROXHAM station, TUNSTEAD, WORSTEAD station, WITHERGATE *GR 2927*, NORTH WALSHAM station, LYNGATE. East of pond at ANTINGHAM. GUNTON station, SOUTHREPPS, NORTH REPPS, CROMER station.

- **RELATED ROUTES:** From WORSTEAD can divert to BENGATE *GR 306274* for excellent WEAVER'S WAY and extensions (56 miles in all). MOSTLY footpath and Bridleway.
- **RECONNOITRED:** November 1976, RNH

G12

- **THE PEDDARS WAY (THETFORD to KINGS LYNN)**
- **COUNTY:** NORFOLK
- **QUIETNESS:** ***
- **MILEAGE:** 31 to CASTLE ACRE, 52 Thetford to the Sea
- **DIRECTION:** south to north
- **T RAIN STATIONS and TIMETABLES:** THETFORD *GR TL8683*, KINGS LYNN *GR TF6220*, SHERINGHAM *GR TG1543*. BUS HUNSTANTON. Car parks at each end of long distance path and elsewhere. 12, 17, 18, 21, 22 (there is also a private steam railway from SHERINGHAM to HOLT, for timetable and other details phone 01263-822045. The trains take bicycles.
- **MAP(S):** OS 144, 132
- **WEATHER FORECAST:** 0891-500408
- **TOURIST INFORMATION OFFICE:** KINGS LYNN 01553-763044
- **PUBLICATIONS:** Peddars Way Association Guide and Accommodation List, indispensable companion for B and B facilities with map references

East Anglia G12/14

- **ACCOMMODATION:** See above
- **PLACES OF INTEREST:** A cycling alternative for the NORTH NORFOLK coastal Path from HOLME by the Sea to CROMER is found in Route G14
- **ROUTE:** track

Note: Very occasional pushing needed as this is basically a Long Distance Footpath, but none the less enjoyable.
From THETFORD station — overnight in B and B gives an early start. Town: pleasant pedestrian precinct. From roundabout at **GR 880828** A1066 for 3 miles **(danger)** south east to RUSHFORD **GR 9281** then east to start of PEDDARS WAY (KNETTISHALL HEATH CP). Long Distance Path goes almost due north over Little Ouse, A1066, and river THET and skirting military DANGER AREA. First diversion from the footpath is after SOUTH PICKENHAM **GR 8604** whence go through NORTH PICKENHAM **GR 8606** to avoid footpaths, resuming the Long Distance Path at **GR 863067**. CASTLE ACRE welcome accommodation at Old Red Lion **GR 818151** on the Way. Route easily followed north to HOLME NEXT THE SEA car park and other facilities **GR 6943**. For return: Bus service for HUNSTANTON (4 miles), KINGS LYNN (17 miles) SHERINGHAM (33 miles) (all these places with YH).
- **RECONNOITRED:** December 1988, RNH

G13

- **NORFOLK BYWAYS (KINGS LYNN to NORTH WALSHAM)**
- **COUNTY:** NORFOLK
- **QUIETNESS:** **
- **MILEAGE:** 60 (allow two days at least)
- **DIRECTION:** west to east
- **TRAIN STATIONS and TIMETABLES:** KING'S LYNN **GR 6220**, NORTH WALSHAM **GR TG2829**, 21, 22, 11, 17
- **MAP(S):** OS 132, 133
- **WEATHER FORECAST:** 0891-500408
- **TOURIST INFORMATION OFFICE:** KING'S LYNN 01553-763044, NORWICH 01603-666071 (Evenings: 761082)
- **PUBLICATIONS:** Leaflets WEAVERS WAY (BLICKLING to end) Tourist Information and County Council: wealth of cycle routes from County Council

- **ACCOMMODATION:** YH at KING'S LYNN **GR TF6119**
- **PLACES OF INTEREST:** CASTLE RISING (English Heritage): SANDRINGHAM, BLICKLING HALL (National Trust), MANNINGTON HALL (roses): ask Tourist Information
- **ROUTE:** road

KING'S LYNN. Stay overnight for early start (YH and good range of B and B from Tourist Information). Town roads to SOUTH WOOTTON **GR 6422** then minor road to NORTH WOOTTON. East to CASTLE RISING **GR 666246** (English Heritage): over river BABINGLEY to A149 **(danger)**. North east minor road to SANDRINGHAM **GR 6928** DODDSHILL. North east to SHERNBORNE **GR 7132**, FRING, DOCKING, BURNHAM MARKET **GR 8342**; east to HOLKHAM PARK (cycling allowed on all 'hard roads'); enter by north gates **GR 892436** or side gate **GR 868433**; leave by south gate or Golden Gates (east) and east to WIGHTON **GR 9439**. BINHAM GR 9839; (Now OS 133) FIELD DALLING; SAXLINGHAM **GR 0239**; LETHERINGSETT (good B and B GLAVENSIDE **GR 063387**). Go south keeping east of THORNAGE and south east to HUNWORTH. Continue south east by minor roads to LITTLE BARNINGHAM **GR 136334**, where go south west and east to MANNINGTON HALL (famous rose garden, walks and Tourist Information). Then south to ITTERINGHAM to start of WEAVERS WAY at BLICKLING PARK **GR 162297**; past Hall (National Trust) along B1354 for half a mile to pick up WEAVERS WAY at bridge over railway **GR 186276**; then reasonably plain cycling to NORTH WALSHAM station.
- **RECONNOITRED:** November 1988, RNH

G14

- **KINGS LYNN to SHERINGHAM and CROMER**
- **COUNTY:** NORFOLK
- **QUIETNESS:** **
- **MILEAGE:** 60 to SHERINGHAM, 65 to CROMER
- **DIRECTION:** south west to north east
- **TRAIN STATIONS and TIMETABLES:**

KING'S LYNN **GR 624201**, SHERINGHAM **GR 157431**, CROMER **GR 214432**, 22, 17
- **MAP(S):** OS 132, 133
- **WEATHER FORECAST:** 0891-500408
- **TOURIST INFORMATION OFFICE:** KING'S LYNN 01553-763044, HUNSTANTON 0485-532610. Others (during holiday season only) at SHERINGHAM and CROMER.
- **PUBLICATIONS:** HMSO *Peddar's Way*; Holiday Guides from CROMER AND SHERINGHAM
- **ACCOMMODATION:** YHs at KING'S LYNN, HUNSTANTON and SHERINGHAM. Many other B and B, caravans and camp sites in this holiday area, especially during summer season.
- **PLACES OF INTEREST:** A route through the justly renowned holiday areas of north Norfolk
- **ROUTE:** road

From KING'S LYNN station, north by A1078 to road junction **GR 643224**. Minor road to NORTH WOOTTON, **GR 6424**. Minor road to CASTLE RISING **GR 6624** (tea at Post Office in summer and good pub). Join A149 at **GR 673246** and north for 500 metres. North east by B1439 WEST NEWTON **GR 6927** (Sandringham Royal Estate and House). Minor road to ANMER, **GR 7429**. Minor road to SHERNBOURNE, **GR 7132**. Minor road INMER Farm, **GR 7034** north to SEDGEFORD **GR 7036** minor road RINGSTEAD 'Gintrap' pub. Camping Barn to east at Courtyard Farm **GR 7240**. YH via track over RINGSTEAD DOWNS to HUNSTANTON). From RINGSTEAD east via CHOSELEY FARM on minor road all the way to BURNHAM MARKET, **GR 8342** ('Humble Pie' shop). North by minor road to BURNHAM OVERY STAITH, **GR 8444**. Either (1) A149 **(busy)** to north entrance of HOLKHAM PARK, **GR 891440** and due south through Park. Or (2) for quieter route, return to BURNHAM OVERY TOWN, then east on B1155 to west gate of HOLKHAM PARK at **GR 8643** (gate open weekdays 9-6) to join north to south Drive through magnificent Park to south gate, passing Triumphal Arch. East at **GR 883391**, minor road Crabbe Castle Farm, **GR 9039**. North on B1105 near WIGHTON, **GR 9340** via byway at **GR 933423**

to A149. East on A149 (a little over half a mile). At **GR 944427** north by bridleway to join north NORFOLK COASTAL LONG DISTANCE PATH at WARHAM GREENS, **GR 943438**. East along Coastal Path, because of wetness may need to leave at **GR 973440**, south to STIFFKEY, **GR 9743** (`Red Lion' pub). A little under two miles on A149 (now OS 134) east to MORSTON, **GR 0043**. Rejoin Long Distance Path to BLAKENEY, **GR 0243**. Either (1) A149 coast road to SHERINGHAM (two adjoining stations). Or (2) Quieter inland route, all on minor roads. GLAVEN; minor road over SALTHOUSE HEATH to cross A148 at **GR 101398**. Minor road to GRESHAM, **GR 1638**. Minor road to SUSTEAD, **GR 1937**. Minor road to METTON, **GR 2037** to join minor road WEAVERS WAY to CROMER station.
- **RELATED ROUTES:** G11, G12, G13
- **RECONNOITRED:** 1990, JH, MBC

G15

- **OLD CITY (CAMBRIDGE) and NEW CITY (MILTON KEYNES)**
- **COUNTY:** CAMBRIDGESHIRE, BEDFORDSHIRE, BUCKINGHAMSHIRE
- **QUIETNESS:** ***
- **MILEAGE:** 72 (two or more days)
- **DIRECTION:** Mainly east to west (an exception to usual directions - don't forget to ask for forecast!)
- **TRAIN STATIONS and TIMETABLES:** CAMBRIDGE **GR TL4657**, MILTON KEYNES **GR SP8438**, 21, 65, 66
- **MAP(S):** OS 154, 153, 152
- **WEATHER FORECAST:** 0891-500408
- **TOURIST INFORMATION OFFICE:** CAMBRIDGE 01223-322640, BEDFORD 01234-215226, MILTON KEYNES 01908-691995
- **PUBLICATIONS:** Tourist Information and CAMBRIDGESHIRE County Council leaflet on Wimpole Way (2nd edn 1990) and BEDFORSHIRE County Council Three Shires Way (1990) (the latter is a must)
- **ACCOMMODATION:** YHs at CAMBRIDGE (near station) and MILTON KEYNES. Accommodation list from Tourist Information.
- **PLACES OF INTEREST:** See items in text.

This is primarily a bridleway (rough stuff), enjoyable **only** when dry underfoot. See route G6 for tarmac alternative. The Wimpole Way opened in 1988. The Three Shires Way opened 7 October 1990.
• **ROUTE:** track

Part 1: Cambridge to Grafham Water, OS 154
From CAMBRIDGE station the spectacular CARTER cycle bridge near station starts Cycleway north west to city centre. Then due west by GARRET HOSTEL LANE over river CAM and 'THE BACKS' (Queens Road A1134) Cycle Traffic lights **GR 444585**, then due west to well signposted WIMPOLE WAY; over M11 at **GR 420588**; through COTON **GR 4058** west (south of HARDWICK **GR 3758**) south of HIGHFIELD (briefly OS 153) to minor road at **GR 326571** north of BOURN **GR 3257**. North north east to cross A45 to KNAPWELL (now OS 153). Minor road to ELSWORTH (at 'The POACHER' pub **GR 317636**). Minor road west north west to B1040. South east over old A14 to road junction **GR 276623**. East on minor road to YELLING **GR 2662** north at crossroad **GR 2462** go to GRAVELEY **GR 2464** minor road to OFFORDS to cross river OUSE at **GR 2167**. Cycle pavement (official) to BUCKDEN **GR 1967**; ramped subway under A1 to B651 to GRAFHAM WATER and start of THREE SHIRES WAY to TATHALL END near HANSLOPE in BUCKINGHAMSHIRE. For later use there is a further 12 mile bridleway circling the reservoir at SHOOTERS HOLLOW **GR 177672**; on all visits find time to cycle the track alongside the reservoir retaining wall. From SHOOTERS HOLLOW, minor road go north west to GRAFHAM **GR 1669**. (B and B, 2 Breach Road).

Part 2: Grafham to Milton Keynes, OS 153
North on minor road, then west at **GR 160697** to take bridleway north west at **GR 145696**, north west of old railway bridge. Under pylons to minor road and through EASTON **GR 1471**. West north west SPALDWICK **GR 1272** west and south west past MOLLY ROSE Lodge (B and B and horses) at **GR 093717**. B660 west at TILBROOK GRANGE **GR 0871**; minor road south of COVINGTON **GR 0570** from A45 crossing bridleway on bare earth to minor road go to SHELTON **GR 0368**. South west YIELDEN **GR 0167**; due south first made up, then earth, to minor road KNOTTING

GR 0063; then generally bridleway west to cross A6 **(care)** at **GR 985629** and SHARNBROOK SUMMIT bridge on FORTY FOOT LANE (woods and SANTA POD DRAG RACING TRACK; a saving grace is a water tap at **GR 959611** in a very dry region). Pleasant Picnic Area at minor road **GR 603597** (now OS 152). South west (Boundary BEDFORDSHIRE and NORTHANTS) to NUNWOOD and THREE SHIRES WOOD **GR 9156** where BUCKINGHAMSHIRE comes in; cross A428 **(care)** at **GR 906544**. South through LAVENDON GRANGE **GR 9053** over B565 to quiet crossing of river OUSE at **GR 9052** (last met at OFFORD CLUNY **GR 2167**). CLIFTON REYNES **GR 9051** south west to PETSOE END **GR 8949** over A509 west and south (several gates). RECTORY Farm **GR 8848** go west to FILGRAVE **GR 8748**. Minor road go to TYRINGHAM and over river OUSE again **GR 8546**. North west on B526 then go south south west, east of GAYHURST Church (beloved of Sir Hugh Casson and others). Choice A: THREE SHIRES WAY proper signposted generally west to cross below M1 at **GR 839459** Dairy Farm and grass track north west to TATHALL END **GR 821467** here meet SWANS WAY 65 mile bridleway. Route from NORTHAMPTON to GORING and STREATLEY ON THAMES — route F8. Choice B: Cyclists may prefer to cross M1 at **GR 848451** for HAVERSHAM **GR 8243**. Both routes meet at road junction below H of HAVERSHAM on map **GR 822430** go south to double roundabout near WOLVERTON station at **GR 823415** and pick route to bridge over canal at **GR 829410** (west of WINDMILL on south); then MILTON KEYNES leisure cycle route past 'concrete cows' under A422 to MILTON KEYNES's hospitable YH at BRADWELL **GR 832395**.
• **RECONNOITRED:** 13 and 14 October 1990 (on mountain bike during fine dry spell), RNH

G16

• **LONDON (KING'S CROSS) to CAMBRIDGE via EPPING FOREST**
• **COUNTY:** LONDON, ESSEX, CAMBRIDGESHIRE

- **QUIETNESS:** **
- **MILEAGE:** 66. Add 5 for EPPING FOREST YH.
- **DIRECTION:** south west to north east
- **TRAIN STATIONS AND TIMETABLES:** LONDON KING'S CROSS, CAMBRIDGE
- **MAP(S):** OS 154, 177, 166, 167
- **WEATHER FORECAST:** 0891-500407
- **TOURIST INFORMATION OFFICE:** LONDON, VICTORIA 0171-730 3488, REGENTS STREET, CAMBRIDGE 01223-322640
- **PUBLICATIONS:** British Waterways Board leaflets re REGENTS CANAL, OS/Nicholson *Guide to Waterways* (South), 5th Edn 1991
- **ACCOMMODATION:** Seven YHs LONDON, also EPPING FOREST, CAMBRIDGE
- **PLACES OF INTEREST:** LONDON and CAMBRIDGE speak for themselves. The middle part of the route coincides with excellent annual Charity Ride Granada Wheel Appeal for World Wide Fund for Nature. Permit needed for cycling the canal towpath.
- **ROUTE:** road

Part 1: London (King's Cross) to Epping Forest YH, OS 177 (21 miles — mostly canal towpath)

From KING'S CROSS station *GR TQ3083* north to bridge over Regents Canal at *GR 303835* follow north side of canal east to start of ISLINGTON tunnel; keep going east to MAYGOOD Street and cross LIVERPOOL Road and ISLINGTON High Street to DUNCAN Street, the canal towpath resumes all the way to junction with HERTFORD UNION BRANCH (DUCKETTS) at *GR 357833* (two sides of VICTORIA PARK) go north east under A102(M) to join LEE NAVIGATION. Fine wide towpath with good barriers for cycle access, go north — all locks are clearly named. Towpath changes from west to east side at STONEBRIDGE LOCK *GR 356905*. Go a little over six miles from junction with HERTFORD CUT to PICKETTS LOCK *GR 363937*. The vast reservoirs on the Ordnance Survey map are not visible from towpath owing to high grassed embankments (sheep grazing in season) leave towpath at Ely Road A110 south of King George's reservoir to CHINGFORD, go north on A112 at *GR 376948*. Diversion for EPPING FOREST YH follows, recommended: leave A112 at *GR 37795*. YARDLEY LANE past school entrance to Forest. Bridleway, WOODMANS RIDE, east crosses minor road at SEWARDSONE BURY, north east by bridleway and cross minor road at *GR 401967*, go past Field Study Centre and north east to KING'S OAK pub at *GR 4198*. Helpful Conservation Centre nearby (full range of maps and other guides). YH lies to the north west at *GR 407984*.

Part 2: Epping Forest to Cambridge (45 miles, all minor roads)

To resume route, go generally north north west to road junction at *GR 386990* to regain A112 north over M25 (now OS 166). Cross A121 WALTHAM ABBEY at *GR 3800*, go north on B194 LOWER NAZEING (now OS 167), north on minor road signed to ROYDON *GR 4110*, north west to STANSTEAD ABBOTS *GR 3911* (briefly on OS 166 again) then go north west on B180 to HUNSDONBURY back on OS 167 to HUNSDON *GR 4114* then to WIDFORD, HADHAMS MUCH and LITTLE, crossing A1250 at *GR 4422*, north by minor road to CLAPGATE *GR 4425* and north north east to STOCKING PELHAM *GR 454292*. Go to BERDEN *GR 4629* then east and north to CLAVERING *GR 4732* crossing B1038 go north west by minor road between Windmills to ROAST GREEN *GR 4632*, go to FURTHER FORD END (now OS 154). LOWER GREEN *GR 4334*, LITTLE CHISHILL to SHAFTENHOE END *GR 4038* and north east over B1039 to GREAT CHISHILL. At *GR 424390* go north west to join B1368, and north east over A505 to FOWLMERE *GR 4245*, Nature Reserve, and north west to FOXTOW *GR 4148* then to BARRINGTON *GR 3949* and north north east to HASLINGFIELD *GR 4052*: **Either** leave by minor road north to A603 at BARTON *GR 4055* and then CAMBRIDGE **or** *GR 4153* to bridleway over M11 at *GR 424550* into GRANTCHESTER *GR 4355*; then minor road at NEWNHAM and CAMBRIDGE or walk on footpath on west of river CAM to CAMBRIDGE YH station: good signed cycle routes to City Centre and King's College Chapel.

- **RECONNOITRED:** July 1991, RNH

G17

- **ICKNIELD WAY CYCLE ROUTE**
- **COUNTIES:** BUCKINGHAMSHIRE, BEDFORDSHIRE, HERTFORDSHIRE, ESSEX, CAMBRIDGESHIRE, SUFFOLK, NORFOLK
- **QUIETNESS:** ** and *** mostly minor roads
- **MILEAGE:** 110 approx
- **TRAIN STATIONS AND TIMETABLES:** Tring (OS 165, *GR SP9512*) 66, Cheddington (OS 165, *GR SP9218*) 66, Leagrave (OS 166, *GR TL0624*) 52, Hitchen (OS 166, *GR SP9512*) 24, Letchworth (OS 166, *GR TL2132*) 25, Ashwell (OS 153, *GR TL2938*) 25, Great Chesterford (OS 154, *GR TL5042*) 21, Newmarket (OS 154, *GR TL6462*) 15, Thetford (OS 144, *GR TL8683*) 18, Harling Road (OS144, *GR TL9787*) 18
- **MAP(S):** OS 165(1991), 166(1990), 153(1992), 154(1991), 155(1991), 144(1990)
- **WEATHER FORECAST:** 0891-500 4 06 (West), 07 (Mid), 08 (East)
- **TOURIST INFORMATION OFFICES:** (selected) Dunstable 01582 471012, Luton 01582-401579, Hitchin 01462 434738, Cambridge 01223 322640
- **PUBLICATIONS:** Elizabeth Barrett, *The Icknield Way Path, A Guide for Horse riders, Cyclists and Others.* Wimpole Books, Pips Peace, Kenton, Stowmarket, £4.00 inc P&P. Tel: 01728 860429. Leaflets from Tourist Information Offices.
- **ACCOMMODATION:** Only YH on route is Ivinghoe at start. YHs near route: Saffron Walden (4 miles, Cambridge (13 miles) and Brandon (9 miles).
- **PLACES OF INTEREST:** Consult Tourist Information and Publications
- **ROUTE:** Icknield Way Route. Ivinghoe/Tring to Harling Road near Thetford. Road and trail.

Part 1: Ivinghoe/Tring to Letchworth, OS 165, 166 (26 miles)

Ivinghoe YH OS 165 *GR SP944162* is three miles from Tring station and two miles from Cheddington station. Leave Ivinghoe north east for Beacon GR 9617 — start of Ridgeway National Trail.

Choice (A): Bridleway route — Crabtree Cottage *GR 9517* crossing minor road and A4166 Edlesborough to road junction *GR 977191* **(critical point)**.

Choice (B): Tarmac — leave Ivinghoe north east by B489 to north west on A4146 briefly to road junction *GR 9718* to minor road north east to join Choice (A).

COMBINED ROUTE: To north east minor road crossing river Ouze *GR 9819* north east Dolittle Mill and Wellhead to north west Church End *GR 992214* **(critical point)** to Byway north east (now OS 166) Beecroft (Dunstable) *GR TL0022* to minor road north east crossing A5 **(care)** to north east A5120 crossroads Houghton Regis *GR 017238* **(critical point)**, to minor north east crossing M1 and railway to Lower Sundon *GR 0527* to north east Streatley *GR 0728* to minor road south east crossing A6 at *GR 076279* **(critical point)**, to bridleway east *GR 094280* to south east to Icknield Way Galley Hill to north east to minor road to Telegraph Hill *GR 1128* to north east crossing B655 (stagger) to north east Pirton *GR 1431* to east and south east to join Way *GR 170308* **(critical point)** to north east crossing A600 Ickleford *GR 1831* to north east minor road over river Hiz Cadwell *GR 1832* to north and east minor road Letchworth to south east (station) *GR 2132*. The World's First Garden City. Vision of Ebenezer Howard led to Britain's new and expanded towns after the war of 1939-1945.

Part 2: Letchworth to Great Chesterford near Saffron Walden, OS 166, 153, 154 (24 miles)

Leave Letchworth south of railway by minor road and footbridge over A1(M) *GR 2333* (now OS 153) to Baldock station *GR 2434* to north east minor road Bygrave *GR 2635* to Ashwell *GR 2639* (attractive village, museum, source of river Cam) to north east Icknield Way Path all way south of Litlington *GR 3142* (now OS 154) to east north east over A1198 (old A14) Harcamlow Way under railway to A10 north east briefly Melbourn *GR 3844*, leave by minor road south east over A505 and new path to Icknield Way Path *GR 4041* to east north east Icknield Way Path to road junction south of Ickleton Granges *GR 460416*, critical point, to north east minor road over M11 to Ickleton *GR 4943* to south east Great Chesterford *GR 5042*, (station); Saffron Walden YH lies three miles to south east on B184.

Part 3: Great Chesterford to Newmarket, OS 154 (24 miles)

Leave Great Chesterford by minor road north east over B184 to minor road north east Grave Hall Farm muddy stretch *GR 5344* to north east crossing A604 Linton *GR 5646* (shop etc.) to north east by B1052 over Roman road 'Via Devana' (divert here for Cambridge YH 13 miles via Gog Magog Hills *GR 4954*) to B1052 Balsham official route from west end of village by tracks and bridleway to north east Green End Farm *GR 5953* to north east by tracks and minor road departing from official route to Underwood Hall *GR 6157* crossing B1061 at *GR 628587*.

[Choice: If not visiting or staying at Newmarket, quiet route continues north east by minor roads to Cheveley *GR 6861* — good pub — to east crossroads *GR 6560* (critical point), to north west by Hadrian Stud *GR 6561* to north west crossing railway to B1061 Newmarket famous as a centre of race horse breeding and training. Racehorse museum. N.B. Cycling is **NOT** permitted on the numerous 'Horse Walks'.

Part 4: Newmarket to East Harling near Thetford, OS 154 (155) 144 (36 miles)

Leave Newmarket by B1063 south east to minor road *GR 654629* (critical point), to minor road south east past Dunchurch Lodge Stud to Cheveley Park *GR 6760* to Cheveley to north to B1063 to east Ashley *GR 6961* to north east over B1085 to north east Gazeley (official route goes via Moulton *GR 6964*) to north Needham Street *GR 7265* to minor road under old A45 now A14 and railway Slade Bottom *GR 7267* to north Herringswell *GR 7169* to north east minor road (now OS 155 — a little less than four miles) to Tuddenham *GR 7371* to north east minor road over river Lark to Icklingham *GR 7773* (now OS 144 — two and a half mile overlap). Leave Icklingham by Icknield Way track *GR 774727* (critical point), north east Shravedell Heath *GR 7977* (critical point), to east over B1106 [nearest point to Brandon YH *GR TL786864* — 9 miles] to east 'Duke's Ride' Barrow Clump Buildings *GR 8377* to south east new path to Four Corners *GR 8376* to north east and south east New Zealand cottages *GR 8576* crossing A134 (stagger) D House to north east Icknield Way Path to A1088 Euston *GR 8979* to north west leave A1088 by minor road *GR 896794* (critical point), for one mile only to south east

and east by Trig Point *GR 9279* over minor road to north east Icknield Way Path now Peddars Way to minor road to east Hall Farm *GR 9680* to north over river Little Ouse to north past Riddlesworth Hall school *GR 9681* crossing A1066 to north north east and north north west through forest crossing river Thet *GR 9585* to minor road north east Bridgham *GR 9586* to minor road north west Church *GR 9587* to east Harling Road station *GR 9787* and end of route.

• **RECONNOITRED:** 1994, part BMS party, part RNH

G18

• **LONDON to YORK**
This route is included by kind permission of the Cyclist's Touring Club.
Note: The CTC's 50th York Rally took place at KNAVESMIRE racecourse in June 1994 with a record attendance of 43,000. The CTC organized a ride from LONDON as a strenuous two day event starting at BOREHAMWOOD, with an overnight stop in the attractive village of COLSTERWORTH at the Travel Lodge, OS 130 *GR SK9324* (Lincs). The route which follows here is modified to start in central LONDON, is in easier stages, and uses youth hostels where available, starting with the attractive pair 'Ham' and 'High' in north LONDON. This route also diverts to call on the CTC's Bidlake Memorial Garden on the old Great North Road near SANDY, OS 153 *GR 164487* to recall that once the bicycle was the fastest carriage on that road.

• **COUNTIES:** LONDON BOROUGHS, HERTFORDSHIRE, BEDFORDSHIRE, CAMBRIDGESHIRE, LINCOLNSHIRE, NOTTINGHAMSHIRE, SOUTH YORKSHIRE, NORTH YORKSHIRE.

• **QUIETNESS:** ** mainly minor roads, all tarmac

• **MILEAGE:** 250 approximately. See under stages for variations.

• **DIRECTION:** south to north

• **TRAIN STATION AND TIMETABLES:** (selection) LONDON KING'S CROSS (OS 176, *GR TQ3083*), ST ALBANS (OS 166, *GR TQ1507*), STAMFORD (OS 141, *GR TF0206*), LINCOLN (OS 121, *GR SK9770*),

SELBY (OS 105, **GR SE6132**), YORK (OS 105, **GR SE5951**), 26, 52, 53.
- **MAP(S):** OS 176 (1990), 166 (1990), 153 (1992), 142 (1991), [141], 130 (1990), [121 (1992)], 120 (1992), 112 (1992), [111 (1988)], 105 (1990). If staying in LONDON the A-Z is good value from £3.00. Ideal is `On Your Bike' Map of London Cycling Campaign £4.50 post free from LCC, 3 Stamford Street, London SE1 9NT, Tel: 0171-928 7220.
- **WEATHER FORECAST:** 0891-500-4, Bedfordshire/Hertfordshire 07, Lincolnshire 13, Yorkshire 17
- **TOURIST INFORMATION OFFICES:** (selection) ST ALBANS 01727-865411, BEDFORD 01234-215226, LINCOLN 01522-512971, SELBY 01757-703263, YORK 01904-621756
- **PUBLICATIONS:** Consult Tourist Information
- **ACCOMMODATION:** Youth hostels at LONDON, THURLBY, LINCOLN, YORK. Elsewhere contact Tourist Information.
- **PLACES OF INTEREST/COMMENTS:** Iveagh Bequest Kenwood House, Hampstead Heath (Adams House, Rembrandt, peaceful grounds, free — OS 176 **GR 273976**). Shuttleworth Collection (old aeroplanes). STAMFORD fine town in stone, LINCOLN Cathedral and cycle museum (see text).
- **ROUTE:**

Part 1: London (King's Cross) to St Albans via youth hostels at Ham and High, OS 176, 166 (29 miles)
From central LONDON (King's Cross) to youth hostels at HAMPSTEAD and HIGHGATE (Ham and High).
From King's Cross station OS 176 **GR TQ3083** first right and south west on footway (Euston Road — A501) past St Pancras station and British Library site. Right, north, at Ossulton Street **GR 300827**, official cycle route to KENTISH TOWN (A400) via Purchese Street. Go straight on at Goldington Street and Crescent and straight on at College Place in Kentish Town Road A400. Go left, north west, at Kelly Street **GR 288846 (critical point)**, right, north east, at Grafton Road and straight on at Gospel Oak station **GR 2885**. Left at Savernake Road to footbridge with ramp over railway at **GR 277857 (critical point)** into

Parliament Hill (Hampstead Heath). **DAYLIGHT ONLY.**
Choice A: For HAMPSTEAD YH go left, north west, on tarmac track across Heath to official cycle route **GR 274862** then by track east north east over Heath and straight on across track (memorial stone to 1987 gale) to Spaniards Road B519 **GR 165876 (critical point)**. Right on B519 footway to pedestrian crossing, MOUNT TYNDAL **GR 266871 (critical point)** crossing B519 push briefly on footpath (some rustic wooden steps) down to Wildwood Road **GR 263872 (critical point)**. Left on Hampstead Way then right on Wellgarth Road and youth hostel at **GR 258873**.
Choice B: To HIGHGATE youth hostel. From footbridge into Parliament Hill **GR 277857**, go north east on cycle route, Highgate Road **GR 283862, (critical point)**. Go north north east to Millfield Lane **GR 283865**, divert right at Merton Lane **GR 278867** and left to youth hostel **GR 281877**.
Resuming the Route: Choice A: From HAMPSTEAD youth hostel retrace to Wildwood Road, leave by Kingsley Way **GR 263883 (critical point)** (north west of Hampstead golf course).
Choice B: From HIGHGATE YH retrace to Millfield Lane **GR 283865**, go right, B519, Hampstead Lane and left near Spaniards Inn. Go right to Winnington Road **GR 266875** to Holne Chase and right to Kingsley Way **GR 263885**. Both routes — From Kingsley Way to straight on crossing A1 **(care)** then straight on to Ossulton Way to A504. Left **(care)** over new crossing of A406 (North Circular Road), right at Rosemary Avenue **GR 257900** to Station Road and straight on crossing A598 **(care)**, FINCHLEY central station **GR 2590**. Straight on at Dollis Park and left at Lyndhurst Gardens to reach Dollis Road (via the fenced footpath in playing field) **GR 244909 (critical point)**. Go to Holders Hill Circus **GR 244912** then minor road west north west to Devonshire Road and north west to Sanders Lane. North north west to Milespit Hill then the B552 (The Ridgeway) **GR 228926**. Go north west to Highwood Hill **GR 2193** and north east on A5109 and rejoin B552 then go north west, now OS 166, three and three quarter mile overlap, to BARNET GATE **GR 2195**. North east on A411 on minor road north to ROWLEY GREEN **GR 2196** go over A1 to minor road east of BOREHAMWOOD

GR 2097 to road junction Well End *GR 205985* **(critical point)**. North east and north to RIDGE *GR 2100*, go over M25 SOUTH MIMMS *GR 2201* to minor road on east of A1(M) WATER END *GR 2304*. West over A1(M) by minor road to COLNEY HEATH *GR 2006*, footbridge over A414. Minor roads to ST ALBANS *GR 1507* (Abbey, Roman remains etc.)

Part 2: St Albans to Kimbolton, OS 166, 153 (56 miles)

Leave ST ALBANS on B651 to north east to SANDRIDGE *GR 1710*. North east B851 through WHEATHAMPSTEAD *GR 1714*, KIMPTON *GR 1718* and WHITWELL *GR 184212* **(critical point)** then north west on minor road (LILLEY BOTTOM) crossing A505 to LILLEY *GR 1126*. Minor road (winding) to HEXTON *GR 1030* and north on minor road to HIGHAM GOBION *GR 1032*. North east to SHILLINGTON *GR 1234*, now OS 153, go north east to MEPPERSHALL *GR 1336* over A507 to SHEFFORD *GR 1439*. North west on B658 road junction *GR 135398* **(critical point)**, go north to IRELAND *GR 1311* then north to OLD WARDEN *GR 1343*. Aeroplane museum and Swiss garden (well worth a visit). Minor road north east ICKWELL to NORTHILL to HATCH *GR 1547*. Here divert on B658 briefly to CTC Bidlake Memorial near SANDY *GR 164487*. Then A603 **(care)** briefly to road junction *GR 150490* **(critical point)**. Go north to BLUNHAM *GR 1551* then west over river Ouse, GREAT BARFORD *GR 1352* crossing A428 to minor road north west and north to COLMWORTH *GR 1058*, to LITTLE STAUGHTON to road junction *GR 103633* **(critical point)** easily missed. West and north (if you go east, GRAFHAM WATER beckons — ideal cycle circuit for children), go to minor road to join B660 near PERTENHALL *GR 0865* and north east to join A45 **(care)** then west to KIMBOLTON *GR 0967*.

Part 3: Kimbolton to Colsterworth (or Thurlby YH), OS 153, 142, 141, 130 (53 miles to Colsterworth, 47 miles to Thurlby)

From KIMBOLTON *GR 0967*, leave north west on A45 to B660 at *GR 0968*. North to CATWORTH *GR 0873*, go north, now OS 142, crossing A14 (old A604) at BRINGTON *GR 0875*. North and north east to OLD WESTON *GR 1077* and B660 to WINWICK *GR 1080* to GREAT GIDDING *GR 1283*. Minor road (not B660) to Cow Pasture Farm

GR 1384 and north west over B660 minor road to LUTTON *GR 1187*. North east and north to crossroads *GR 115926* **(critical point)** and minor road north west to ELTON *GR 0893* village. Minor road crossing river Nene *GR 0894*, go north west and north to YARWELL *GR 0697* to WANSFORD *GR 0799*. Minor road at *GR 090996* **(critical point)** and minor road to SOUTHORPE *GR 0803* then north to BARNACK *GR 0704*. North west B1443 to PILSGATE *GR 0605*, go north west, now OS 141, to STAMFORD *GR 0307* (location for BBC TV's 'Middlemarch' 1994). Leave town by minor road near cemetery *GR 023075* **(critical point)**. North to LITTLE CASTERTON *GR 0109*, now OS 130, crossing river Gwash *GR 0210* go north east to join B1176 north of RYHALL *GR 0310*.

Here Choice A: To COLSTERWORTH for Travel Lodge or bed and breakfast. North on B1176 to crossroads *GR 0213* **(critical point)** then north west by minor road to CASTLE BYTHAM *GR 9818*. West north west hugging old railway then crossing A1 to SOUTH WITHAM *GR 9219*. North to NORTH WITHAM to COLSTERWORTH *GR 9324*.

Choice B: To THURLBY YH. From RYHALL *GR 0310* road junction south of river *GR 034100* **(critical point)**. Minor road east north east crossing railway at GREATFORD *GR 0811* go generally north to BRACEBROUGH *GR 0813* to WILSTHORPE *GR 0913* to OBTHORPE, to THURLBY YH, OS 130, *GR 097168*. To rejoin main route, leave THURLBY on minor road west to MANTHORPE *GR 0716* to WITHAM ON THE HILL *GR 0516*. North west to LITTLE BYTHAM, *GR 0017*, go west to CASTLE BYTHAM *GR 9818* (main route), then as Choice A above to COLSTERWORTH *GR 9324*.

Part 4: Colsterworth to Newark (with alternative Lincoln YH), OS 130, 121 (Newark 35 miles, Lincoln 58 miles)

Choice A: To NEWARK. Leave COLSTEWORTH *GR SK9324* west on B676 STAINBY *GR 9122* to BUCKMINSTER *GR 8722*. Go north west to SPROXTON *GR 8524*, to SALTBY to CROXTON KERRIAL *GR 8329*. North west to KNIPTON *GR 8231*, north to BELVOIR (castle), road junction *GR 817337* **(critical point)** then north west and north over GRANTHAM canal to BOTTESFORD *GR 8039*. North north west over A1 to road junction north of LONG BENNINGTON

East Anglia G18

GR 834454 **(critical point)**, over river Witham and wind round to DRY DODDINGTON *GR 8546* to CLAYPOLE *GR 8448* then on minor road west and north west to BALDERFIELD to join A6065 *GR 825496*, now OS 121, to NEWARK *GR 8053*.

Choice B: Continuing on minor roads to LINCOLN from NEWARK, make for THE HOLLIES *GR 8252*, go east crossing A1 then minor road north to CODDINGTON *GR 8354*, to STAPLEFORD *GR 8757*, to BASSINGHAM *GR 9159*. Go north east over river Witham to HADDINGTON *GR 9163* then south and north to HYKEHAM *GR 9465*, to LINCOLN *GR 9771* (castle and cycle museum). YH on south east outskirts of city *GR 980700*. From LINCOLN to rejoin main route at CLAYWORTH, OS 120, *GR SK7288*, leave LINCOLN, OS 121, south west area of BOULTHAM *GR 9669*. Minor road north west over A1180 and railway to SKELLINGTHORPE *GR 9271*, north west to SAXILBY *GR 8975* then south south west to BROADHOLME *GR 8974*. South west over B1190 to THORNEY *GR 8572* to join A57 **(care)**, go west just over two miles crossing river to DUNHAM ON TRENT *GR 8174*. West and north to LANEHAM *GR 8076* to RAMPTON *GR 7978* to TRESWELL *GR 7879*. North to WORTH LEVERTON to STURTON LE STEEPLE *GR 7984* and north west, now OS 120, just over a mile overlap. North west crossing railway to NORTH WHEATLEY *GR 7585* then north west to CLAYWORTH *GR 7288* (main route).

Part 5: Newark to Thorne, OS 121, 120, 112, (111) (Newark to Thorne 58 miles, Lincoln to Thorne 39 miles)

Leave NEWARK, OS 121 *GR 8053* north west crossing river Trent *GR 7954*. Go north north west by Great North Road to SOUTH MUSKHAM, road junction *GR 790574* **(critical point)** then minor roads to BATHLEY *GR 7759* to NORWELL *GR 7761*. North east to CARLTON ON TRENT *GR 7964* over A1 then north and north west B1164 to SUTTON ON TRENT to WESTON *GR 7767* and north west to CLAYWORTH *GR 7288* (main route).

Part 6: Thorne to York via Selby, OS (111), 105 (38 miles)

Leave THORNE by minor road north to MOORENDS *GR 6915*. Road junction at Greenland farm *GR 6919* **(critical point)**, go west north west over M18, now OS 105, to A614 and north over M62 to EAST COWICK

to SNAITH *GR 6422*. North A1041 to CARLTON *GR 6424* to CAMBLESFORTH *GR 6426* to SELBY *GR 6132*. Leave by B1223 north west to WISTOW *GR 5935* to CAWOOD *GR 5737* crossing river Ouse B1222, north east to STILLINGFLEET *GR 5940*. Go north to NABURN *GR 5945*, go by SUSTRAN's cycle track (landscaped) all the way to KNAVESMIRE racecourse *GR 5947* if going to CTC Rally. If not, divert after crossing river Ouse at *GR 5946* **(critical point)** and keep to riverside path, Ebor Way, all the way to YORK except for a small diversion.

AREA H

West Country

Avon, Somerset, Devon, Cornwall, Wiltshire and West Dorset

H1

- **AVONMOUTH to BATH via BRISTOL**
- **COUNTY:** AVON
- **QUIETNESS:** ***
- **MILEAGE:** 10 BRISTOL, 26 BATH
- **DIRECTION:** west to east
- **TRAIN STATIONS and TIMETABLES:** AVONMOUTH *GR ST5178*, BATH *GR ST7564*, 133, 134
- **MAP(S):** OS 172, 173
- **WEATHER FORECAST:** 0891-500405
- **TOURIST INFORMATION OFFICE:** BRISTOL 0117-9260767
- **PUBLICATIONS:** Leaflet from SUSTRANS or Tourist Information
- **ACCOMMODATION:** BRISTOL YH *GR ST5872*, BATH YH *GR ST7664*
- **PLACES OF INTEREST:** Extension BATH to BRADFORD-ON-AVON and TROWBRIDGE by canal towpath
- **ROUTE:** track

AVONMOUTH *GR 5178*. Over AVON bridge (cycletrack) to PILL, HAM GREEN Hospital, CHAPEL PILL Farm *GR 537762*. South bank of AVON to BRISTOL. Two of Brunel's master-pieces, Suspension Bridge and SS Gt Britain *GR 578724*. The SUSTRANS trailway (through tunnels) to BATH. BATH SPA station.
- **RELATED ROUTES:** Severn Bridge WS2
- **RECONNOITRED:** 1984, RNH

BODMIN PARKWAY *GR SX1164*, 135, 51 (Bus 141)
- **MAP:** OS 200
- **WEATHER FORECAST:** 0891-500404
- **TOURIST INFORMATION OFFICE:** BODMIN 01208-76616
- **PUBLICATIONS:** Leaflet Tourist Information or County Council
- **ACCOMMODATION:** Consult Tourist Information
- **PLACES OF INTEREST:** A delightful extra is to take ferry PADSTOW to ROCK *GR 9275*, then Cornish lanes nearest estuary to CARLYON *GR 9575* and GUTT bridge at *GR 9775* and B3314 back to Wadebridge. 1991: Trail now extended to WENFORDBRIDGE *GR 0875*. Colour leaflet including some best of BETJEMAN.
- **ROUTE:** track

By NIGHT RIVIERA (starts from Waterloo most nights, reservations essential) gives early start at BODMIN PARKWAY station *GR 1164*. (If round trip of 24 or 36 miles is too far, break journey or take bus to WADEBRIDGE). Minor lanes by CUTMADOC *GR 0963*. South west of BODMIN to NANSTALLON and TRAIL at 'B' of BOSCARNE. *GR 034675*. Then superb purpose-built cycle trailway to WADEBRIDGE. Minor diversions at old station to traffic lights then continue north west to PADSTOW.
- **RECONNOITRED:** December 1986, RNH

H2

- **BODMIN PARKWAY to PADSTOW**
- **COUNTY:** CORNWALL
- **QUIETNESS:** ***
- **MILEAGE:** 24 WADEBRIDGE, 36 PADSTOW
- **DIRECTION:** Varied
- **TRAIN STATIONS and TIMETABLES:**

H3

- **PENZANCE to LAND'S END and to ST IVES**
- **COUNTY:** CORNWALL
- **QUIETNESS:** *
- **MILEAGE:** 30 minimum
- **DIRECTION:** east to west and south west to north east

- **TRAIN STATIONS and TIMETABLES:** PENZANCE **GR SW4747**, ST IVES **GR SW5140**, 51, 135, 144
- **MAP:** OS 203
- **WEATHER FORECAST:** 0891-500404
- **TOURIST INFORMATION OFFICE:** PENZANCE 01736-62207, ST IVES 01736-796297
- **ACCOMMODATION:** PENZANCE YH (18th century Mansion) **GR 457302**
- **PLACES OF INTEREST:** If wind unfavourable try PENZANCE-HAYLE (H4) or BODMIN PARKWAY-PADSTOW (H2). Visit the St Ives Tate Gallery, overlooking sandy beach, with its wonderful architecture and sculpture.
- **ROUTE:** road

PENZANCE station NIGHT RIVIERA gives early start. A30 (busy in season) to LAND'S END (no charge). Coast Road B3306 via ST JUST (with minor diversion at TREGESEAL 3732 for the map reader) to ST IVES. ST IVES Victorian seaside resort, sandy beach to yourself. Barbara HEPWORTH sculpture at Guildhall.
- **RELATED ROUTES:** H4 and H5
- **RECONNOITRED:** November 1984, RNH

H4

- **MOUNT'S BAY to ST IVES BAY**
- **COUNTY:** CORNWALL
- **QUIETNESS:** **
- **MILEAGE:** 11, + 8 for Mousehole
- **DIRECTION:** south west to north east
- **TRAIN STATIONS and TIMETABLES:** PENZANCE **GR SW4747**, ST IVES **GR SW5140**, 135, 51, 144
- **MAP:** OS 203
- **WEATHER FORECAST:** 0891-500404
- **TOURIST INFORMATION OFFICE:** See route H3
- **ACCOMMODATION:** YH at PENZANCE **GR 457302**
- **PLACES OF INTEREST and NOTE:** NIGHT RIVIERA gives early start. At Hayle leave time to explore the Estuary, including King George Memorial Walk **GR 5638**; now mature planting. The YHA sign at **GR 566384** is now only nostalgic. MOUSEHOLE

diversion from PENZANCE via NEWLYN and PENLEE (of lifeboat memory) to MOUSEHOLE — delightful hill and seaside village. The whole is a really quiet route off-season only.
- **ROUTE:** road

PENZANCE station; A30 to handsome wooden footbridge **GR 485312**. Long Distance Path: pushing on sea side of railway to car park at MARAZION **GR 513312**. North east by minor lane to farm **GR 519319**; cart track through three gates (pushing); cross A394; GWALLON; ROSEVIDNEY **GR 5334**; ST ERTH (station one mile if needed); CHENHALLS. Under A30(T) to HAYLE and station.
- **RELATED ROUTES:** H3 and H5
- **RECONNOITRED:** RNH

H5

- **PENZANCE to CARBIS BAY**
- **COUNTY:** CORNWALL
- **QUIETNESS:** *
- **MILEAGE:** 10 — hilly
- **DIRECTION:** south west to north east
- **TRAIN STATIONS and TIMETABLES:** PENZANCE, CARBIS BAY **GR SW5238**, 51, 135, 144
- **MAP:** OS 203
- **WEATHER FORECAST:** 0891-500404
- **TOURIST INFORMATION OFFICE:** PENZANCE 01736-62207
- **ACCOMMODATION:** PENZANCE YH
- **ROUTE:** road

PENZANCE station or YH — make for B3311. North north east viewpoint at Castle Gate **GR 4934**. Before NANCLEDRA go east and north east by minor roads to BRUNNION **GR 5036**. Then north east to LONGSTONE and CARBIS BAY station.
- **RELATED ROUTES:** H3, H4
- **RECONNOITRED:** December 1987, RNH

H6

- **REDRUTH to NEWQUAY**
- **COUNTY:** CORNWALL
- **QUIETNESS:** *

- **MILEAGE:** 18
- **DIRECTION:** south west to north east
- **TRAIN STATIONS and TIMETABLES:** REDRUTH *GR SW7042*, NEWQUAY *GR SW8161*, 51, 135, 142
- **MAP(S):** OS 203, 200, (204)
- **WEATHER FORECAST:** 0891-500404
- **TOURIST INFORMATION OFFICE:** NEWQUAY 01637-871345
- **ACCOMMODATION:** Consult Tourist Information
- **PLACES OF INTEREST:** If A3075 too busy, explore the maze of minor roads lying west of it
- **ROUTE:** road

Out of REDRUTH by minor road over A30 to NORTH COUNTRY *GR 6943*. Branch to right (north east) to MAWLA *GR 7045* and make for MOUNT HAWKE *GR 7147*. East to A30 at THREE BURROWS. Take A3075 to GOONHAVEN and NEWQUAY.
- **RECONNOITRED:** December 1987, RNH

H7

- **TWO RIDES BASED on PLYMOUTH The TAMAR and PLYM VALLEYS**
- **COUNTY:** DEVON
- **QUIETNESS:** *
- **MILEAGE:** 14 or 30
- **DIRECTION:** north west to south east mainly
- **TRAIN STATIONS and TIMETABLES:** DEVONPORT *GR SX544558*, GUNNISLAKE *GR SX4271*, 135, 139
- **MAP:** OS 201
- **WEATHER FORECAST:** 0891-500404
- **TOURIST INFORMATION OFFICE:** PLYMOUTH 01752-264849
- **PUBLICATIONS:** Card re PLYM Valley
- **ACCOMMODATION:** YH PLYMOUTH *GR SX4655*
- **PLACES OF INTEREST:** Abound in and near PLYMOUTH. Contact Tourist Information.
- **ROUTE:** track

(1) Try for early morning train DEVONPORT station up the TAMAR Valley to GUNNISLAKE *GR 4271*. Cycle by A390 (fairly quiet off-season) to LISKEARD (14 miles). Station back to PLYMOUTH station; walk due south by open spaces to the HOE. Tourist Information

on the way. (2) PLYM VALLEY SUSTRANS PROJECT starts near LAIRA bridge *GR 502543* to east of bridge on B3416. *GR 522567*: up delightful wooded BICKLEIGH VALE to GOODAMEAVY *GR 5264*, just within DARTMOOR NATIONAL PARK. Trail with fine viaducts, probably the best in the country — designed for cyclists by cyclists (SUSTRANS Project, 35 King Street, Bristol). Return downhill all the way. 16 miles round trip is all too short.
- **RELATED ROUTES:** H11, H17
- **RECONNOITRED:** November 1986, RNH

H8

- **YEOVIL JUNCTION to TEMPLECOMBE or GILLINGHAM**
- **COUNTY:** DORSET
- **QUIETNESS:** *
- **MILEAGE:** 13 or 21
- **DIRECTION:** west to east
- **TRAIN STATIONS and TIMETABLES:** YEOVIL JUNCTION *GR ST5714*, TEMPLECOMBE, GILLINGHAM *GR ST8026*, 160
- **MAP:** OS 183
- **WEATHER FORECAST:** 0891-500403
- **TOURIST INFORMATION OFFICE:** SHERBORNE 01935-815341
- **PLACES OF INTEREST:** SHERBORNE town and Castle
- **ROUTE:** road

YEOVIL JUNCTION south west to STOFORD east to BRADFORD ABBAS to SHERBORNE, Castle (English Heritage). MILBORNE PORT *GR 6718* north east to Church to HENSTRIDE BOWDEN, fine descent to TEMPLECOMBE station (reopened by local effort). If time permits, minor roads to GILLINGHAM.
- **RELATED ROUTES:** H10
- **RECONNOITRED:** Summer 1987, RNH

H9

- **ST MARY'S, ISLE OF SCILLY:** an introductory visit
- **COUNTY:** ISLES OF SCILLY
- **QUIETNESS:** ** out of season
- **MILEAGE:** Up to 15-20
- **DIRECTION:** Various

- **TRAIN STATIONS and TIMETABLES:** N/A, 135, 51 (BI Helicopters, Penzance).
- **MAP(S):** OS 203 and local map, Tourist Information
- **WEATHER FORECAST:** 0891-500404
- **TOURIST INFORMATION OFFICE:** PENZANCE 01736-62207, SCILLY ISLES 01720-422536
- **ACCOMMODATION:** YH PENZANCE a good base
- **NOTES:** Transport: No sea route off-season, but folded cycles welcome on helicopter
- **ROUTE:** track

In the course of a winter's day of short daylight one can explore most of the tarmac roads of ST MARY'S at ease. No signposts as the locals know their way and visitors' cars are discouraged — 'Ancient Burial Chamber' is the most prominent sign. The circuit of the garrison promontory *GR 8910* is rideable, and with some push you can explore OUTER HEAD at extreme south of island and follow coastal path through PORTHLOO to HALANY POINT and the north. HOLY VALE *GR 9211* and the Nature Trail should not be missed. Use large scale map.

- **RELATED ROUTES:** Others from PENZANCE
- **RECONNOITRED:** December 1987, RNH

B and B in town and vicinity available from Tourist Information. South on B3092 to EAST STOUR, STOUR PROVOST, TODBER *GR 7919* minor road south south east to join B3091 to MANSTON at junction *GR 822152*. Choice: (1) South to HAMMOON and A357 at NEW CROSS GATE *GR 812125* when south east for four miles on A357 **(not quiet)** to DURWESTON *GR 8508* or (2) NOT cycled: south east to CHILD OKEFORD *GR 8312* and try bridleway at *GR 853113* to STOURPAINE *GR 8609* crossing river STOUR by MILL to DURWESTON. Route continues south east minor road and through BRYANSTON PARK (famous school) along permissive bridleway to BLANDFORD FORUM (TOURIST INFORMATION and refreshments). Careful map reading at join of sheets *GR 888064* take No Through Road for cars across bypass to LANGTON LONG BLANDFORD *GR 8905*. TARRANT CRAWFORD; CRAWFORD bridge on river STOUR *GR 918020*; south by B3075 to A31. South west for 1 mile **(not quiet** — no way through CHARBOROUGH PARK). At MARSH station *GR 9098* go south by B3075 for over five miles of good country, some wooded, to A351 on outskirts of WAREHAM; avoid the A road by judicious use of the old road.

- **RELATED ROUTES:** H8
- **RECONNOITRED:** November 1988, RNH

H10

- **GILLINGHAM, BLANDFORD, WAREHAM**
- **COUNTY:** DORSET
- **QUIETNESS:** **
- **MILEAGE:** 31
- **DIRECTION:** north to south
- **TRAIN STATIONS and TIMETABLES:** GILLINGHAM *GR ST8026*, WAREHAM *GR SY9188*, 160, 158
- **MAP(S):** OS 183, 194, 195
- **WEATHER FORECAST:** 0891-500403
- **TOURIST INFORMATION OFFICE:** BLANDFORD FORUM 01258-454770
- **PLACES OF INTEREST:** Consult Tourist Information
- **ROUTE:** road

GILLINGHAM: Overnight stay for early start;

H11

- **DARTMOOR NATIONAL PARK**
- **COUNTY:** DEVON
- **QUIETNESS:** **
- **MILEAGE: Hilly**; TOPSHAM-BELLEVER 30, BELLEVER-PLYMOUTH 29
- **DIRECTION:** east to west mainly
- **TRAIN STATIONS and TIMETABLES:** TOPSHAM *GR SX9688*, EXETER-PLYMOUTH *GR SX4755*, DEVONPORT, 135, 137, 145
- **MAP(S):** OS 192, 191, 201, 202
- **WEATHER FORECAST:** 0891-500404
- **TOURIST INFORMATION OFFICE:** EXETER 01392-265297, BOVEY TRACEY 01626-832047, PLYMOUTH 01752-264849/264851
- **PUBLICATIONS:** PLYM VALLEY TRAILWAY from Tourist Information

PLYMOUTH; *Bellever Forest* from Forestry Commission

- **ACCOMMODATION:** Good YHs at EXETER (TOPSHAM), BELLEVER and PLYMOUTH (DEVONPORT station), also STEPS Bridge *GR 802882*
- **PLACES OF INTEREST:** A good introduction to DARTMOOR National Park. See HMSO guide and Tourist Information for more material.
- **ROUTE:** road and track, start OS 192

If alighting at EXETER ST DAVID'S or CENTRAL make for the river or canal and quiet route (daylight) on south west side (Country Park) to bridge A379 *GR 9489* for YH or start of ride. From TOPSHAM station minor roads north west to YH at LOWER WEAR *GR 941897* choose overnight stay for early start; then endure A379 (pavements) for one and a half miles to road junction *GR 921887*. Thereafter delightful minor roads **(some hilly)** SHILLINGFORD ST GEORGE *GR 9087*. WEBBERTON CROSS *GR 8887*. LAWRENCE CASTLE *GR 8786* (Views, closed winter). South west TRUSHAM and into Dartmoor National Park (OS 191) *GR 8582*. CROCOMBE bridge (good B and B); south west entering National Park to FIVE LANES *GR 8380*, and downhill to BOVEY TRACEY National Park Authority and TOURIST INFORMATION at PARKE *GR 805786*, on west and south west taking minor road (bridleway) at *GR 778774* to see HAYTOR VALE village. Onwards past HAYTOR ROCKS and miles of unfenced moorland (SEVEN LORDS LAND) and downhill to WIDECOMBE IN THE MOOR *GR 7176*. Then careful map reading to LOWER CATOR *GR 6876* and north west to CLAPPER BRIDGE and BELLEVER *GR 6577* (YH simple and hospitable). Forest walks. Explore the forest gravel tracks. The north to south track through *GR 646783* is good but east to west (THE LICHWAY West point) impassable in winter. Resume route south west of POSTBRIDGE at *GR 646787* go south west on B3212 to PRINCETOWN (cafe in winter). Five miles on B3212 beyond PRINCETOWN, after crossing dismantled railway, take minor road at *GR 546694* to enjoy magic tracks around BURRATOR RESERVOIR. Circumnavigate clockwise, going east at *GR 54769 3*, you may have to lift over dam approaches at *GR 557681*, but it's worthwhile.

Then at second dam exit *GR 552680*, go south to MEAVY *GR 5467* and skirting CALLISHAM *GR 5366* and generally south (hospitable B and B at GREENWELL Farm *GR 535659* to LOWER GOODAMEAVEY *GR 5264* (now OS 201/202). Here starts the best Trailway in Britain, thanks to the SUSTRANS Project and the Plymouth City Fathers — the BURRATOR Reservoir. The cycleway guides you to LAIRA bridge *GR 5054* and eventually a sheltered route to PLYMOUTH HOE, from where open space leads to station. Meanwhile care and some walking advisable.

- **RELATED ROUTES:** H7, H15
- **RECONNOITRED:** December 1989, RNH

H12

- **THE WESSEX RIDGEWAY:** PEWSEY to AVEBURY and SWINDON
- **COUNTY:** WILTSHIRE
- **QUIETNESS:** **
- **MILEAGE:** 29
- **DIRECTION:** south west to north east
- **TRAIN STATIONS and TIMETABLES:** PEWSEY *GR SU1660*, SWINDON *GR SU1485*, 116, 125
- **MAP:** OS 173
- **WEATHER FORECAST:** 0891-500405
- **TOURIST INFORMATION OFFICE:** AVEBURY 01672-539425 (part year, answering machine), SWINDON (all year) 01793 530328
- **PUBLICATIONS:** HMSO Guide to Ridgeway also covers extension to GORING. For a bridleway route GORING-IVINGHOE BEACON (ICKNIELD WAY) see *The Bridleways of Britain*, A Whittett, 1986, Route 1.
- **PLACES OF INTEREST:** See guides in publications and Tourist Information
- **ROUTE:** track

From PEWSEY station *GR SU1660*, minor road over railway. North east to crossroads. 142 WILCOT *GR 1461* to ALTON PRIORS and BARNES *GR 1063*; north east towards LOCKERIDGE, but left point 174 at *GR 132663*. EAST KENNET (see LONG BARROW); SILBURY HILL *GR 1068*;AVEBURY *GR 1070*. Pick up RIDGEWAY Long Distance Path at A4 junction *GR 1168* or Track junction. *GR 1270*:

well defined track; flint and rutted in parts, generally north to BARBURY CASTLE (critical point) (kite flying 2nd Sunday in month). Public convenience shelter: south east to minor road *GR 193746* Near WESTFIELDS Farm north DRAYCOT FOLIAT *GR 1877*. CHISELDON *GR 1879*. HODSON over M4 to Old Town. New Town and SWINDON station.
• **RECONNOITRED:** AVEBURY-CHISELDON section September 1989, RNH

H13

• **CREWKERNE to BRUTON, FROME or WARMINSTER**
• **COUNTY:** SOMERSET, WILTSHIRE
• **QUIETNESS:****
• **MILEAGE:** 41
• **DIRECTION:** south west to north east
• **TRAIN STATIONS and TIMETABLES:** CREWKERNE *GR ST4508*, BRUTON *GR ST6834*, 123, 160
• **MAP(S):** OS 193, 183
• **WEATHER FORECAST:** 0891-500405
• **TOURIST INFORMATION OFFICE:** YEOVIL 01935-71279
• **PUBLICATIONS:** *Cycling in South Somerset*, District Council or Tourist Information
• **ACCOMMODATION:** Consult Tourist Information
• **PLACES OF INTEREST:** MONTACUTE HOUSE (National Trust) *GR ST4917*; FLEET AIR ARM MUSEUM *GR ST5523*; ROSIE'S CIDER *GR ST6926*; ALFRED'S TOWER, STOURHEAD and LONGLEAT
• **ROUTE:** road

(Based on District Council Publication *Share the secret of South Somerset*). From CREWKERNE station A356 east of MERRIOTT to WEST CHINNOCK *GR 4613*, minor road north to CHISELBOROUGH and NORTON-SUB-HAMDON *GR 4716*, A3088, minor road south east to HAMHILL COUNTRY PARK *GR 4916* (now OS 183) minor road to MONTACUTE (National Trust) *GR 4917*; go south west and west by minor roads to YEOVIL (station at *GR 5716* if needed). Exit north by A359. At *GR 556176* minor road north to MUDFORD SOCK *GR 5519* go to ASHINGTON *GR 5621* north west to LIMINGTON *GR 5422*,

YEOVILTON (Fleet Air Arm Museum) and north east and east on B3151; one and a half miles to minor road south east to BRIDGEHAMPTON *GR 5624*, QUEEN CAMEL *GR 5924* — over A359 to cross railway at *GR 603252*; minor road west to SUTTON MONTIS, CADBURY CASTLE *GR 6225*, COMPTON PAUNCEFOOT, BLACKFORD, MAPERTON east and north east LATTIFORD *GR 696266* on A357/B3145 junction WINCANTON *GR 7128* — exit by B3081 go to minor road at *GR 712296* to RECTORY Farm, CHALTON MUSGROVE *GR 7331*, to HARDWAY — then 3 choices: (1) TO BRUTON: minor road near NORTH BREWHAM south west to BRUTON station *GR 6832*. (2) TO FROME: north to NORTH BREWHAM *GR 7236* go east on minor road to road junction YARNFIELD GATE *GR 7637* go north to GAREHILL *GR 7740* minor road north west over railway to junction *GR 7642*, minor road to cross railway again to B3092. North to FROME. (3) TO WARMINSTER: From HARDWAY *GR 7234*. East on minor road **(hilly)** ALFRED'S TOWER *GR 7435* with wonderful view after walking up steps. (National Trust limited opening March to November). Into WILTSHIRE go east to KILMINGTON COMMON *GR 7735*; divert one and a half miles south for STOURHEAD (National Trust) and STOURTON. Return north by minor road or B3092 MAIDEN BRADLEY *GR 8038* go to HORNINGSHAM *GR 8141* for LONGLEAT House and Park *GR 8143* (open all year including cafe). Resume to NEWBURY *GR 8241*. Minor road north west and take one of several quiet routes (avoiding both A362 and A350) to WARMINSTER *GR ST8745* (station).
• **RELATED ROUTES:** H8, H14, H15
• **RECONNOITRED:** 1990, RNH

H14

• **AXMINSTER to CASTLE CARY or BRUTON**
• **COUNTY:** SOMERSET
• **QUIETNESS:** **
• **MILEAGE:** 50 to CASTLE CARY, add 5 miles for BRUTON
• **DIRECTION:** south west to north east
• **TRAIN STATIONS and TIMETABLES:** AXMINSTER *GR SY2998*, CASTLE CARY *GR ST6333*, 135, 160

- **MAP(S):** OS 182, 183, 193
- **WEATHER FORECAST:** 0891-500405
- **TOURIST INFORMATION OFFICE:** (Part year) AXMINSTER 01297-34386, CHARD 01460-67463, ILMINSTER 01460-57294
- **PUBLICATIONS:** *Cycling in South Somerset*, District Council
- **ACCOMMODATION:** Consult Tourist Information, STREET YH 5 miles to north of route at *GR 453302*
- **PLACES OF INTEREST:** BARRINGTON COURT (National Trust) *GR 397182*, LYTE'S CARY MANOR (National Trust) *GR 529269* - 14th to 16th centuries
- **ROUTE:** road

(Based on District Council leaflet *Share the secret of South Somerset*, with permission). AXMINSTER *GR SY2998*. Leave north east by A358 go to WEYCROFT *GR 3000* go to junction *GR 312013* north east minor road go to WADBROOK and HOLDICH *GR 3402*; go north east and north west to CHARD JUNCTION *GR 3404* and PERRY ST due north over B3167 and A30 to 'Farm' of Tudbeer Farm *GR 345093* go to minor road north east of CHARD Reservoir *GR 3410* CRICKET MALHERBIE *GR 3611* and OXENFORD Farm, DOWLISH WAKE *GR 3712*, go north to KINGSTONE, north west then north east to ILMINSTER (Tourist Information) *GR 3614*. North east by B3168 to PUCKINGTON *GR 3718* go to BARRINGTON, south east to SHEPTON BEAUCHAMP *GR 4017*. East SOUTH PETHERTON. Minor road north east and north west to EAST LAMBROOK *GR 4219* SOTHAY. North to KINGSBURY EPISCOP *GR 4321* go to THORNEY, MULCHELNEY, LANGPORT *GR 4226*. East and north east to WAGG *GR 4326* go to PITNEY *GR 4428* north west past church and clockwise minor road (on OS 182 for one mile only) to Park at *GR 453302* (nearest point to STREET YH Swiss style chalet at *GR 480345* — usually open April-October inclusive) go south east to SOMERTON *GR 4928* (OS 183) CARY station *GR 4928*. B3153 for one mile go south east to CHARLTONS and north east to KEINTON MANDEVILLE *GR 5530*. East along B3153 — over A37 and minor road to FODDINGTON *GR 5829*. Minor road go east to NORTH BARROW *GR 6029*. Minor road north east COCKHIL *GR 6231* to CASTLE CARY(station) *GR 6333*. If time permits, route continues east

via HADSPEN *GR 6532* and COLE to BRUTON station at *GR 688348*.
- **RELATED ROUTES:** H8, H13, H15
- **RECONNOITRED:** 1990, RNH

H15

- **TOPSHAM (EXETER) to CHELTENHAM via WHIMPLE, CASTLE CARY, FROME and BRADFORD-ON-AVON**
- **COUNTIES:** DEVON, SOMERSET, WILTSHIRE, GLOUCESTERSHIRE
- **QUIETNESS:** **
- **MILEAGE:** 13 to WHIMPLE, 56 to CASTLE CARY, 17 to FROME, 11 to BRADFORD-ON-AVON, 50 to CHELTENHAM
- **DIRECTION:** south west to north east
- **TRAIN STATIONS and TIMETABLES:** TOPSHAM *GR SX9688*, CHELTENHAM *GR SO9322*. Intermediate stations at WHIMPLE, CASTLE CARY, BRUTON, FROME and BRADFORD-ON-AVON, 123, 127, 135, 160.
- **MAP(S):** OS 192, 193, 183, 173, 163
- **WEATHER FORECAST:** 0891 500405
- **TOURIST INFORMATION OFFICE:** (All year) Exeter 01392-265297, Malmesbury 01666-823748, Cheltenham 01242-522878
- **PUBLICATIONS:** Many local and west country guide books
- **ACCOMMODATION:** YHs at EXETER (TOPSHAM), STREET, DUNTISBORNE ABBOTS and CLEEVE HILL (four miles from CHELTENHAM station)
- **PLACES OF INTEREST:** Too many to list: CHELTENHAM SPA, MALMESBURY, STREET and other places; BRADFORD-ON-AVON is the birthplace of Moulton Bicycles
- **ROUTE:** road

Part 1: Topsham to Whimple (13 miles)
From TOPSHAM Station to EBFORD *GR 9888*. Minor road to WOODBURY *GR 0187*. Minor road WOODBURY SALTERTON *GR 0189*. Minor road go to MARSH GREEN *GR 0493*. Minor road go to WHIMPLE *GR 0497* (station).
Part 2: Whimple to Castle Cary (56 miles)
From WHIMPLE minor road to TALATON *GR 0699*. Minor road over A373 at *GR 111029*.

Minor road to WESTERHOPE FARM *GR 1205*. Minor road to SMEATHARPE *GR 2011*. North by minor road to HOLMAN CALVEL *GR 2216* (Now OS 193). Minor road to BLACKWATER *GR 2615*. Minor road to BROADWAY *GR 3215*. Minor road to CAD GREEN *GR 3417*. Minor road B3168 to BARRINGTON *GR 3818*. Minor road to SHEPTON BEAUCHAMP *GR 4017*. Minor road to NEW CROSS *GR 4119*. Minor road to B3165. At *GR 479285* minor road to B3151 go to KINGSDON *GR 5126* (Now OS 183). Minor road to CHARLTON ADAM *GR 5328*. Minor road to BABCARY *GR 5628*. Minor road to NORTH BARROW *GR 6029*. Minor road to CASTLE CARY.

Part 3: Castle Cary to Frome (17 miles)
From CASTLE CARY minor road to HADSDEN *GR 6532*. Minor road to BRUTON (station) *GR 6834*. Minor road to NORTH BREWSHAM *GR 7236*. Minor road to GARE HILL *GR 7840*. Minor road to crossroads at *GR 759436*, minor road to TYTHERINGTON *GR 7745*. Minor road, go to FROME (station) *GR 7848*.

Part 4: Frome to Bradford-on-Avon (11 miles)
From FROME go to OLDFORD *GR 7850* (If A361 busy try longer minor roads). LULLINGTON *GR 7851*. Minor road to WOOLVERTON *GR 7954*, minor road to RODE *GR 8054* (now OS 173). B3109 to BRADFORD-ON-AVON (station) *GR 8260*.

Part 5: Bradford-on-Avon to Cheltenham (50 miles)
From BRADFORD-ON-AVON B3109 go to BRADFORD LEIGH *GR 8362*. North on B3109 to CORSHAM *GR 8670*. Minor road to BIDDESTONE *GR 8673*. Minor road to YATTON KEYWELL *GR 8676*. Minor road including Fosse Way to NORTON *GR 8884*. Minor road to MALMESBURY *GR 9387*. B4104 to LONG NEWNTON *GR 9192*. Minor road to CHERRINGTON *GR 9098* (Now OS 163). Minor road east of SAPPERTON *GR 9403* (Canal Tunnel and 'Tunnel House Inn' — good pub) and west of DUNTISBOURNE ABBOTS *GR9707*. (YH) Go to WINSTONE *GR 9509*. Minor road to ELKSTONE *GR 9612*, COWLEY *GR 9614*. Minor road to join B4070 for CHELTENHAM *GR 9322* station.

- **RECONNOITRED:** Stephen Essex, Cycling Officer of Manchester City Council

- **The Towpath of the restored KENNET and AVON canal.** This is open to cyclists with permits, **but great care is needed**.
- **COUNTY:** WILTSHIRE, BERKSHIRE
- **QUIETNESS:** ***
- **MILEAGE:** (All to stations except the first) DEVIZES 13, PEWSEY 25, HUNGERFORD 41, NEWBURY 51, READING 70
- **DIRECTION:** west to east
- **TRAIN STATIONS and TIMETABLES:** Start BRADFORD ON AVON *GR ST8260*, End READING *GR SU7173*, with 9 intermediate stations, 116, 117 (obtain leaflet of local services)
- **MAP(S):** OS 173, 174, 175
- **WEATHER FORECAST:** 0891 500 405/406
- **TOURIST INFORMATION OFFICE:** BRADFORD ON AVON 012216-5797, NEWBURY 01635-30267, READING 01734-566226, DEVIZES 01380-729408 (answering machine in winter)
- **PUBLICATIONS:** (1) OS Nicholson's guide to waterways, South, 5th Edn 1991: history, architecture, every lock, bridge and pub! (2) Less detail: Pictorial map of Kennet and Avon canal, (Geo Projects 1990). Many other publications: Canal Trust Devizes and Tourist Information.
- **ACCOMMODATION:** Tourist Information supply ample list; very few B and B signs on canal itself
- **PLACES OF INTEREST:** Numerous. See text and Tourist Information. CROFTON pumping station *GR SU2662* for boys of all ages. Note that on this canal the locks and bridges are not numbered on the ground. In general, in the following description the locks mentioned thus 'SEEND Lock' are those named on the site; some are sponsored (for instance by 'SAMFARMER').
- **ROUTE:** track

Part 1: Bradford on Avon to Devizes (13 miles)
BRADFORD ON AVON — an exquisite small town in natural stone, as well as the home of MOULTON BICYCLES. From station *GR ST8260*, south on B3109 to join towpath on north side of canal. To north outskirts of TROWBRIDGE (canal over railway) *GR 8559*. SEMINGTON. Under A350. 'SEMINGTON UPPER Lock'

GR 9060. 'SEEND Lock' No. 18 GR 930614.
Over old railway and below pylons LOWER
FOX HANGERS Bridge Lock 22 GR 9561 to
begin a series of locks, numbers 22-27. West
of road B3101 and the famous CAEN HILL
FLIGHT numbers 29-44. West of DEVIZES
restored from total dereliction and reopened
by the Queen in August 1990, Plaque
GR 912616. DEVIZES — plenty of interest
and good B and B at HILLCREST GR 005610.

Part 2: Devizes to Newbury (38 miles)
To COATE Bridge GR 0162 rebuilt 1990 by
Wiltshire County Council in a style that is
sympathetic to the canal design. At HORTON
Bridge GR 0363 optional use of minor road to
cut out loop of canal if change of surface
desired or to go to phone box. Quiet miles of
towpath with swing bridges and no classified
roads. HONEYSTREET WHARF well
preserved GR 1061. LADY'S bridge (built
STONE classical; JOHN RENNIE bowing to
the wishes of Lady SUSANNAH GR 1260 —
compare the Earl of Essex bridge on GRAND
UNION route G8. BRISTOW station and
PEWSEY WHARF GR 1561 for station.
'WOOTTON RIVERS Lock' GR 1962. 'HEATHY
CLOSE Lock' Number 52 GR 203632.
'BRIMSLADE Lock' GR 2163. 'CADLEY Lock'
number 54 GR 2063 under A346 to BRUCE
TUNNEL - complex of road, railway, Tunnel
GR 2363. The SAVERNAKE FOREST Hotel.
Lock 58 'SAM FARMER Lock' GR 256621.
CROFTON PUMPING Station and WILTON
WATER GR 2662 (oldest working BEAM
ENGINE). Check 'STEAM DAYS' - leave time
to explore). 'CHURCH Lock' GREAT BEDWYN
GR 2764 for station 'FROXFIELD MIDDLE
Lock'. GR 302674 (Marks and Spencer).
'MARSH Lock' west of HUNGERFORD station
GR 3268 'KINTBURY Lock' GR 3867.
'DREWEAT'S Lock' GR 410673. 'GREENHAM
Lock' west of NEWBURY. (Good TOURIST
INFORMATION at WHARF, open unsociable
hours). Station.

Part 3: Newbury to Reading (19 miles)
Under HAM bridge GR 4967; under railway.
THATCHAM GR 5266 station. MIDGHAM
station. (OS 175 starts). THEALE GR 6470.
Station: virtual 'Lake District' to Reading;
towpath ends at road bridge (dual carriageway) GR 7172. Pick your way by quiet streets
due north to station GR 7173. No towpath in
centre of town. The location of the junction
with river Thames can be seen from station

marked by the Gasometer.
* **RELATED ROUTES:** J14, J1, J12
* **RECONNOITRED:** September 1990, RNH

Condition of Towpath
Over 66 miles some variety in the surface
condition of the towpath is to be expected and
welcomed. All 66 miles are rideable by a 75
year old on a mountain or shopper bike
(September 1990 — a dry summer). Especially
advisable to heed the wind forecast and go
when dry underfoot, preferably in the close
season for coarse fishing (16 March-15 June),
although most anglers are tolerant. The surface
of the towpath varies from grass or gravel wide
enough for three abreast, single file riding
through nettles and brambles for a few short
stretches (wear gloves!). Major repairs and
works by BWB going on all the time —
September 1990 west of MIDGHAM station
GR 5766; the thick clay and silt from the canal
placed on the towpath has cracked to form a
miniature Giant's Causeway, but there is a
useful 'permitted' diversion in a field. Towpath
cycling must be the done thing since Angela
Rippon was seen on a cycle in the run-up to the
Queen's re-opening of the canal in August 1990.
From current local reports and from my own
knowledge (1937-1939), the whole towpath
has never been so good for 50 years — so try it
(RNH), if you have a permit (MZB). Towpaths,
are not, as a rule, public footpaths or bridleways,
so there are a limited number of stiles, usually in
pairs, where a road crosses the canal (to deter
access by motor cycles). The permit to cycle
allows you to use the towpath 'as you find it'. In
the 66 miles from Bradford-on-Avon to Reading
there are about 40 stiles or gates, mostly in pairs.
For Senior Citizens it is easier if two persons do
the lift over.

H17

* **DEVON — Coast to Coast
  (north to south)**
* **COUNTY:** DEVON
* **QUIETNESS:** **
* **MILEAGE:** 60+, two days+
* **DIRECTION:** north to south
* **TRAIN STATIONS and TIMETABLES:**
  BARNSTAPLE GR SS5532, PLYMOUTH

GR SX4755, 135, 136
- **MAP(S):** OS 180, 191, 201. Make sure your OS 180 shows new A39 road at *GR 5029* south of INSTOW.
- **WEATHER FORECAST:** 0891-500404
- **TOURIST INFORMATION OFFICE:** BARNSTAPLE 01271-47177, PLYMOUTH 01752-264849
- **ACCOMMODATION:** Half Thatch Cottage BRAUNTON *GR 4836*, YH at INSTOW *GR 483303*
- **PLACES OF INTEREST and NOTES:** Route based on Railway Path Project *Routes in the making* 1983, p.7 with permission and thanks. Making the start at ILFRACOMBE: To meet the rule of this book of public transport being available at the start, this route was drafted with the start at Barnstaple station. National Express Coaches have gone public on the carriage of folded and bagged cycles on their coaches; it is strongly recommended that the start be made from ILFRACOMBE, as in the original SUSTRANS route. The route is the direct minor road (fine old drove/ridge road) running south from behind the YH at *GR SS524476* go over B3343 at Hore Down Farm *GR 5343* diverting at MARWOOD for magical gardens *GR 5437* go to Springfield Cross *GR 5435* go to Bradiford *GR 5534* to BARNSTAPLE (adds 11 miles). YH at Ilfracombe one of the few remaining owner-managed.
- **ROUTE:** track

Part 1: Barnstaple, Braunston, Instow, Okehampton
From BARNSTAPLE station *GR SS5532* north east to cross river TAW and river YEO to reach TRAILWAY (marked Coastal Path on recent OS) to BRAUNSTON via the car park of Rugby Club (POTTINGTON) at *GR 551335*. Towpath hugs estuary most of the way to VELATOR *GR 4835*; go to BRAUNSTON *GR 4836*, and back by towpath to Barnstaple station where towpath and coastal path goes north west and south west by TAW estuary to INSTOW *GR 4730* leave at *GR 473303* to reach YH at WORLINGTON *GR 483303* (Victorian mansion with sea views). Leaving YH west go to road junction *GR 494305* south east over A39 *GR 5029* go to HOLMACOTT *GR 5028* go to LOWER LOVACOTT *GR 5227* south to STONY

CROSS go to ALVERDISCOTT *GR 5125* south west and south east at road junction *GR 515321* **(critical point)** go to HUNTSHAW CROSS *GR 5322* go south east six miles to road junction north west of MIDDLEMOOR CROSS *GR 606167* south west to join B3217 to garage/shop DOLTON BEACON *GR 5913* go south east on B3220 (now OS 191) go past STAFFORD MOOR Trout Fishery *GR 5911* go to LOOSEDON CROSS *GR 5909* minor road go south east over FOURWAYS CROSS *GR 6107* minor road south east to MOOREND *GR 6304* go generally south minor road go to crossroads *GR 634035* **(critical point)** and SAMPFORD COURTENAY *GR 6301* (award winning village). B and B. Minor road, go south over B3215 BELSTONE CORNER *GR 6298*, south by minor road to start of OKEHAMPTON by-pass at *GR 6294*: west through quieter OKEHAMPTON (cream tea November Sunday at 'Coffee Pot' Arcade).

Part 2: Okehampton to Yelverton
Leave OKEHAMPTON by 'old' road *GR 586948* west on B3218 for four miles go south at THORNDON CROSS *GR 5393*. Minor road gives magic descent to WEEKS Farm *GR 5191* (B and B) go south then minor road to A30, go to BRIDESTOWE go generally south east minor road to junction *GR 528889* **(critical point)** go south south west by ancient lanes (rough with 'clapper' bridges) over B3278 (now OS 201; nearly six miles overlap) BATTISHILL *GR 5085* minor road to LYDFORD *GR 5184* (GORGE Walk, National Trust, closed winter) go to minor road to old railway bridge at *GR 5083*: make for BRIDLEGATE at *GR 503830* **(critical point)**; then push south west along footpath south east of BURN Cottage over open moor to minor road at *GR 193816*. WEST BLACKDOWN go south then east on unfenced road to MARY TAVY *GR 5079*. ALTERNATIVES: (A) Minor roads south east to cross river TAVY by CLAM footbridge (old Bristol Coach road) *GR 510784* to PETER TAVY *GR 5177*. (B) from MARY TAVY minor road go north east to HORNDON, pub and B and B 'ELEPHANTS NEST' at *GR 516800* - sixteenth century 'New' Inn shown on OS 2.5″ - by minor road go south east by stony minor road over river TAVY by cart bridge *GR 5279*; note ancient milepost at *GR 525794*. South west by minor road to PETER TAVY. *Both routes* go generally south to cross B3357 at MOORSHOP *GR 5174*;

minor road south open moor to road junction **(critical point)** *GR 516720* go south east by minor road over river to WALKHAMPTON * *GR 5369* go south west minor road and B3212 go to YELVERTON *GR 5267*.

Part 3: Yelverton to Plymouth
From YELVERTON roundabout go south west on A386 (footway) to junction with old mineral Tramway *GR 516672* footpath to CLEARBROOK one a half miles **(critical point)** by side of DRAKES LEAT contour round CHUB TOR *GR 5166* go south on tramway route but leave it to go anti-clockwise to car park at *GR 518652* go to minor road down to old railway bridge at GOODMEAVY *GR 528646*. Then route through tunnel (cycle lights) and all way by best trailway in Great Britain to PLYMOUTH with its expanding provision of cyclepaths (renewed thanks to the City Fathers). Cycle route to PLYMOUTH station not yet trouble free but improving at every visit.

* **NOTE;** At WALKHAMPTON *GR 5369* consider (if time and energy permits) a circuit of BURRATOR RESERVOIR (as in route H11) — a man-made beauty spot, thanks again to the City Fathers.
* **RELATED ROUTES:** H11
* **RECONNOITRED:** November 1990, RNH and help of S and PS of YELVERTON

H18

* **AVON CYCLEWAY**
* **COUNTY:** AVON (GWENT)
* **QUIETNESS:** **
* **MILEAGE:** Total 108; see also under each part
* **DIRECTION:** See under each part
* **TRAIN STATIONS and TIMETABLES:** CHEPSTOW, YATE, BATH SPA, YATTON, 56, 125, 133, 134
* **MAP:** OS 172
* **WEATHER FORECAST:** 0891-500405
* **TOURIST INFORMATION OFFICE:** BATH, 01225-462831, BRISTOL 01272-260767
* **PUBLICATIONS:** *Avon Cycleway* essential companion for these routes
* **ACCOMMODATION:** YHs BRISTOL and BATH
* **PLACES OF INTEREST:** See publications and consult Tourist Information. The

excellent circular AVON CYCLEWAY (by kind permission of Avon County Council) and the LINK routes are here adapted to meet the features of this book, namely rail access and wind assisted. All four routes are by road.
* **ROUTE:** mostly road

H18A: Avon Cycleway North, Chepstow to Yate via Thornbury and Chipping Sodbury, OS 172; 28 miles, direction north west to south east
From CHEPSTOW station *GR ST5393* pick estate roads and paths just west of railway to BULWARK *GR 5392* to join Severn bridge cycleway at *GR 537916* over magnificent bridges to east end and to B4461 ELBERTON **(critical point)** *GR 6088* for signed Avon Cycleway: winding minor roads on edge of LITTLETON on Severn to KINGTON *GR 6190* go to THORNBURY. *GR 6490*: signed quiet route crosses B4061 at *GR 644909* and crisscrosses via CROSSWAYS *GR 6590* over A38 and M5 (MILBURY HEATH) *GR 6790* north east CROMHALL *GR 6990* south on B4058 for one mile road junction CROMHALL COMMON *GR 6989* south go to WICKWAR *GR 7288* go to minor road east to INGATSTONE COMMON to crossroad *GR 765877* **(critical point)** go south to HAWKESBURY *GR 7686* and south to HORTON *GR 7584* go south west through TOTTEROAK to CHIPPING SODBURY *GR 7282*: select quiet roads to YATE station at *GR ST702826* (not marked on some OS maps before 1990).

H18B: Avon Cycleway East, Bath to Yate, OS 172; 18 miles, direction south to north
From BATH SPA station *GR ST7564* take towpath of Kennet and Avon Canal west to BRASSMILL LANE and start of Railway Path at *GR 7264* (if you do not hold Canal Cycling Permit, take route in Avon Cycleway leaflet Churchill Bridge, Green Park Road). Follow railway path route to BITTON station *GR 6769* and WARMLEY station *GR 6773* to RODWAY HILL *GR 6675*. Here leave railway path for SHORTWOOD *GR 6776* east and north north east on B4465 through PUCKLECHURCH *GR 5976* over M4 go to WESTERLEIGH HILL *GR 705793* **(critical point)** leave AVON Cycleway by minor road north to YATE station at *GR ST7082*.

H18C: Avon Cycleway South, Yatton via The Chews to Bath, OS 172; 28 miles, direction west to east
From YATTON station *GR ST4266* south east by B3133 to minor road north east CLAVERHAM go north and north east to BROCKLEY ELM Farm *GR 468675* (critical point) to join AVON Cycleway go south east over A370 go east south east DOWNSIDE to LULSGATE BOTTOM *GR 5165* over A38 go to minor road south east to road junction in FELTON *GR 526654* (critical point) go south east WINFORD MANOR *GR 5364*. Go south east three miles CHEW STOKE *GR 5661* minor road, east and north towards CHEW MAGNA south east at *GR 577626* go to MOORLEDGE *GR 5862*, north to STANTON DREW and north east 'UPPER STANTON DREW' *GR 6062* over A37 at PENSFORD *GR 5263* minor road PUBLOW *GR 6264* go to WOOLLARD and COMPTON DANDO *GR 6464* and BURNETT over B3116 to SALTFORD *GR 6867* to join BRISTOL BATH Cycleway and towpath of Kennet and Avon Canal to BATH (for further description of this see route H18B above).

H18D: Avon Cycleway West, Yatton to Chepstow via Clevedon and Avon and Severn Bridges, OS 172; 34 miles, direction south to north
From YATTON station *GR ST4266*, minor road over KENN MOOR *GR 4268* to road junction *GR 425697* (critical point) to join Avon Cycleway go to Clevedon Court (National Trust, pottery etc). *GR 4271*: circuit of Clevedon to sea front, then trace north east by minor road from *GR 416722* (critical point) five miles to CLAPTON WICK *GR 4472* and CLAPTON in GORDANO *GR 4773* go under M5 to PORTBURY *GR 5075* go to LODWAY to reach AVON bridge *GR 5176* go to SHIREHAMPTON and LAWRENCE WESTON *GR 5478* go to BLAISE HAMLET *GR 5679*. North west under M5. HALLEN *GR 5480* north east EASTER COMPTON *GR 5782* go to B4055 north west. At MARSH COMMON *GR 565834* (critical point) north east and east through AWKLEY *GR 5985* over M4 to OLVESTON *GR 6087* minor road and B1461 to SEVERN bridge and quiet route via BULWARK *GR 5392* to CHEPSTOW (GWENT) *GR ST5393*. (For further notes on CHEPSTOW approach see route **Avon Cycleway North** above).
• **RECONNOITRED:** RNH

H19

• **WILTSHIRE CYCLEWAYS divided into six routes between BR Stations**
• **COUNTY:** WILTSHIRE
• **QUIETNESS:** **
• **MILEAGE:** 246 total; see after each section
• **DIRECTION:** Various, see below
• **TRAIN STATIONS and TIMETABLES:** BRADFORD-ON-AVON, SWINDON, SALISBURY, GILLINGHAM, CHIPPENHAM, BEDWYN as detailed below, 125, 116, 123, 160
• **MAP(S):** OS 173, 174, 183, 184, (172)
• **WEATHER FORECAST:** 0891-500405
• **TOURIST INFORMATION OFFICE:** AMESBURY 01980-622833, BRADFORD-ON-AVON 012216-5797, CHIPPENHAM 01249-657733, MALMESBURY 01666-823748, MERE 01747-861211, SALISBURY 01722-334956, SWINDON 01793-530328, TROWBRIDGE 01225-777054
• **PUBLICATIONS:** *Wiltshire Cycleways* 1988 and 1992, County Council (used with permission) and Tourist Information
• **ACCOMMODATION:** Consult Tourist Information and YH SALISBURY
• **PLACES OF INTEREST:** Numerous — consult Tourist Information
• **ROUTE:**

Wiltshire Circular Cycleway Route and two cross county routes of Wiltshire County Council here adapted for rail access and wind assisted features of this book. Where the official county routes are followed, neat white on blue signs are frequent, but please always use the OS map as signs may be vandalised or incomplete.

H19A: Wiltshire Cycleway — North part, Bradford-on-Avon via Malmesbury to Swindon, OS 173; 41 miles, direction south to north and west to east
From BRADFORD-ON-AVON station OS 173 *GR 8260* leave time to see town (Tourist Information at new Museum); leave by B3107 'MELKSHAM' to take minor road at *GR 828610* north east go to B3109 BRADFORD LEIGH *GR 8362*. East and north east GREAT CHALFIELD *GR 8663* go to ATWORTH *GR 8666* minor road north to east edge of CORSHAM crossing railway at *GR 8769* go north by west of CORSHAM PARK over A4

north to BIDDESTONE *GR 8673* minor road north YATTON KEYNELL *GR 8676* over M4 by minor road to join FOSS WAY *GR 8581* for over two miles, then minor road to NORTON *GR 8884* north east go to FOXLEY go to MALMESBURY *GR 9387*. Leave by minor road east to MILBOURNE; GARSDON *GR 9687*; generally east quiet minor road for over seven miles to road junction near LYDIARD PLAIN *GR O56864* **(critical point)**. Then south and north east to Pub (BOLINGBROKE ARMS) *GR 0785* go north on B4041 and minor road east to LYDIARD MILLICENT *GR 0986* go south east to SHAW, WESTLEA *GR 1284* to join Trailway south west of SWINDON *GR 1284*. Trace way to station at *GR 1485*.

H19B: Wiltshire Cycleway — East, Salisbury — Gt Bedwyn — Swindon, OS 184, 174, (173); 33 miles to Gt Bedwyn, 57 miles to Swindon, direction south to north
From SALISBURY station OS 184 *GR SU1330*; north of Ring Road and river AVON go to minor road north west past OLD SARUM *GR 1332*; cross AVON bridge *GR 1232* and north through all three WOODFORDS to cross river AVON *GR 124372* to GREAT DURNFORD *GR 1338*, minor road north east over A345 and east of AMESBURY over A303 *GR 1642* through BULFORD *GR 1643* and north north west minor road along valley side six miles to FITTLETON *GR 1549* go north east minor road over five miles miles EAST EVERLEIGH *GR 2053* go east on A342 and minor road over A338 CADLEY *GR 2454* go north east (now OS 174) six miles to cross A346 *GR 2760*. If time permits, divert to towpath of Kennet and Avon Canal at *GR 2662* (WILTON WATER and CROFTON PUMPING STATION — especially on the occasional 'steam days'). Go to north west edge of WILTON *GR 2661* and south and north east over canal and railway to GREAT BEDWYN *GR 2764* (station) go north east FROXFIELD *GR 2968* go north west and north to RAMSBURY *GR 2771*. North west STOCK LANE *GR 2373*. North east ALDBOURNE *GR 2675* go to minor road through NORTH FIELD BARN *GR 2677* go under M4 minor road north west WANBOROUGH and LIDDINGTON *GR 2081*. (Now OS 173). Minor road north of M4 and under A419 BADBURY WICK *GR 1881* to SWINDON B4006 and minor roads to station at *GR SU1485*.

H19C: Wiltshire Cycleway — South, Gillingham via Berwick St John —

Salisbury, OS 183; 29 miles, direction west to east
From GILLINGHAM station OS 183 *GR ST8126* north on B3092 to minor road at *GR 806268* go north east two miles at crossroads *GR 827289* south east KNAPP HILL *GR8526* go east on minor roads over A350 go to SEM HILL *GR 8827* (now OS 184) go south east DONHEAD ST MARY *GR 9024* and to minor road over A30 to BERWICK ST JOHN *GR 9422* go north east to EBBESBOURNE WAKE *GR 9924* BROAD CHALKE go to BISHOPSTONE go to STRATFORD TONY *GR 0926* go north by minor road past Racecourse go to NETHERHAMPTON *GR 1029* go to QUIDHAMPTON *GR 1031* go east by minor road BEMERTON *GR 1230* to station.

H19D: Wiltshire Cycleway — West, Gillingham — Bradford-on-Avon — Chippenham via Stourhead and Longleat, OS 183, 173; 45 miles, direction south west to north east
From GILLINGHAM station OS 183 *GR ST8126*, B3092 north to minor road at *GR 806268* go to minor road north east to crossroads *GR 8228 **. North to MERE *GR 8132* go west B3092 under A303 STOURTON *GR 7834* STOURHEAD, National Trust, magnificent gardens) go to B3092 MAIDEN BRADLEY *GR 8039* go north east minor road HORNINGSHAM for LONGLEAT PARK *GR 804417*. House open every day except Christmas: cyclists welcome on all hard roads (except Safari Park!). No charge in Winter. Exits several including PICKET POST GATE *GR 843441*, no longer a gate. Our exit near STALLS Farm *GR 8044*, go to minor road north to DERTFORDS *GR 8145*. CORSLEY HEATH *GR 8245* north via LYE'S GREEN *GR 8246* CHAPMANSLADE go north east on A3098 to DILTON MARSH station *GR 8550* north and north west minor road go to FAIRWOOD *GR 8451* go to RUDGE *GR 8251* minor road RODE *GR 8053*. Over river FROME. Minor road at *GR 803543* **(critical point)** go to TELLISFORD *GR 8055* (now OS 173) (ignore one mile on OS 172) go north to FARLEIGH HUNGERFORD *GR 8057* go north east to WESTWOOD *GR 8059* go to AVONCLIFF (station and fine DUNDAS aqueduct) minor road east on north of railway to BRADFORD-ON-AVON *GR 824606* (if time use river and canal side tarmac track to Tithe Barn and

89

Bradford). Leave BRADFORD-ON-AVON by B3107 signed 'MELKSHAM' go north at *GR 828610* by minor road to BRADFORD LEIGH *GR 8362* east and north east GREAT CHALFIELD *GR 8663* go to ATWORTH *GR 8666* go north to NESTON *GR 8668* (leave Wiltshire Cycleway) east to THE RIDGE *GR 8768* north and south east GASTARD *GR 8868* north east over railway to EASTON *GR 8970* go north east to CHIPPENHAM station *GR 9273*.

* NOTE: Well informed local cyclists have doubts about the Wiltshire County Council use of B3092 Mere *GR 8132* to Maiden Bradley (traffic and poor visibility). For a quiet winding alternative go west at WHITE HILL *GR 8230* over B3095 to ZEALS *GR 7831* go north minor road STOURTON, Stourhead (National Trust) *GR 7734*, go to KILMINGTON COMMON *GR 7736* go to YARNFIELD GATE go to north turning east at *GR 771383* to resume route at Maiden Bradley *GR 8031*.

H19E: Mid Wilts — Vale of Pewsey, Bradford on Avon via the Vale of Pewsey to Great Bedwyn, OS 173, 174; 42 miles, direction west to east
From BRADFORD-ON-AVON OS 173 *GR ST8260*, over bridge go to B3107 'MELKSHAM' go north by minor road at *GR 828610* (critical point) to north east to BRADFORD LEIGH and to minor road east and north east GREAT CHALFIELD *GR 8663*; go to ATWORTH *GR 8665* and go north by minor road to NESTON *GR 8668* go east THE RIDGE *GR 8768* go to GASTARD *GR 8868* go north and south east just before railway at *GR 890699* go over railway and by A350 to LACOCK *GR 9168* go east to BOWDEN HILL and SANDY LANE *GR 9668* go south east on A342 and minor road to HEDDINGTON *GR 9966* go north STOCKLEY *GR 0067* east to BLACKLAND *GR 0168* go south and south east minor road over A361 to BISHOPS CANNING *GR 0364* go to HORTON *GR 0463* go to ALTON BARNES *GR 1062* go to DRAYCOT FITZ PAYNE *GR 1462* over A345 go to MILKHOUSE WATER *GR 1761* go to north east WOOTON RIVERS *GR 1962* (now OS 174). Either keep to winding (signed) Cycleway for three miles to SAVERNAKE HOTEL at *GR 236633* or follow towpath on south of Kennet and Avon Canal. From Hotel, both routes then north east to road junction Point 167 at *GR 254660* (critical point) south east

to GREAT BEDWYN station *GR SU2864*. If you care for a bit of off-road riding (shorter but steeper), go straight on at road junction TURNPIKE Farm *GR 982664* and follow the 'old Bath Road' to BEACON HILL. Fork off at *GR 002654* to OLIVER'S CASTLE and on the ROUNDWAY *GR 0163* go to roundabout on A361 *GR 023630* go to minor road to HORTON to rejoin route.

H19F: Wiltshire Cycleway cross county — South, Frome to Salisbury via Longleat and the Wylye Valley, OS 183, 184; 32 miles, direction north west to south east
From FROME station OS 183 *GR ST7847*, minor road through FELTHAM Farm *GR 7946* ELLIOTS GREEN *GR 7945* DERTSFORDS *GR 8145* south to LONGLEAT PARK by STALLS Farm *GR 8043*. Longleat House, Cafe and Park open every day except Christmas; cyclists may use hard roads, excluding Safari Park lying north of the Estate; no charge in Winter. HORNINGSHAM *GR 8241* south east and north east CROCKERTON *GR 8642* A350 to minor road at *GR 367432* (critical point). Now OS 184. South east SUTTON VENY *GR 9042* and minor road south east through river WYLYE VALLEY go to STOCKTON, WYLYE *GR 0037* go to GREAT WISHFORD *GR 0735* go south east on minor road WILTON *GR 0931*. QUIDHAMPTON *GR 1130* go to BEMERTON *GR 1230* and SALISBURY Cathedral south east to station and YH.

- **RELATED ROUTES:** H1, H12, H15, H16
- **RECONNOITRED:** RNH; NAS of Edington and JG of Trowbridge

---

H20A

- **DORCHESTER to YEOVIL**
- **COUNTY:** DORSET
- **QUIETNESS:** **
- **MILEAGE:** 24 (38 for LULWORTH YH)
- **DIRECTION:** south east to north west
- **TRAIN STATIONS and TIMETABLES:** DORCHESTER WEST *GR ST6890*, YEOVIL JUNCTION *GR ST5714* with 3 intermediate stations within reach, 123, 160
- **MAP:** OS 194
- **WEATHER FORECAST:** 0891-500403
- **TOURIST INFORMATION OFFICE:** DORCHESTER 01305-267992, YEOVIL 01935-71279

- **PUBLICATIONS:** *Cycling in West Dorset* from District Council
- **ACCOMMODATION:** Consult Tourist Information
- **PLACES OF INTEREST:** Dorchester Museum among many others
- **ROUTE:**

From DORCHESTER WEST station OS 194 *GR ST688902* trace the Roman Road over railway at *GR 685907* go north west BRAD-FORD PEVEREL *GR 6593*, crossing river FROME *GR 6493*, over A37 and bridge over railway to minor road at *GR 644943* go north west by minor road close to river SYDLING WATER all way to SYDLING ST NICHOLAS *GR 6299* go north and west at crossroads *GR 632003* (critical point) go north west over A37 *GR 6100* go west and over railway SANDHILLS *GR 5800* go north west RAMPISHAM *GR 5602*. Go to UPHALL and all way north to CLARKHAM CROSS *GR 5507* (critical point) go west HALSTOCK *GR 5308* go north to SUTTON BINGHAM *GR 5411* under railway go north east on minor road, divert north west for EAST COKER. Go over A37 to BARWICK *GR 6313* and YEOVIL JUNCTION station.

If you are youth hostelling the following is a quiet all minor road route from LULWORTH COVE YH *GR SY8380*, built by the efforts of MICHAEL DOWER — later director-general of the Countryside Commission — and others): west north west to DAGGERS GATE *GR 8181* go north WINFRITH NEWBURGH *GR 8084* over A352 to BLACKNOLL and TADNOLL *GR 7986* go to REDBRIDGE *GR 7888*, MORETON station nearby, go west north west over B3390 to WEST STRATFORD *GR 7289* and DORCHESTER. 14 miles making total LULWORTH to YEOVIL 38 miles.

N.B. At LULWORTH note the Ministry of Defence leaflet (1992) *Walks over Ministry of Defence Lands* gives guidance on access in August and at weekends to LULWORTH RANGE (AONB and SSI); nothing is said about cycling.

H20B

- **UPWEY (WEYMOUTH) to CREWKERNE**
- **COUNTY:** DORSET

- **QUIETNESS:** **
- **MILEAGE:** 32
- **DIRECTION:** south east to north west
- **TRAIN STATIONS and TIMETABLES:** UPWEY *GR SY6783*, CREWKERNE *GR SY4508*, 158, 160
- **MAP(S):** OS 194, 193
- **WEATHER FORECAST:** 0891-500403
- **TOURIST INFORMATION OFFICE:** WEYMOUTH 01305-772444, AXMINSTER 01297-34386
- **PUBLICATIONS:** *West Dorset cycle rides* from District Council
- **ACCOMMODATION:** YH BRIDPORT and consult Tourist Information
- **ROUTE:**

OS 194 UPWEY station at *GR SY6783*; A354 for half mile to road junction *GR 667827* (critical point) go to NOTTINGTON *GR 6682* then north and west for three miles to join B3157 at road junction *GR 6783* (critical point) go for over one mile to road junction south west to RODDEN *GR 6184* go south west in circle by minor roads ABBOTSBURY *GR 5785* (Village of abundant interests — swans and peacocks among others) — a walk up to St Catherine's Chapel is a change, go to coast road B3157 by View Point *GR 5685* go to SWYRE *GR 5288* — divert north east for simple YH at LITTON CHENEY *GR 5490* go on B3157 (now OS 193) to BURTON BRADSTOCK *GR 4989* and BRIDPORT *GR 4692*. YH (well adapted from a factory) go north alongside river BRIT crossing to west side at BRADPOLE *GR 4794* go north past WOOTH Manor (visited by Celia Fiennes in her 17th century diary) go north by minor road WAYTOWN *GR 4697* go to NETHERBURY (a lovely village) join A3066 at *GR 477000* go north BEAMINSTER go west north west BROADWINDSOR *GR 4302* go north on B3164 to take minor road *GR 439029* (critical point) to LITTLE WINDSOR *GR 4404*, go north east to A3066 at MOSTERTON *GR 4505* to join A356 go north west to CREWKERNE station.

If B3164 is busy try the small minor roads through SEABOROUGH *GR 4206* for quiet (but **hilly**) approach to CREWKERNE — not reconnoitred personally.

- **RECONNOITRED:** RNH

H20C

- **AXMINSTER to SHERBORNE**
- **COUNTY:** DORSET
- **QUIETNESS:** **
- **MILEAGE:** 33
- **DIRECTION:** south west to north east
- **TRAIN STATIONS and TIMETABLES:** AXMINSTER *GR SY2998*, SHERBORNE *GR ST6416*, 145
- **MAP(S):** OS 193, (194), (183)
- **WEATHER FORECAST:** 0891-500403
- **TOURIST INFORMATION OFFICE:** AXMINSTER 01297-34386, SHERBORNE 01935-815341
- **PUBLICATIONS:** *West Dorset cycle rides* from District Council
- **PLACES OF INTEREST:** See text and consult Tourist Information
- **ROUTE:** road

From AXMINSTER station OS 193 *GR SY2998*, follow town roads to road junction on A35 at *GR 303984* **(critical point)** go east STAMMERY HILL go to minor road (not B road) at BLACKPOOL CORNER *GR 3398* go to minor road north east SCOUSE Farm *GR 3498* go over river BLACKWATER *GR 3500* go to THORNCOMBE *GR 3703* go north north west by Church go to FORDE ABBEY *GR 3605* go north east over railway WINSHAM *GR 3706* go south east on B3162 under railway and cross B3165 go east to DRIMPTON *GR 4105* go south east LITTLE WINDSOR *GR 4404* go north east MOSTERTON (A3066) taking minor road at Church *GR 457056* **(critical point)** (here make for CREWKERNE station if need be). Continue route east by minor road to CHEDINGTON *GR 4805* crossing A356 at WINYARD'S GAP, National Trust *GR 4906* (now OS 194), go to minor road north east all way to HALSTOCK *GR 5308* follow minor road north to SUTTON BINGHAM *GR 5411*; go north east over A37 and railway to STOFORD *GR 5613* (divert north to YEOVIL Junction station if need be) go east under railway BRADFORD ABBAS *GR 5814* (now OS 183), north east and east to SHERBORNE *GR 6316* (two castles, school and museum, friendly Tourist Information).

- **RECONNOITRED:** RNH

AREA J

South

Hampshire, Isle of Wight, East Dorset, Berkshire, Buckinghamshire and Oxfordshire

Introduction to all New Forest Routes — J1, 5 and 6

The New Forest ('New' in 1066) is a paradise for the rail-access cyclist seeking quiet, safe, segregated routes in lovely varied wooded landscape with access from no less than seven stations with names such as HINTON ADMIRAL. There are some 100 miles of firm gravel tracks, free of cars. The Forest is owned by the Crown, and there are few legal rights of way (as shown on OS maps) and no signposts, but the generous access policy for individual cyclists is summarised by the Forestry Commission letter (September 1990) from Queen's House LYNDHURST:
'Cycling within the Forest off Public Highways (Roads and Bridleways) is subject to the FC Byelaws. Access by cyclist is permitted on made up gravel tracks only in daylight hours by individuals and families. Organized cycling events are subject to formal permission and cross country cycling is not permitted at all.'
If you intend to make much use of this cycling paradise it is advisable to get a copy of the *New Forest Recreational Management Map* (scale 1:25000) from Queen's House for use with the other relevant maps. It names every car park, and is a great aid to navigation.

J1

- **SWAY to BEAULIEU ROAD through the NEW FOREST**
- **COUNTY:** HAMPSHIRE
- **QUIETNESS:** ***
- **MILEAGE:** To BROCKENHURST 19, to BEAULIEU ROAD 26.
- **DIRECTION:** south west to north east
- **TRAIN STATIONS and TIMETABLES:** SWAY *GR SZ2798*, HINTON ADMIRAL BEAULIEU ROAD *GR SU3406*, 158
- **MAP(S):** OS 196, Outdoor Leisure 22:

New Forest and *Explore the New Forest* (see below)

- **WEATHER FORECAST:** 0891-500403
- **TOURIST INFORMATION OFFICE:** LYNDHURST 0170328-2269
- **PUBLICATIONS:** *Explore the New Forest* is essential for enjoyable map reading in the maze of tracks, as there are no signposts (it resembles war-time map reading in this respect only). Also Whitbread's Circular Cycle Route and CTC series of Forest Rides.
- **ACCOMMODATION:** BURLEY YH *GR SU2202*: ideal situation
- **PLACES OF INTEREST:** Abundant — see guides
- **ROUTE:** track

SWAY station *GR 2798*. Minor road to SET THORNS INCLOSURE *GR 268991*. Track winds to minor road *GR 263004*. West to BURLEY *GR 2103*, north east by old forest track to 'CROSS' (Canadian Memorial) *GR 239094*. Track east and south east near stream 'HIGHLAND WATER', to road *GR 267077* near MILLYFORD bridge, west and south by track to road west of KNIGHTWOOD OAK *GR 264064*, south east and south on east of RHINEFIELD ORNAMENTAL DRIVE to PC *GR 267046*, east by POUNDGILL INCLOSURE and clockwise route to BOLDERFORD from *GR 291042* and south west minor road to BROCKENHURST station. Go a little over a mile east on B3055 to track at *GR 319023* **(critical point)**, east and then north to cross railway at *GR 334035*; north to B3056. Short ride south east to BEAULIEU ROAD station.

- **RELATED ROUTES:** J5 and J6
- **RECONNOITRED:** June 1986, RNH

J2

- **YARMOUTH-THE NEEDLES-COWES-RYDE**
- **COUNTY:** ISLE OF WIGHT
- **QUIETNESS:** *
- **MILEAGE:** 22 to COWES, 32 to RYDE
- **DIRECTION:** west to east mainly.
- **TRAIN STATIONS and TIMETABLES:** LYMINGTON PIER *GR SZ3395*, PORTSMOUTH HARBOUR *GR SU6200*, 158, 160, 167, 156
- **MAP:** OS 196
- **WEATHER FORECAST:** 0891-500403
- **TOURIST INFORMATION OFFICE:** NEWPORT 01983-525450 generous information on cycling in the Isle of Wight
- **PUBLICATIONS:** Consult Tourist Information
- **ACCOMMODATION:** YH TOTLAND BAY *GR 324866*
- **PLACES OF INTEREST:** Include YARMOUTH Castle (English Heritage)
- **ROUTE:** track

LYMINGTON PIER station to YARMOUTH A3054 and B3322 to ALUM BAY (walk to NEEDLES) return via TOTLAND. From FRESHWATER, Causeway and old railway bridle and cycleway to B3401. WELLOW *GR 3888* NINGWOOD *GR 4089*. A3054 to SHALFLEER: minor road to PORCHFIELD *GR 4491*. COWES (floating bridge and terminals at both EAST and WEST COWES, WEST COWES does not take unfolded cycles). EAST COWES A3021 (OSBORNE HOUSE), road Junction *GR 516934* south east on minor road to WOOTON BRIDGE. Cross Creek at north to FISHBOURNE for car ferry to PORTSMOUTH or bridleway at *GR 557928* (Isle of Wight COASTAL PATH to BINSTEAD and RYDE. Cycles not allowed on Pier Railway (old London Transport rolling stock); take care on wooden planks on Pier). Catamarans to PORTSMOUTH HARBOUR station: may not accept cycles on summer Saturdays.
- **RELATED ROUTES:** J4 and J8
- **RECONNOITRED:** November 1984, RNH

J3

- **ORDNANCE SURVEY — MAKERS OF THE BEST MAPS IN THE WORLD.** A conducted tour at a venue with an attractive hinterland.
- **COUNTY:** HAMPSHIRE
- **QUIETNESS:** *
- **MILEAGE:** 4
- **DIRECTION:** Various
- **TRAIN STATIONS and TIMETABLES:** SOUTHAMPTON *GR SU4112* or MILLBROOK *GR SU3713*, 158, 165
- **MAP:** OS 196
- **WEATHER FORECAST:** 0895-500403
- **TOURIST INFORMATION OFFICE:** SOUTHAMPTON 01703-221106, try also 0703-775555 x 608
- **PUBLICATIONS:** See route J1
- **ACCOMMODATION:** YH SOUTHAMPTON *GR 415156*
- **PLACES OF INTEREST:** Consult Tourist Information
- **ROUTE:** road

SOUTHAMPTON *GR SU387128*, ROMSEY ROAD, MAYBUSH, SOUTHAMPTON SO9 4DU. Tours (about 2 hours) twice daily 10.00 and 14.00 most weekdays. No charge. Book well in advance. If time permits, explore some of the 100 miles of firm gravel tracks in the New Forest — free of cars.
- **RELATED ROUTES:** New Forest and Isle of Wight routes
- **RECONNOITRED:** 1984, RNH

J4

- **RYDE to COWES via OSBORNE HOUSE**
- **COUNTY:** ISLE OF WIGHT
- **QUIETNESS:** **
- **MILEAGE:** 9 from RYDE; 5 from FISH-BOURNE
- **DIRECTION:** east to west
- **TRAIN STATIONS and TIMETABLES:** PORTSMOUTH HARBOUR (for ferry), SOUTHAMPTON (via ferry), 123, 156, 158, 165, 167, 187, 188 (167 includes ferries to the Isle of Wight)
- **MAP:** OS 196
- **WEATHER FORECAST:** 0891-50040310

- **TOURIST INFORMATION OFFICE:** NEWPORT (all year) 01983-562905, RYDE 01983-562905 and COWES 01983-291914
- **PUBLICATIONS:** Free holiday brochures etc., *Cycling on the IOW*, from NEWPORT Tourist Information
- **ACCOMMODATION:** Many — see Tourist Information offices
- **PLACES OF INTEREST:** Osborne House. Most of the island is cycle-friendly, but be prepared for hills.
- **ROUTE:** road

Part 1: Crossing to the island, 4 miles
From PORTSMOUTH Harbour station, aircraft-like catamarans will take cycles to RYDE Pier in 15 minutes; limited space in high season. Nicer car ferry takes 45 minutes, plenty of space and no folding, from nearby Gunwharf **GR 633000**. Lands in rural FISHBOURNE — recommended. From COWES, take Red Funnel car ferry to SOUTHAMPTON, then short ride to station. All ferries carry cycles free.

Part 2: Ryde to Cowes, 8 miles (Fishbourne to Cowes 5 miles)
From Pierhead beware of slippery pier and at Esplanade station (Tourist Information) west on way marked Coastal Path to **GR 582924**. Walk across golf course to QUARR Road **GR 5692**. B3325 (FISHBOURNE riders join here) south west to WOOTTON bridge. By minor roads to BROCKS COPSE Road, **GR 5392**. Minor road over A3021 to WHIPPINGHAM. Minor road to OSBORNE HOUSE (English Heritage) entrance **GR 512946**. B3321 to EAST COWES for SOUTHAMPTON ferry or floating bridge to WEST COWES; town centre, also ferry to SOUTHAMPTON.
- **RELATED ROUTES:** COWES-NEWPORT CYCLEWAY. From WEST COWES floating bridge via Arctic Road to **GR 497948** for start of Cycleway on old railway alongside west bank of river MEDINA to NEWPORT. Return by same route. Wild life, river views, highly recommended.
- **RECONNOITRED:** 1990, REK

J5

- **BROCKENHURST to BEAULIEU ROAD via FOREST TRACKS**
- **COUNTY:** HAMPSHIRE

- **QUIETNESS:** ***
- **MILEAGE:** 15 on forest tracks
- **DIRECTION:** south west to north east
- **TRAIN STATIONS and TIMETABLES:** BROCKENHURST **GR SU3002**, BEAULIEU ROAD **GR SU3406**
- **MAP:** OS 196
- **WEATHER FORECAST:** 0891-500403
- **TOURIST INFORMATION OFFICE:** LYNDHURST 01703-2269
- **PUBLICATIONS:** *Explore the New Forest*
- **ACCOMMODATION:** YH at BURLEY on the edge of the Forest **GR 220028** and consult Tourist Information
- **PLACES OF INTEREST:** See Publications
- **ROUTE:** track

For early start stay overnight in the BROCKENHURST area **GR 3002**, make for Forest bridleway **GR 303003**. East and south east before ROYDON MANOR **GR 3100** to crossroads at **GR 318994**. East generally to BOLDRE church **GR 324994**. Memorial to HMS HOOD. One third of a mile north by minor roads or tracks DILTON Farm **GR 3300**; minor diversion edge of fields; edge of Forest; East remains of Airfield, south east to explore BEAULIEU HEATH; model aircraft flying area. Return to find STOCKLEY COTT north of Airfield **GR 344019**. Half mile north on B3055 to corner; take gravel track north east to junction **GR 348024** north to gate and level crossing **GR 3403**; north north west through DENNY LODGE INCLOSURE; watch for track junction **GR 342047**; north east through WOODFIDLEY passage **GR 3405** over BISHOP'S DYKE at **GR 348053**; very sandy track to SHATTERFORD car park close to BEAULIEU ROAD station **GR 349064**. These names are taken from 1:25,000 Leisure Sheet; they are also in *Explore the New Forest*, HMSO.
- **RELATED ROUTES:** J1, J6
- **RECONNOITRED:** December 1989, RNH

J6

- **NEW FOREST BURLEY YH to WINCHESTER YH.** See introduction to area J routes for the excellent cycling opportunities in the New Forest.
- **COUNTY:** HAMPSHIRE
- **QUIETNESS:** ***

- **MILEAGE:** 12 to BURLEY YH, further 31 SHAWFORD station. Add 4 for WINCHESTER; total 47.
- **DIRECTION:** south west to north east
- **TRAIN STATIONS and TIMETABLES:** NEW MILTON *GR SZ2495*, SHAWFORD, WINCHESTER *GR SU4729*, 158
- **MAP(S):** OS 195, 185, 196
- **WEATHER FORECAST:** 0891-500403
- **TOURIST INFORMATION OFFICE:** LYNDHURST 01703-2269, WINCHESTER 0192-840500 (recorded message outside office hours)
- **PUBLICATIONS:** Book: *Explore the New Forest*, HMSO, an essential companion; the large-scale map (1:25000) overprinted with the Forest gravel tracks is vital for enjoyment.
- **ACCOMMODATION:** Ample list from Tourist Information including YH at BURLEY and WINCHESTER
- **PLACES OF INTEREST:** See *Explore the New Forest*. Near Winchester is the Watercress Line Steam Railway, and the Marwell Zoo for endangered species.
- **ROUTE:** track

NEW MILTON station (or SWAY) BURLEY ROMSEY SHAWFORD WINCHESTER
From NEW MILTON station go north on B3058 for a quarter mile. At *GR 243955* go east alongside open space and then north by minor road to footpath near Danestream Farm *GR 253968* (one stile). Push due north to cross minor road to gravel path at *GR 252983*. Stile giving entry to Forest, go east along greensward and track on south boundary of Forest to car park (BOUNDWAY HILL) at *GR 2698*. Then north east over stream at *GR 264987*, through SET THORNS enclosure and cross minor road to car park (LONGSLADE BOTTOM) and dismantled railway; east along this for one third of a mile. North through HINCHESLEA WOOD *GR 2700* to car park (HINCHESLEA) *GR 270014* then north by Red Hill to car park (WHITE MOOR) at *GR 277025*. Here north north west by minor unfenced road to PUTTLES bridge. Forest Walks (well presented), on north to RHINEFIELD Cottage *GR 266043*; go west through Rhinefield Sandys Inclosure on main road A35, south west **with care for one mile** pass car park MARKWAY and to WILVERLEY POST *GR 242020*. Go north west by track

past CLAY HILL car park *GR 232025* to BURLEY YH at *GR 220029*.
From BURLEY YH to SHAWFORD and WINCHESTER largely by car-free tracks, 31 miles
Minor road to BURLEY GRANGE and road junction at *GR 220043* along minor road north east just past Forest Office at *GR 230049*. Take track north by gate 175 through BURLEY OUTER RAILS inclosure; after crossing three streams, the last called BLACKENSFORD BROOK at *GR 239063*, at HART HILL track junction *GR 243063* go north west and north through NORTH OAKLEY inclosure. Well-signposted Forest Walks meet at *GR 238075*. Care at *GR 243083* go east and cross one minor road (BOLDERWOOD HILL) to another minor road along which go south east to car park and Viewpoint HIGHLAND *GR 247083*. Just beyond at Spot height 99 take track north east through HIGHLAND WATER INCLOSURE **(care map reading)** to FORD beyond ACRES DOWN HOUSE at *GR 270099*. Then minor road through NEWTON, MINSTEAD. (Now OS 186) Crossing A337 to BARTLEY *GR 3012* to join A336 and minor road north to WINSOR *GR 3113* north east and east to road junction *GR 334148* go north to bridleway which crosses M27 at *GR 3316* on to MOOR COURT, SKIDMORE, LEE MANOR Farm *GR 3617** to A27 (short length footway) to ROMSEY (neither TOURIST INFORMATION nor Broadlands House open in Winter). Exit by A31 few yards first railway bridge minor road east to A27 at *GR 307200* NUTBURN go north east to FLEXFORD and HOCOMBE *GR 4323*. Crossroads A33 at *GR 4522* and make for bridge under railway and over canal *GR 468225* and push along ITCHEN Navigation to SHAWFORD station. Further river or canal side paths recommended (not reconnoitred) to WINCHESTER station and YH.
* If you wish to omit ROMSEY (no cafe in Winter) and avoid main roads take minor road via ASHFIELD *GR 367188* to HOE Farm NORTH BADDESLEY to rejoin above route at road junction *GR 395199* NUTBURN.
- **RELATED ROUTES:** J1, J5, J2, J4
- **RECONNOITRED:** December 1988, RNH

J7

- **PILGRIMS WAY CYCLE ROUTE**
  (close to **NORTH DOWNS WAY**)
  WINCHESTER to CANTERBURY
- **COUNTY:** HAMPSHIRE, SURREY, KENT
- **QUIETNESS:** *
- **MILEAGE:** WINCHESTER to HINDHEAD
  42, HINDHEAD to TANNER'S HATCH 28,
  TANNER'S HATCH to KEMSING 39,
  KEMSING to CANTERBURY 51. Total 160.
- **DIRECTION:** west to east
- **TRAIN STATIONS and TIMETABLES:**
  WINCHESTER *GR SU5132*,
  CANTERBURY EAST *GR TR1457*
  and numerous intermediate stations.
  Winchester 158, Canterbury 212.
- **MAP(S):** OS 185, 186, 187, 188, (178),
  189, 179
- **WEATHER FORECAST:** 0891-500402
- **TOURIST INFORMATION OFFICE:**
  WINCHESTER 01962-840500, FARNHAM
  01252-715109, GUILDFORD
  01483-444007, ROCHESTER
  01634-843666, MAIDSTONE
  01622-673581, CANTERBURY
  01227-766567 (WINCHESTER, FARNHAM
  and ROCHESTER have answering
  machines outside office hours)
- **PUBLICATIONS:** Countryside Commission
  leaflet and book of maps
- **ACCOMMODATION:** YHs on or near route.
  On the route: (1) WINCHESTER
  GR SO4829. (2) HINDHEAD *GR 892368*
  Simple YH 4 miles from FRENSHAM
  PONDS Country Park. (3) TANNERS
  HATCH near DORKING see text of route,
  GR 104515 28 miles from Hindhead. (4)
  KEMSING near Sevenoaks *GR 555588*. (5)
  CANTERBURY *GR 157570*. NEAR ROUTE
  (6) HOLMBURY ST MARY 3 miles south of
  route *GR TQ104452*. Useful if taking the
  A25 choice of route — divert at SHERE
  GR 0748 or ABINGER HAMMER *GR 0947*.
- **PLACES OF INTEREST:** Numerous.
  Consult Tourist Information and guides.
  Adapted from route prepared for St Paul's
  Bedford (sponsored ride 1982) accom-
  modation was in Church halls. This version
  aims at YH. Please report suggested
  improvements.
  *Beware: This route is a good deal less
  quiet than most in this book, and care
  should be taken when using the minor*

*roads, especially those serving the M25.
The route involves some walking along
footpaths so as to reach churches and
other features on the Pilgrims Way.
This route is based on staying at Youth
Hostels (three of them of simple traditional
type). Consult Tourist Information for ample
alternative B and B accommodation.*
- **ROUTE:** road and track

**Part 1: Hampshire OS 185, 186, Winchester
to GR 7948 Crondall near Farnham**
WINCHESTER *GR SU4730*: YH in National
Trust watermill in town centre. North east
minor road under M3 junction 9 EASTON
GR 5132 (diversion to see MARTYRWORTHY
GR 5132). Then keep south of river ITCHEN,
AVINGTON *GR 5332*, OVINGTON *GR 5631*,
south of NEW ALRESFORD to BISHOP'S
SUTTON *GR 6131*, GUNDLETON *GR 6133*,
BIGHTON *GR 6134*, north east MEDSTEAD
GR 6637 (now OS 186). North east to BEECH
GR 6938, ALTON minor roads to CUCKOO
CORNER *GR 7341*, MILL COURT, UPPER
FROYLE *GR 7542*, LOWER FROYLE; then
WELL *GR 7646*, CRONDALL *GR 7948* and
south east to
**Part 2: Surrey Farnham to Tatsfield Court
Farm near Westerham, OS 186, 187**
DIPPENHALL *GR 8146* to FARNHAM
GR 8446 (station). Here starts the official
'North Downs Way'.
**Choices between FARNHAM and
GUILDFORD**
(A) Close to North Downs Way: From station
GR 8446 walk along official long distance
path to bridge over river WEY at *GR 860465*.
Minor roads to THE SANDS *GR 8846*. North
to SANDY CROSS; east to SEALE *GR 8947*,
PUTTENHAM *GR 9347*, COMPTON *GR
9547*, north east 'TRACKWAY' *GR 9748*
to GUILDFORD.
(B) Avoid Farnham town by minor roads
from DIPPENHALL *GR 8146* over A31
BOUNDSTONE *GR 8344* to FRENSHAM
PONDS (Country Park, National Trust).
GR 8440 (simple YH at HINDHEAD five miles
to south east, then MILL BRIDGE *GR 8442*
and north east minor roads CHARLESHILL
GR 8944 and north east over WARREN POND
GR 9045 to join route A at PUTTENHAM
GR 9347. From GUILDFORD take 'WEY
SOUTH' footpath to road junction *GR 998484*,
east to CHANTRIES and ST MARTHA'S HILL

GR TQ0248 (now OS 187) and NEWLANDS CORNER *GR 0449*. Public convenience, teas. **Choice for route between NEWLAND'S CORNER *GR 0449* and GODSTONE *GR TQ3552*** (A) By road A25 (reported wide and fairly safe February 1990) through pleasant towns and villages: ABINGER HAMMER *GR 0947*, WESTCOTT, DORKING, BUCKLAND,REIGATE, REDHILL, BLETCHINGLEY, GODSTONE. (B) Minor roads diverting to TANNER'S HATCH YH 'unique traditional hostelling experience': spartan, open all months. A25 (see SILENT POOL *GR 0648*). Road junction *GR 068483* north and north east COMBE 2 FOREST *GR 098516* then south east and east DOG KENNEL GREEN *GR 1250*; RANMORE COMMON. Note track junction *GR TQ138504* for rough track to TANNER'S HATCH YH in 1,000 acre National Trust POLESDEN LACY estate. Retrace to RANMORE COMMON Road go north west pushing on long distance path or by minor roads including WESTHUMBLE *GR 1651* to crossing river MOLE either near roundabout and Hotel *GR 172518* or 500 yards south at footbridge *GR 174514* **(steep ascent)** to BOXHILL Country Park *GR 1751*. North east PEBBLE COOMBE *GR 2153*, B2032 KINGSWOOD *GR 2456* south of CHIPSTEAD take minor road south east to HOOLEY *GR 2856*. Then trace DEAN LANE *GR 288558* to ALDERSTEAD HEATH *GR 3055*. East to CHALDON; crossroads north to CHURCH (dates from AD 1086 and possesses interesting mural) *GR 3055*. Resume North Downs Way south of SIX BROTHERS FIELD *GR 3154*, WHITE HILL over M25 by BRIDLEBRIDGE *GR 342527*. GODSTONE *GR 3552*. Make for minor road over A22 and M25 *GR 3552*. FLINTHALL Farm north east BOTLEY HILL *GR 3955*. HILL PARK *GR 4355*, BETSOMS Farm (now OS 188). **Part 3: Kent N of Westerham GR TQ4454 to Canterbury, OS 188, (178), 189, 179** North east and north skirting CHEVENING PARK to KNOCKHOLT *GR 4859* south east to cross A21 and M25 *GR 5058*, north east OTFORD, *GR 5159* east to KEMSING YH *GR 555588*, (limited opening). East HEAVERHAM, WROTHAM *GR 6059*, north east by Church under M20 and A20. TROTTISCLIFFE *GR 6360* south east and east RYARSH *GR 6759*, BIRLING,

SNODLAND *GR 7061*, north avoiding A228; CUXTON *GR 7066*. Find access *GR 716673* to MEDWAY Bridge (foot or cyclepath) *GR 7266*. South IVY COTTAGE *GR 7265*, BURHAM *GR 7262* over A229 BOXLEY *GR 7759*, DETLING *GR 7958*, BROAD ST *GR 8356*, HOLLINGBOURNE *GR 8455* (now OS 189). Pick minor roads to avoid A20(T) to HARRIETSHAM *GR 8652*. LENHAM *GR 8952*, WARREN ST *GR 9252*, south east 'TRACKWAY' Road to B2077, north east over A251, SHOTTENDEN *GR 0454*, CHILHAM *GR 0653* crossing river STOUR BAGHAM *GR 0753*, south east of CHARTHAM *GR 1055*, north east to CANTERBURY East station at *GR 145574* and YH at *GR 157570*.
- **RELATED ROUTES:** J6, K1, K5, K7
- **RECONNOITRED:** 1982, STP B

J8

- **COWES to NEWPORT and FISHBOURNE**
- **COUNTY:** ISLE OF WIGHT
- **QUIETNESS:** **
- **MILEAGE:** 17
- **DIRECTION:** north to south and south west to north east
- **TRAIN STATIONS and TIMETABLES:** SOUTHAMPTON *GR SU4112* for Town Quay for ferry *GR 4110*. End PORTSMOUTH Harbour from ferry at Gunwharf, 156, 158.
- **MAP:** OS 196
- **WEATHER FORECAST:** 0891-500403
- **TOURIST INFORMATION OFFICE:** NEWPORT 01983-525450
- **PUBLICATIONS:** ISLE OF WIGHT Tourist Guide
- **ACCOMMODATION:** Consult Tourist Information
- **PLACES OF INTEREST:** Interesting ferry trips; the sea and shipping; steam railway
- **ROUTE:** track

From WEST COWES FERRY TERMINAL, *GR 497963* south through town to Arctic Road for start of Trailway. Runs alongside river Medina (views and yachts) to NEWPORT (island capital; Isle of Wight Museum, Carisbrooke Castle nearby). From roundabout at end of Industrial Estate south east over river. Leave by Staplers Road *GR 503893*. Right at junction *GR 522897*, Blacklands Road.

Join bridleway at KNIGHTS CROSS, *GR 536897*. North at *GR 543900*, crossing steam railway to WOOTON station. Coastal Path or A3054 to FISHBOURNE CREEK *GR 556931*, for ferry to PORTSMOUTH.

Extension for steam railway
(Tel: 01983 882204)
At junction *GR 543900*, east and south east on bridleway to join minor road. East to HAVENSTREET STEAM RAILWAY CENTRE *GR 5589*. To WOOTON bridge by HAVENSTREET. At junction *GR 564907* north on Firestone Copse Road, then Coastal Path or A3054 to ferry.
Car ferry takes cycles free. Arrives at PORTSMOUTH Gunwharf. Harbour station half mile to north.

- **RELATED ROUTES:** J2, J4, J8
- **RECONNOITRED:** 1990, REK

J9

- **WEYMOUTH (DORSET) to BOSTON (LINCOLNSHIRE) via SALISBURY, OXFORD, MARKET HARBOROUGH, STAMFORD and SPALDING with short diversions for Youth Hostels at RIDGEWAY (WANTAGE), OXFORD, MILTON KEYNES or BADBY and THURLBY**
- **COUNTY:** DORSET, WILTS, BERKSHIRE, OXFORDSHIRE, BUCKINGHAMSHIRE NORTHAMPTONSHIRE, LINCOLNSHIRE
- **QUIETNESS:** **
- **MILEAGE:** Total 310 **to be ridden in short stages with numerous overnight stops**, WEYMOUTH-SALISBURY 60, SALISBURY-OXFORD 71, OXFORD-STAMFORD 99, STAMFORD-BOSTON 42. To Youth Hostels WEYMOUTH-CRANBORNE 46, CRANBORNE-SALISBURY 17, SALISBURY-RIDGEWAY (WANTAGE) 64, RIDGEWAY-OXFORD 33, OXFORD-BADBY 47, BADBY-THURLBY 65, THURLBY-BOSTON 32
- **DIRECTION:** south west to north east
- **TRAIN STATIONS and TIMETABLES:** WEYMOUTH (OS 194, GR SY6779), BOSTON (OS 131, GR TF3244) with numerous intermediate stations including SALISBURY, BEDWYN, OXFORD,

NORTHAMPTON, MARKET HARBOROUGH, STAMFORD and SPALDING, 19, 27, 49, 53, 68, 116, 158
- **MAP(S):** OS 194, 195, 184, 174, 164, 152, 141, 130, 131
- **WEATHER FORECAST:** 0891-500403/406/417
- **TOURIST INFORMATION OFFICE:** WEYMOUTH 01305-772444, BLANDFORD FORUM 01258-454770, SALISBURY 01722-334956, OXFORD 01865-726871, NORTHAMPTON 01604-22677, MARKET HARBOROUGH 01858-462649, STAMFORD 01780-55611, SPALDING 01775-725468, BOSTON 01205-356656
- **ACCOMMODATION:** YH SALISBURY (open all year), THE RIDGEWAY (near WANTAGE), (OXFORD), (BADBY), (THURLBY — limited opening), and consult Tourist Information (brackets indicate near, but not on, the route)
- **PLACES OF INTEREST:** English Heritage OLD SARUM, National Trust TOLPUDDLE, SALISBURY (Montpessow House and Joiners Hall), STOWE landscape Gardens (a must). See also text and consult Tourist Information.
- **ROUTE:**

The route is divided into four stages, each ending at stations. JS reconnoitred it in five days to SPALDING, staying at SALISBURY, LAMBOURN, KIDLINGTON and WEST HADDON *GR SP6371*. Many will spread it out over a longer period as places of interest abound.

Part 1: Weymouth to Salisbury, OS 194 (60 miles)
From WEYMOUTH station *GR SY6779* south and east to B3157 CHARLESTOWN *GR 6579*, north to PUTTON, north east to join A354 at *GR 6682* for short length to old road **(steep, rough)** *GR 669848* **(critical point)**, crossing A354 to minor road east south east and north east to BROADMAYNE *GR 7286*, go south east on A352 to roundabout *GR 7485*, north east B3390 over level crossing and divert to MORETON Church *GR 806894* — engraved windows by WHISTLER; resume B3390 north east over river FROME to crossroads AFFPUDDLE HEATH *GR 8092* **(critical point)**, go east by minor road bearing north east over river PIDDLE passing watercress farm to BERE REGIS *GR 8494*, north east

A31 briefly to minor road at **GR 8596**, north east to WINTERBORNE KINGSTON, north to join A354 **GR 8501**, north east to BLANDFORD FORUM **GR 8806**, now OS 195. Leave by B3082 east to join minor road **GR 9106 (critical point)**, generally east around HUGSTOCK (old airfield) obelisk **GR 9506** to WITCHAMPTON, join B3078 **GR SU0005**, north east for 9 miles CRANBORNE **GR 0513**, north east, now OS 184, to DAMERHAM NORTH END **GR 1016**, north east minor road to ROCKBOURNE **GR 1118**, north west crossroads **GR 0921** (critical point) go north east to join A354 **GR 1023** to north COOMBE BISSETT **GR 1026**, east to HOMINGTON and north at ODSTOCK **GR 1426**, north by minor road to SALISBURY YH at **GR 149299**.

Part 2: Salisbury to Oxford, OS 184, 174, 164 (71 miles)
Out of SALISBURY avoid A345 and take Wiltshire Cycleway to STRATFORD sub CASTLE road junction **GR 131325**. * **(Critical point)**, go north east past OLD SARUM over A345 by minor road north east to WINTERBOURNE **GR 1835**, minor road to IDMISTON **GR 1937** then A338 for 16 miles to COLLINGBOURNE DUCIS **GR 2453**.
* If the 16 miles of A road is unacceptable a good and only slightly longer route is route H19B, summarized as follows: From **(critical point) GR 131325** OLD SARUM follow up AVON valley (Wiltshire Cycleway) GREAT DORNFORD **GR 1338**, east of AMESBURY **GR 1641**, north through BULFORD **GR 1743**, north to crossroads **(critical point)** HAXTON **GR 152496**, north east on minor road to join A342 at EVERSLEIGH **GR 2053**, go east and join minor road to cross A338 at COLLINGBOURNE DUCIS **GR 244541** to resume main route thus:
Over A338 at **GR 2454** to CADLEY and north at SHEARS INN crossroads **GR 2553 (critical point)**, now OS 174, to (signed WEXCOMBE) north and north east minor road over A338 at **GR 2760** by minor road north west to WILTON **GR 2661** (divert east to WINDMILL or north west to CROFTON Pumping station especially if it is a 'steam day'), north east by minor road over Kennet and Avon Canal **GR 2763**, GREAT BEDWYN **GR 2764**, north east FROXFIELD **GR 2968** to short length on A4 **(care)** then minor road north and east to cross river KENNET **GR 3270**, CHILTON FOLIAT, north on B4001 under M4 to join B4000 north

west and north east to LAMBOURN **GR 3278**, north on B4001 past the gallops VIEWPOINT **GR 3485**, north east and north to join B4507, east to WANTAGE **GR 3987**. Leave by BELMONT and west end of GROVE **GR 394900**, go over railway to DENCHWORTH **GR 3891**. North CHARNEY BASSETT (place of interest, CHARNEY MANOR) **GR 3894**, now OS 164, (three mile overlap), go north to cross A420 **GR 3897**, north and east by minor road to LONGWORTH to join A415 **GR 4099**, go north to cross river THAMES NEWBRIDGE, going east at **GR 404015 (critical point)**, to NORTHMOOR, BABLOCK HYTHE **GR 4304**, north west to STANTON HARCOURT **GR 4105**. If time permits, divert to COTSWOLDS LEISURE PARK. Go to B4449 EYNSHAM **GR 4309**. For Oxford break here go to B4044 via north HINKSEY to a good cycle city. Go to minor road CASSINGTON, over railway YARNTON. OXFORD with YH at HEADINGTON **GR 533074**.

Part 3: Oxford to Stamford, OS 164, 152, 141 (99 miles)
Cross A34 at roundabout **GR 474131**, minor road 'Yarnton Lane' weave way through KIDLINGTON over A423 and A43 much rebuilt to minor road to ISLIP **GR 5214** and minor road north east, six miles MERTON **GR 5717**, north east to AMBROSDEN and BLACKTHORN **GR 6219**, cross A41 north east, minor road under railway to MARSH GIBBON **GR 6423**, north east to CHARNDON **GR 6724**, north past Three Bridge Mill **GR 6726** and continue north, now OS 152, to GAWCOTT **GR 6831**, north east over bypass to BUCKINGHAM **GR 7034** (if time, divert to STOWE Gardens — National Trust, open all year on some days. Leave by A413. MAID'S MORETON **GR 7035** go to minor road, north east LECKHAMPSTEAD **GR 7237**, north east WICKEN **GR 7439**. North, north west and north east to PAULERSPURY **GR 7145**, PURY END, west and north east over A5 **(care)** at **GR 7047**. Follow north east SHUTLANGER **GR 7249** to STOKE BRUERNE (Mecca for Canal enthusiasts). Resume minor road over tunnel north to BLISWORTH **GR 7253**, north west to GAYTON **GR 7054**. If you visit NORTHAMPTON approach by arm of the Grand Union Canal **GR 7256**; over M1 at **GR 7058**, KISLINGBURY **GR 6959** to crossroads **GR 7061, (critical point)** north west on Roman Road to NOBOTTLE, LITTLE BRINGTON **GR 6663**, north to GREAT

BRINGTON (divert for ALTHORP — seat of the SPENSERS), north EAST HADDON, now OS 141, to RAVENSTHORPE *GR 6670*, reservoir to GUILSBOROUGH *GR 6772*, north west to COLD ASHBY *GR 6576*, north east on B4036 NASEBY *GR 6878*, north to minor road (Battlefield AD 1645) to SIBBERTOFT *GR 6882*, north east to MARSTON TRUSSELL *GR 6985*, A427 at LUBENHAM *GR 7087* north on minor road FOXTON *GR 7086* (ten famous canal locks). East at road junction *GR 699895*, **(critical point)** and east over A6, canal and (divert to MARKET HARBOROUGH station. B and B, shops, museums and other interests), go to GREAT BOWDEN *GR 7488* and *GR 746891* **(critical point)**, pick up quiet minor road north east to WELHAM *GR 7692*, generally east and north east to WESTON BY WELLAND *GR 7791* and by B664 to MEDBOURNE *GR 7992*, south east and east DRAYTON, GREAT EASTON *GR 8493*, circuit of EYEBROOK reservoir if time; briefly A6003, join B672 at CALDECOTT *GR 6693* go on B672 to MORCOTT *GR 9200* and east on A47 to minor road at WINDMILL *GR 9300*, east BARROWDEN *GR 9400*, north east by minor road, cross A47 and WR GEESTON *GR 9804* go to KETTON, north east on A6121 to TINWELL *GR 0006* and STAMFORD *GR 0307* — Burghley House and other attractions.
Part 4: Stamford to Boston, OS 141, 130, 131 (42 miles)
If not visiting the town, take minor road north crossing A1 by bridge (A606) then minor road to B1081 road junction *GR 004006* (critical point), TOLL BAR, north east on minor road (now OS 130) to BELMESTHORPE *GR 0410*, north east to GREATFORD *GR 0812*, **(critical point)**. At road junction *GR 100128* note that simple YH lies at THURLBY *GR 097168* (4 miles quiet lanes), north east by minor road to cross A15 with **care** BASTON *GR 1113* north east alongside COUNTER DRAIN through TONGUE END *GR 1618*, north east, now OS 131, to minor road and north east to SPALDING. Leave SPALDING by minor road north east SPRINGFIELDS *GR 2624* on south east of river WELLAND (Marsh Road) — open fen country. At WRAGG MARSH House *GR 3030* take bridleway on river bank to cross river at FOSDYKE bridge *GR 3132*, then a maze of minor roads to BUCKLEGATE *GR 3335* and to FRAMPTON *GR 3239*, over the river to BOSTON.

- **RELATED ROUTES:** This long route crosses seven others in this book: see map
- **RECONNOITRED:** 1989 and other times, James L Slater

J10

- **EXPLORING the VALE of AYLESBURY - BLETCHLEY to OXFORD**
- **COUNTY:** BUCKINGHAMSHIRE, OXFORDSHIRE
- **QUIETNESS:** **
- **MILEAGE:** 40
- **DIRECTION:** north east to south west (the opposite direction to usual but can be ridden in reverse)
- **TRAIN STATIONS and TIMETABLES:** MILTON KEYNES, BLETCHLEY *GR SP8633*, OXFORD *GR SV5006*, 65, 66, 116
- **MAP(S):** OS 165, 164
- **WEATHER FORECAST:** 0891-500406
- **TOURIST INFORMATION OFFICE:** AYLESBURY 01296-382308, OXFORD 01865-726871
- **ACCOMMODATION:** YH BRADWELL VILLAGE (MILTON KEYNES) *GR SP8339*, OXFORD YH *GR SP5307*
- **ROUTE:** road

BLETCHLEY station, south west to NEWTON LONGVILLE *GR 8431*. DRAYTON PARSLOW, SWANBOURNE, GRANBOROUGH, follow north west of QUAINTON, KINGSWOOD *GR 6919*, cross A4, and continue west of WOOTON UNDERWOOD to BRILL *GR 6513*, OAKLEY, WORMINGHALL, south west of WATERPERRY, HOLTON, now OS 164. Bridleway at *GR 590067* to SHOTOVER HILL and minor road to city centre and station.
- **RELATED ROUTES:** J12, J13
- **RECONNOITRED:** RNH, November 1983

J11

- **AYLESBURY to KINGHAM**
- **COUNTY:** BUCKINGHAMSHIRE, OXFORDSHIRE
- **QUIETNESS:** **
- **MILEAGE:** 47

- **DIRECTION:** east to west (this is also in an unusual direction but can be ridden in reverse)
- **TRAIN STATIONS and TIMETABLES:** AYLESBURY *GR 8113*, KINGHAM *GR 2522*, 114, 126
- **MAP(S):** OS 165, 164, 163
- **WEATHER FORECAST:** 0891-500406
- **TOURIST INFORMATION OFFICE:** AYLESBURY 01296-382308, STOW ON THE WOLD 01451-31082
- **ACCOMMODATION:** Consult Tourist Information and YH CHARLBURY (old glove factory with tenterhooks — cycle hire available here)
- **ROUTE:** road

From AYLESBURY south west on A418 to road junction *GR 7912*. Keep south west to crossroads *GR 772100*, north east over A418 to CUDDINGTON *GR 7311*. West and north west CANNON'S HILL ASHENDON *GR 7014*, WOTTON UNDERWOOD *GR 6816*, LUDGERSHALL *GR 6617*, PIDDINGTON *GR 6417*, LOWER ARNCOTT *GR 6018*. AMBROSDEN, now OS 164, (five and a half miles overlap) *GR 6019*, south west to MERTON *GR 5717*, ISLIP *GR 5214*, B4027 north west to BLETCHINGDON *GR 5017*, west to GIBRALTER WIER, WOOTTON *GR 4420*, GLYMPTON *GR 4221* to OVER KIDDINGTON on A34(T) at crossroads *GR 408221*, then by minor road to road junction **(critical point)** *GR 401216*, (notices Ditchley Park Private) used for Foreign Office functions (for example, Premier and Chancellor Kohl 1992) go to track south west through sign of 'Grim's Ditch' (OS 1985 Edn) skirting on south east side of woods past Lodge Farm *GR 3919* to join B4437, go west. The local network of rights of way has been changed since the OS of 1985. To CHARLBURY YH at *GR 361198*, station to south west. North west on B4026 SPELBURY *GR 3521* CHADLINGTON *GR 3322*, now OS 163, CHURCHILL *GR 2824*, south west to KINGHAM station *GR SP2522*.
- **RELATED ROUTE:** E7
- **RECONNOITRED:** 1989, E and JB

J12

- **FENNY STRATFORD to BANBURY**
- **COUNTY:** BUCKINGHAMSHIRE, NORTHAMPTONSHIRE
- **QUIETNESS:** **
- **MILEAGE:** 35
- **DIRECTION:** south east to north west
- **TRAIN STATIONS and TIMETABLES:** FENNY STRATFORD *GR SP882343* or BLETCHLEY *GR 8633*, BANBURY *GR SP4640*, 66, 71, 116
- **MAP(S):** OS 152, 165
- **WEATHER FORECAST:** 0891-500406
- **TOURIST INFORMATION OFFICE:** MILTON KEYNES 01908-691995, BANBURY 01295-259855
- **ACCOMMODATION:** YH at BRADWELL VILLAGE (MILTON KEYNES) *GR 831395*
- **ROUTE:** road

FENNY STRATFORD (or BLETCHLEY), NEWTON LONGVILLE *GR 8431*, DRAYTON PARSLOW *GR 8428*, MURSLEY *GR 8228*, the HORWOODS *GR 7930* and *7731*, north SINGLEBOROUGH *GR 7632*, north DANCER'S GRAVE — THORNTON *GR 7535*, CATTLEFORD bridge LECKHAMPSTEAD *GR 7237*, AKELEY *GR 7037*, CHACKMORE *GR 6835*, STOWE PARK (National Trust) leave by south west WATER STRATFORD *GR 6534*, FINMERE *GR 6332*, north west to FULWELL House *GR 6234*, south west and west to MIXBURY *GR 6034*, EVENLEY *GR 5834*, west to CHARLTON, KING'S SUTTON (station for cutting short), north to UPPER ASTROP *GR 5137*, WARKWORTH *GR 4840*, go to BANBURY station.
- **RECONNOITRED:** 1980s, J and EB

J13

- **BLETCHLEY to MORETON IN MARSH**
- **COUNTY:** BUCKINGHAMSHIRE, OXFORDSHIRE, WARWICKSHIRE, GLOUCESTERSHIRE
- **QUIETNESS:** **
- **MILEAGE:** 54
- **DIRECTION:** east to west (an unusual direction for this book but can be cycled in reverse)

- **TRAIN STATIONS and TIMETABLES:**
  BLETCHLEY *GR 8633* (FENNY
  STRATFORD quieter at *GR SP882343*,
  MORETON IN MARSH *GR SP2032*, 65,
  66, 126
- **MAP(S):** 152, 151, 165, 164
- **WEATHER FORECAST:** 0891-500410
- **TOURIST INFORMATION OFFICE:** STOW
  ON THE WOLD 01451-31082
- **ACCOMMODATION:** YH MILTON
  KEYNES, STOW ON THE WOLD, consult
  Tourist Information
- **PLACES OF INTEREST:** National Trust
  Claydon House in text.
- **ROUTE:** road

From BLETCHLEY (or FENNY STRATFORD)
minor roads south west to DRAYTON
PARSLOW *GR 8428*, SWANBOURNE
GR 8027, WINSLOW *GR 7728*, with good
teashop in bakery, VERNEY JUNCTION
GR 7327, MIDDLE CLAYDON *GR 7225*,
CLAYDON House, known for Florence
Nightingale and others, a National Trust
property; STEEPLE CLAYDON *GR 6927*, west
to TWYFORD *GR 6626*, south west to
POUNDON *GR 6425*, north west at crossroads
GR 624242, point 70 on map, now OS 165,
STRATTON AUDLEY *GR 6026*, over A421
STOKE LYNE *GR 5628*, west to ARDLEY
GR 5427, SOMERTON *GR 4928*, NORTH
ASTON *GR 4728*, DUNS TEW *GR 4528*,
LEDWELL *GR 4128*, GREAT TEW and
LITTLE TEW *GR 3929*, west to cross A361,
now OS 151, to GREAT ROLLRIGHT
GR 3231, west and south west to LITTLE
COMPTON *GR 2630* and north to BARTON
ON THE HEATH *GR 2532*, north GREAT
WOLFORD *GR 2434*, TODENHAM *GR 2335*,
south west to MORETON IN MARSH
GR 2032.

- **RELATED ROUTES:** J12
- **RECONNOITRED:** 1980s, J and EB

J14

- **READING TO TRING via HENLEY,
  PRINCES RISBOROUGH and
  WENDOVER**
- **COUNTY:** BERKSHIRE, OXFORDSHIRE,
  BUCKINGHAMSHIRE
- **QUIETNESS:** **

- **MILEAGE:** 52
- **DIRECTION:** south west to north east
- **TRAIN STATIONS and TIMETABLES:**
  READING *GR SU7173*, TRING
  GR SP9512, 66, 116, 117, 158
- **MAP(S):** OS 175, 165
- **WEATHER FORECAST:** 0891-500406
- **TOURIST INFORMATION OFFICE:**
  READING 01734-566226, HENLEY
  01491-578034, WENDOVER
  01296-6967596 (Reading and Henley have
  answering machines outside office hours)
- **ACCOMMODATION:** YH at BRADENHAM
  GR 828972. Consult Tourist Information for
  B and B.
- **PLACES OF INTEREST:** READING,
  Kennett and Avon Canal. HENLEY,
  THAMES Views and HAMBLEDON LOCK,
  TRING Grand Union Canal. Riding in the
  Thames Valley and the Chilterns.
- **ROUTE:** road

Part 1: Reading to Henley, 13 miles
From READING station make for READING
bridge *GR 727743* and riverside path to
CAVERSHAM bridge, then CAVERSHAM
Church at *GR 7075*, north west along The
Warren to MAPLEDURHAM *GR 6776* (House,
Mill and Country Park), north east by minor
road to TRENCH GREEN *GR 6877*, over
A4074 to KIDMORE END *GR 6979*, SONNING
COMMON *GR 7080*, ROTHERFIELD
PEPPARD *GR 7181*, GREYS GREEN
GR 7282, Greys Court (National Trust).
BROADPLAT *GR 7383*, east south east via
BADGEMORE to HENLEY station *GR 7682*.
Part 2: Henley to Tring, 39 miles
Retrace and resume (BROADPLAT GR 7383).
North to BIX *GR 7285*, north and north west
through PAGES Farm *GR 7287*, west and
north west by track and path to COOKLEY
GREEN *GR 6990* (for smoother route, divert at
BIX north east to B480 to STONOR *GR 7888*,
west to MAIDENSGROVE *GR 7288*, then
north west to rejoin at COOKLEY GREEN).
B480 to WATLINGTON to join the RIDGE-
WAY/ICKNIELD WAY at *GR 694933*, north
east along Way (teas at Hill Farm, *GR 7296*
just before M40). If you think the RIDGEWAY
and ICKNIELD WAY too rough (chalk and flint)
it can be avoided by a smoother route from
STONOR *GR 7388*, north west to CHRISTMAS
COMMON *GR 7193*, then north east by minor
road, now OS 165, over both M40 *GR 7396*

and A4 to KINGSTON BLOUNT *GR 7399*, B4009 to CHINNOR, *GR 773027* south east to BLEDLOW, minor road to SAUNDERTON, minor road to PRINCES RISBOROUGH to join B4444, rejoin B4009 to LITTLE KIMBLE *GR 8206*, east to ELLESBOROUGH, BUTLER CROSS *GR 8407*, WENDOVER station *GR 8607*. East to THE HALE *GR 8907*, minor road to ST LEONARDS *GR 9107*, generally north to LEYLANDS Farm *GR 9007*, LONGCROFT *GR 9108* to join RIDGEWAY long distance path *GR 9109*, north east to HASTOE and WIGGINGTON *GR 9410* crossing A41 to TRING station *GR SP9512*.
- **RELATED ROUTES:** J16
- **RECONNOITRED:** 1990, K Hales

J15

- **WINDSOR to HEMEL HEMPSTEAD via BEACONSFIELD and THE CHALFONTS**
- **COUNTY:** BERKSHIRE, BUCKINGHAMSHIRE
- **QUIETNESS:** **
- **MILEAGE:** 30
- **DIRECTION:** south to north
- **TRAIN STATIONS and TIMETABLES:** WINDSOR, 2 stations, *GR SU9677* (BEACONSFIELD *GR SU9491*), HEMEL HEMPSTEAD *GR TL0405*, 66, 115, 119, 147
- **MAP(S):** OS 175, 176, 166
- **WEATHER FORECAST:** 0891-500406
- **TOURIST INFORMATION OFFICE:** WINDSOR 01753-852010, HEMEL HEMPSTEAD 01442-64451
- **ACCOMMODATION:** YHs at WINDSOR (open almost all year), JORDANS *GR 9791*, IVINGHOE *GR 9416*
- **PLACES OF INTEREST:** WINDSOR, CLIVEDEN, BEACONSFIELD Model Village, HEMEL HEMPSTEAD New Town and others
- **ROUTE:** road

Part 1: Windsor to Beaconsfield, 14 miles
From WINDSOR bridge take towpath north west on north bank, leave towpath go to TAPLOW *GR 904818*, minor road north to CLIVEDEN, National Trust, *GR 9185*, WOOBURN COMMON *GR 9287*, minor road

over M40 to BEACONSFIELD. Then minor roads to station or Model Village, *GR 939914*.
Part 2: Beaconsfield to Hemel Hempstead, 16 miles
East and south east by minor road to JORDANS, Quaker Meeting House and YH at *GR 975911*. Minor road to CHALFONT ST GILES *GR 9893*, Milton's Cottage, now OS 176 (3 mile overlap) and OS 166. A4442 to minor road at *GR 008948*, for minor road to LATIMER *GR 0099*. North east to FLAUNDEN *GR 0100*, VENUS HILL *GR 0102* to HEMEL HEMPSTEAD, station *GR 042059*.
- **RELATED ROUTES:** J16
- **RECONNOITRED:** 1990, K Hales, MBC

Alternative route — WINDSOR to BEACONSFIELD
If Thames towpath is not suitable (eg floods, coarse fishing season, 16th June to 15 March): As before to BOVENEY LOCK *GR 9477*. North by minor road to DORNEY *GR 9279*, Dorney Court, minor road crossing M4 and A4 through BURNHAM to PUMPKIN HILL *GR 941849*, BURNHAM BEECHES (a wise purchase by the City of London in Victoria's reign), minor road to ABBEY PARK Farm *GR 944866*, west to rejoin route to WOOBURN COMMON. This alternative route is between one and two miles shorter than G10.

J16

- **WINDSOR to CHALFONT and LATIMER via IVER and DENHAM**
- **COUNTY:** BERKSHIRE and BUCKINGHAMSHIRE
- **QUIETNESS:** **
- **MILEAGE:** 13 to DENHAM. Total 21 via CHALFONT; 26 via RICKMANSWORTH.
- **DIRECTION:** west to east, then north
- **TRAIN STATIONS and TIMETABLES:** WINDSOR (2 stations) *GR SU9677*, CHALFONT and LATIMER *GR SU9997*, 114, 119
- **MAP:** OS 176
- **WEATHER FORECAST:** 0891-500406
- **TOURIST INFORMATION OFFICE:** WINDSOR 01753-852010
- **PUBLICATIONS:** For canal, Nicholsons/OS *Guide to the Waterways - South*

- **ACCOMMODATION:** YH at Jordans
  GR 975910 3 miles west of route
- **PLACES OF INTEREST:** Although it has
  become a commuting area for London, this
  is still a walking country of hills and beech
  woods, rich in history. At JORDANS is a
  17th century meeting house and William
  Penn's grave.
- **ROUTE:** road

Part 1: Windsor to Denham, 13 miles
From WINDSOR station, B470 to DATCHET
GR 9877, continue B470, crossing M4 and A4,
at *GR 013788*, minor road east and north east
to IVER station. Minor road crossing B470,
A4007 and A412 go to PINEWOOD FILM
STUDIOS and BLACK PARK COUNTRY
PARK, *GR 0184*, minor road to DENHAM
GOLF CLUB station *GR 0287*.

**Part 2A: Denham to Chalfont and Latimer
via Chalfont Common, 8 miles**
From DENHAM GOLF CLUB station north
west via minor road to CHALFONT COMMON,
at junction *GR 001948*, minor road to
CHALFONT and LATIMER station, *GR 9997*.

**Part 2B: Denham to Chalfont and Latimer
via Rickmansworth, 13 miles**
From DENHAM GOLF CLUB station return to
DENHAM station at *GR 043877*, minor road to
DENHAM GREEN, north on minor road to join
towpath of Grand Union Canal at WEST
HYDE, Bridge 177. (Note Fisheries Inn, bar
meals at a fine old pub practically surrounded
by water). North on towpath to leave canal at
Bridge 176, SPRINGWELL LANE *GR 0492*.
Over A412 north west through
RICKMANSWORTH (station) past CATLIPS
Farm *GR 0395*, north west to cross railway for
station at CHORLEYWOOD *GR 0296*, north
over A404 CHENIES, Manor House, *GR 0198*,
west and south to CHALFONT and LATIMER
station, *GR 9997*.

- **RELATED ROUTES:** J15
- **RECONNOITRED:** 1990, K Hales, MBC

AREA K

South East
Kent, Surrey, East and West Sussex

K1

- **LONDON to BRIGHTON**
- **COUNTY:** LONDON, SURREY, SUSSEX
- **QUIETNESS:** Few cars **
- **MILEAGE:** 58
- **DIRECTION:** north to south
- **TRAIN STATIONS and TIMETABLES:** CLAPHAM JUNCTION, BRIGHTON, 186 (special trains back)
- **MAP(S):** OS 176, 187, 198
- **WEATHER FORECAST:** 01891-500402
- **TOURIST INFORMATION OFFICE:** BRIGHTON 01273-23755
- **PUBLICATIONS:** BIKE EVENTS programme annually
- **ACCOMMODATION:** YH at BRIGHTON *GR 300088* (on principle open all year except January)
- **PLACES OF INTEREST:** Consult Tourist Information
- **ROUTE:** road

CLAPHAM COMMON station *GR 288745*, B237, A214, B241, MITCHAM A216, A236, A237, B277, CARSHALTON B278, WOODMASTERNE. CHIPSTEAD minor road south below M25 near GATTON *GR 277537*. Half mile of A23, now OS 187, SOUTH MERSTHAM, below M23 at SOUTH NUTFIELD *GR 316488*, SMALLFIELD *GR 3143*, B2037, B2028 TURNERS HILL, ARDINGLY, LINDFIELD, now OS 198, B2111, minor road SLUGWASH LANE **(take special care)** *GR 352215*, WIVELSFIELD, B2112 DITCHLING *GR 3215*, minor road for short distance past BEACON. East of HOLLINGBURY Castle to BRIGHTON Pier and Marine Parade *GR 3103*. In attendance en route: 12 railway stations, 12 official refreshment points, six cycle repair points and three wet weather points. A triumph of organization — not to be missed. Senior Citizens can look upon this ride as a personal MoT test. Don't forget the British Heart Foundation — some do. Venue of start varies. Consult Bike Events.

- **RELATED ROUTES:** K2, K3
- **RECONNOITRED:** 1985-1990, RNH

K2

- **WORTH WAY and FOREST WAY (THREE BRIDGES (CRAWLEY) to ERIDGE)**
- **COUNTY:** SUSSEX EAST and WEST
- **QUIETNESS ***
- **MILEAGE:** 20
- **DIRECTION:** west to east
- **TRAIN STATIONS and TIMETABLES:** THREE BRIDGES *GR TQ288369*, ERIDGE *GR TQ5434*, 52, 184, 186
- **MAP(S):** OS 187, 188
- **WEATHER FORECAST:** 0891-500402
- **TOURIST INFORMATION OFFICE:** LEWES 01273-483448, CHICHESTER 01243-775888 (29a South Street, Chichester PO19 1AH — new address)
- **PUBLICATIONS:** WORTH WAY (West Sussex County Council), FOREST WAY (East Sussex)
- **ACCOMMODATION:** No YH near; consult Tourist Information
- **PLACES OF INTEREST:** See publications
- **ROUTE:** track (**most** of the canal towpath is open)

From THREE BRIDGES station route of WORTH WAY. South and east under M23 through pleasant woodland and CRAWLEY DOWN (some diversion) to EAST GRINSTEAD station *GR 3838*. Old railway made into minor by-pass aptly named 'BEECHING WAY'. Pick up FOREST WAY proper at *GR 440379*, route is fairly plain cycling (some mud during rainy seasons) to end at *GR 514369*. West of GROOMERBRIDGE minor road east to

junction **GR 526368**. Watch for BRIDLEWAY/TRACK east and soon south over railway and south east minor road to ERIDGE station (scene of Bicycle Belle cream teas after Bike Events rides).
* **RELATED ROUTES:** K3/J7, K1
* **RECONNOITRED:** October 1988, RNH

K3

* **THE PILGRIMS (NORTH DOWNS) WAY,** see route J7

K4

* **GUILDFORD to SHOREHAM ON SEA**
* **COUNTY:** SURREY, WEST SUSSEX
* **QUIETNESS:** ***
* **MILEAGE:** 42
* **DIRECTION:** north to south
* **TRAIN STATIONS and TIMETABLES:** GUILDFORD **GR SU992496** CHILWORTH **GR 0347**, or SHALFORD **GR0047**, provides a more rural start. SHOREHAM **GR 2105**, 148, 156 and 188
* **MAP(S):** OS 186, 187, 198
* **WEATHER FORECAST:** 0891-500 402
* **TOURIST INFORMATION OFFICE:** GUILDFORD 01483-444007
* **PUBLICATIONS:** *The Downs Link* Surrey County Council and Tourist Information
* **ACCOMMODATION:** Few visible on route except ST BOTOLPHS (see text). Consult Tourist Information.
* **PLACES OF INTEREST:** BRAMBER CASTLE (see text)
* **ROUTE:** track

Part 1: Wey Navigation (National Trust), 4 miles

From GUILDFORD station at **GR SU992496**, to reach the WEY NAVIGATION towpath with least traffic first try the metal stairs at north end of WALNUT TREE HOUSE (office block just east of station). If locked (weekends) either go north to no. 99 Walnut Tree Rd (Smithcraft) for narrow (permitted) access or south **braving the traffic** to join the river WEY through modern office block at **GR 995494**. Go

south on towpath mostly on west of navigation. Cross the NORTH DOWNS (PILGRIMS) WAY at handsome footbridge, a former Foot Ferry **GR 994483**. Towpath is National Trust property and throughout well signposted under railway and A248. When A281 is reached at **GR 999463** leave towpath and keep on east of river through SUMMERSBURY (cul de sac for cars only) to join minor road at **GR 006462**. South east and south west to join DOWNS LINK Trailway proper at Double bridge south east of GOSDEN Farm on OS at **GR 004456**.

Part 2: Downs Link Trailway to St Botolphs, 32 miles

The DOWNS LINK Trailway uses the old HORSHAM and DISTRICT Railway Company line of 1865 and the London, Brighton South Coast Railway 1877/9. The route is neatly way-marked by hardwood fingerposts and occasional metal plaques all bearing the logo of an arch with a bold horizontal line. The old station board (BRAMLEY and WONERSH) survives at **GR 009451**. On towards CRAN-LEIGH **GR 0638** on OS 187. The route needs no directions except for departures from the track. Note CRANLEIGH, SNOXHALL Recreation Centre (swimming and refresh-ments) at **GR 063385**. Then BARNARDS station **GR 076350** lovingly restored in private hands. The THURLOW ARMS pub nearby is very welcoming. Continue south east by footpath diversion over BAYNARDS TUNNEL. One third of a mile some pushing, one stile (6 cyclists met on this diversion; the alternative bridle route not tried). After RUDGWICK **GR 0833**, cross A281 and the river ARUN by a TWO-TIERED bridge at **GR 095326**. After going below A29 (STANE ST) at **GR 110311** and A264 in half a mile leave railway by signposted diversion by minor road and follow west side of CHRIST'S HOSPITAL School grounds. Watch for return to railway track on right at **GR 143282**, avoid private drive. At SOUTHWATER **GR 1526** brickworks converted into attractive Country Park with water (end of OS 187; some overlap with 198). Next diversion is at PARTRIDGE GREEN **GR 1919**. Follow signs and minor road south and then east towards HOMELANDS Farm on OS at **GR 194184** to rejoin railway and over river ADUR. Next is HENFIELD **GR 2016** with slight diversion to east of railway past THE BEECHINGS. On over river ADUR again near STRETHAM MANOR **GR 200137**. Soon after watch for signs going west by field track to WYCKHAM Farm **GR 190131**.

Part 3: Quiet roads to sea at Shoreham, 6 miles

Follow flinty gravel road towards BRAMBER Castle, National Trust **GR 1810**. Over A283 to resume short stretch of railway to ST BOTOLPHS **GR 1909** (Church and B and B). Minor road South below LANCING COLLEGE and over A27 (busy) for concession route on east of AIRFIELD and below railway at **GR 208053**. Over A259 to SHOREHAM BEACH and the sea. Retrace by quiet bridge at **GR 216048** to SHOREHAM station.

- **RELATED ROUTES:** PILGRIMS WAY (J7)
- **RECONNOITRED:** August 1990, RNH. Some shade from the canal and railway vegetation in very hot weather.

K5

- **CHICHESTER to PULBOROUGH**
- **COUNTY:** WEST SUSSEX
- **QUIETNESS:** **
- **MILEAGE:** 25
- **DIRECTION:** south west to north east
- **TRAIN STATIONS and TIMETABLES:** CHICHESTER **GR SU8504**, PULBOROUGH **GR TQ0418**, 187
- **MAP:** OS 197
- **WEATHER FORECAST:** 0891-500402
- **TOURIST INFORMATION OFFICE:** CHICHESTER 01243-775888
- **ACCOMMODATION:** YH at ARUNDEL
- **PLACES OF INTEREST:** Goodwood Country Park, Roman Villa BIGNOR, PARHAM House **GR 0614** new brick maze 1991
- **ROUTE:** road

From CHICHESTER station through beautiful city centre, signs to BRIGHTON and A27, north west at roundabout (Motel) **GR 8705**, north to GOODWOOD Airfld, right at **GR 880070**, WESTERTON north east by minor road past GOODWOOD House for four miles to EAST DEAN **GR 9013** (good pub). East and north east UPWALTHAM **GR 9413**. A285 north east, DUNCTON DOWN (viewpoint) **GR 9516**, east at road junction (telephone call box) **GR 960164** to SUTTON **GR 9715**. BIGNOR

GR 9814 (Roman Villa). South east to WEST BURTON **GR 0014** BURY, minor road to HOUGHTON **GR 0111**. B2139 AMBERLEY station and through village to east RACKHAM **GR 0413**, north to WIGGON HOLT COMMON **GR 0516**, A283 north and west to PULBOROUGH.

- **RECONNOITRED:** 1990, B and M

K6

- **DOVER to CANTERBURY (THE NORTH DOWNS, PILGRIM'S WAY)**
- **COUNTY:** KENT
- **QUIETNESS:** **
- **MILEAGE:** 19
- **DIRECTION:** south east to north west
- **TRAIN STATIONS and TIMETABLES:** DOVER PRIORY **GR TR313414**, CANTERBURY EAST **GR TR145575**, 207, 210
- **MAP:** OS 179
- **WEATHER FORECAST:** 0891-500402
- **TOURIST INFORMATION OFFICE:** DOVER 01304-205108, CANTERBURY 01227-766567
- **PUBLICATIONS:** Countryside Commission North Downs Way maps and guide
- **ACCOMMODATION:** YHs at DOVER (open all year) and CANTERBURY (open all year except January)
- **PLACES OF INTEREST:** The Pilgrim's Way of Chaucer's time was for horses. The official North Downs Way Long Distance Path is for walkers; this ride is mainly on quiet Kentish lanes with a few of the firm bridleway stretches. Places of interest abound. The ride is kept short to leave time to view DOVER and CANTERBURY.
- **ROUTE:** track

From DOVER PRIORY station: If going to the CASTLE (Hell Fire Corner Exhibition — a most popular English Heritage property with timed tours); avoid the dual carriageways and push east through old pedestrianized town centre to Castle Hill Road **GR 324416**. For access to North Downs Way make for CONNAUGHT PARK **GR 3142**. Minor road through Cemeteries **GR 317427** past Military School. At minor road over and beyond A2 north west by bridleway to join long distance path at **GR 316446**, leave long distance path to north east at **GR 315463**, minor road to WEST LANGDON **GR 3147**,

north north west by minor road over A256, then tarmac drives past WALDERSHARE House, minor road to GOLGOTHA **GR 2648**, go over railway and a mile of genuine firm woodland bridleway to WOOLAGE VILLAGE **GR 2350** (don't be misled south west to A2). Keep west north west minor road to B2046. North east on B2046 west by farm track just north of Cemetery **GR 222509** (**critical point** as official long distance path was ploughed October 1990) to join good farm track; official long distance path north west to minor road at **GR 202523**, north to **GR 204540**, minor road to BEKESBOURNE **GR 1955**. Minor road and long distance path from **GR 186556** to CANTERBURY. Take care to avoid dual carriageways for Cathedral and station by a little pushing. There are two stations: East is in fact South, and West is in fact North of the City.
- **RELATED ROUTES:** NORTH DOWNS WAY (K3)
- **RECONNOITRED:** October 1990, RNH

Introduction
This is a brief unofficial guide for cyclists riding the 100 miles of the **SOUTH DOWNS WAY, WINCHESTER to EASTBOURNE** with six youth hostels on the way.
The South Downs Way became available to cyclists by a side wind, so to speak. In 1947 a 'Hobhouse' Committee recommended six long distance paths (now called 'National Trails') including the South Downs Way (SDW). The best known is the Pennine Way (which still only remains as a footpath). Legislation followed in 1949 and by 1962/63 the Minister responsible had approved the National Parks Commission's plans for a bridleway, officially opened in 1972. The provision was for horse riders and walkers and it was only in 1968 that an Act said that cyclists may use bridleways, subject to giving way to horses. The route is not designed for cyclists and the cyclists use the bridleway as they find it — very muddy in wet weather. Thus the first edition of the HMSO Guide to the South Downs Way has these discouraging words. 'Cyclists. The South Downs Way is officially open to cyclists except for the Seven Sisters stretch. In fact, not much of the Way is suitable for cycling and any

cyclist undertaking it will have to envisage a great deal of pushing, not only up hills, but over surfaces made difficult by ruts, by long grasses, by stones, and by mud.'
- **THE SOUTH DOWNS WAY — WINCHESTER to EASTBOURNE**
- **COUNTIES:** HAMPSHIRE, WEST SUSSEX, EAST SUSSEX
- **QUIETNESS:** ***
- **MILEAGE:** 100 approximately, plus diversions for bed and breakfast
- **DIRECTION:** north west to south east approximately
- **TRAIN STATIONS AND TIMETABLES:** (selection) WINCHESTER OS 185 **GR SU4729**, PETERSFIELD OS 197 **GR SU7423**, AMBERLEY OS 197 **GR TV0211**, HASSOCKS OS 198 **GR TQ3015**, SOUTHEAST OS 198 **GR TQ4305**, EASTBOURNE OS 199 **GR TV6099**, 51, 158, 189.
- **MAP(S):** 185 (1992), 197 (1992), 198 (1992), 199(1992)
- **WEATHER FORECAST:** 0891-500 4, HANTS 03, SUSSEX 02
- **TOURIST INFORMATION OFFICES:** (selection) WINCHESTER, 01962-840500, PETERSFIELD 01730-268829, ARUNDEL 01903-882268, BRIGHTON 01273-323755, LEWES 01243-483448, EASTBOURNE 01323-411400
- **PUBLICATIONS:** The best of many books is the National Trail Guide *South Downs Way* by Paul Millmore
- **ACCOMMODATION:** Consult Tourist Information, youth hostel at WINCHESTER, ARUNDEL, BRIGHTON (Patcham), TELSCOMBE, ALFRISTON and EASTBOURNE (see references in route description)
- **ROUTE:** track

Part 1: Winchester to Petersfield (or Queen Elizabeth Country Park) OS 185, 197 (25 miles)
The YH at WINCHESTER is an 18th century watermill (National Trust) in Water Lane (opened in 1931) city centre **GR 486293**. For the start of the South Downs Way leave city south by A272 but at crossroads **GR 486288** (**critical point**) (signpost). Go east to footbridge over M3 and A33 at **GR 495288** (**critical point**) then push on footpath to CHILCOMBE **GR 5028** by minor road and another minor

road south east to cross A272 at **GR 5227**. Go north east to crossroads **GR 5328 (critical point)** then south east by track and bridleway south east and south to cross A272 again. Then mostly minor road south east to EXTON **GR 6121** over river Meon **GR 618213 (critical point)** to bridleways over old railway and round south of Old Winchester Hill **GR 6420** to join minor road, follow north to sloping path at **GR 644216 (critical point)**. Push up by ingenious bridleway routes Whitewood farm **GR 6521** and COOMBE CROSS **GR 6620 ***, go south on minor road HMS Mercury **GR 6719**. East on minor road, now OS 197, then east and north east on track to car park (public convenience) **GR 713202**. Push up by bridleway to Queen Elizabeth Country Park (this park was the western terminus of South Downs Way when opened in 1972).

* Note: For diversion to PETERSFIELD for bed and breakfast, divert at COOMBE **GR 6621** go north east to EAST MEON **GR 6822**, now OS 197, and either LANGRISH **GR 7023** or RAMSDEN **GR 7022** to reduce length of A272 into PETERSFIELD **GR SU7423**. To regain the South Downs Way leave south west on old A3 (bypassed) to road junction **GR 736217** to rejoin South Downs Way south of BURITON **GR 7420**.

Part 2: Petersfield (or Queen Elizabeth Country Park) to Arundel YH, OS 197 (30 miles)
Leave PETERSFIELD as above or leave Queen Elizabeth Country Park by bridleway east by Coulters Dean Farm **GR 7419**, go south east crossing B2146 and B2141 **GR 7818**. Then bridleways by winding route HARTING DOWNS **GR 7918** to Monkton House **GR 8317** and east to cross A286 at **GR 8716** south of COCKING, go east to GRAFFHAM DOWN **GR 9216** then south east to cross A285 at **GR 9514** Littleton farm. Track and bridleway to BURTON DOWN **GR 9613** and BIGNOR HILL (National Trust) **GR 9813** then south east to cross A29 **GR 0011** to HOUGHTON **GR 0111 *** and AMBERLEY **GR 0211**. North on B2139 briefly to road junction **GR 026123 (critical point)** north east and then east by bridleway to RACKHAM BANKS **GR 0412** to SPRINGHEAD HILL **GR 0612** (where route from ARUNDEL YH rejoins).

* Note: For diversion to ARUNDEL (castle, wildfowl and YH) leave HOUGHTON **GR 0111**

by minor road south to join bridleway on west bank of river Arun all way round to SOUTH STOKE **GR 0210** — lovely road to OFFHAM **GR 0208** and wildfowl reserve. Go south with castle towering above to ARUNDEL **GR 0106**, station. Youth hostel is Georgian building east of river Arun at WARINGCAMP **GR 0307**. To regain South Downs Way from ARUNDEL YH, take minor road to BURPHAM **GR 0408** to PEPPERING HIGH BARN **GR 0410**. Go north east by bridleway and and byway to rejoin South Downs Way at SPRINGHEAD HILL **GR 0612**.

Part 3: Arundel YH to Patcham (Brighton) YH via Truleigh Hill YH OS 197, 198
From ARUNDEL YH to South Downs Way see above. Resume the South Downs Way at SPRINGHEAD HILL **GR 0612**. Go east, now OS 198, to cross A24 near WASHINGTON **GR 1212**, climb up to CHANCTONBURY RING **GR 1312** then south east to STEYNING BOWL viewpoint **GR 1610** and south on minor road to bridleway **GR 165087 (critical point)**. East and north east and descent through BOTOLPHS **GR 1909** (good bed and breakfast near church) for quiet crossing of river Arun **GR 196093**. Up again to BEEDING HILL **GR 2009** (viewpoint) and past TRUELEIGH HILL YH (Tottington Barn — modern building) **GR 220105**. Go generally east on South Downs Way for two miles then at road junction (club house) **GR 2610**.
Choice A: For tarmac route to PATCHAM (BRIGHTON) YH. Minor road south east and below new A27 to A2038. For YH either follow A2038 north east or trace quieter route through WESTDENE estate **GR 2908**.
Choice B: For quieter off road descent to PATCHAM from club house **GR 2610** to South Downs Way, east past DEVILS DYKE to pick up bridleway at **GR 275115 (critical point)** just east of SADDLESCOMBE for delightful descent by bridleway and minor road south east past aerial mast and under new A27 to A2038 at **GR 296092** and then PATCHAM. Youth hostel at Patcham Place **GR 300088**. Queen Anne mansion leased by generous Brighton Corporation to YHA since 1939 (keen map readers will note that no public rights of way are shown on OS 198 (1992 edition) within the area of Brighton Borough).
Part 4: Patcham YH (Brighton) to Eastbourne YH via Telscombe YH and Alfriston YH, OS 198 and 199 (20 miles)

From PATCHAM YH (BRIGHTON) OS 198 *GR TQ300088* - cross A23 **with care** to minor road north to church *GR 303092*. East to pick up track at *GR 308094* **(critical point)** crossing new A27. Uphill to TEGDOWN HILL *GR 3110* then follow footpath north north east to join minor road north east to DITCHLING BEACON *GR 3313* (the hill featured in the annual London to Brighton Charity Ride and used by the Tour de France, July 1994). Continue east on South Downs Way acorn signs for two miles to track junction near BLACK CAP *GR 369126* **(critical point)**. Here go south west and then south east to BALMER DOWN *GR 3710* and descend to cross below A27 to KINGSTON near LEWES *GR 3808*. Continue by South Downs Way up the downs to FRONT HILL *GR 4006* to RODMELL *GR 4105* then south east to SOUTHEASE *GR 4205* (divert here for TELSCOMBE YH two miles to south west at *GR 405033*, 200 year old cottage). Note station at SOUTHEASE only one precisely on South Downs Way. Go east over river Ouse by railway and A26 up ITFORD HILL *GR 4305* and along the tops to viewpoint at *GR 4605* and on to FIRE BEACON *GR 4805*, now OS 199. Go south east to BOSTAL HILL *GR 4904* to ALFRISTON YH south of town at *GR 518019* comfortable 16th century house (over 40 years a YH). Resume South Downs Way by crossing river Cuckmere by minor road *GR 5203*; up again round TENANTRY GROUND *GR 5402* and down to JEVINGTON *GR 5601* to cross the WEALDWAY path *GR 5700* to the edge of EASTBOURNE where you find the YH — a former golf club house with sea views *GR 588990*. Plenty of choice of routes from YH: (i) the official end of the South Downs Way is at the west end of the promenade *GR TV600971*. This can be reached by town streets. Pick up the bridleway near the current club house *GR 5898*, go south to join B2103 winding down to promenade (cycling permitted); (ii) most travellers will wish to visit BEACHY HEAD *GR 5995*. From B2103 (above) take minor road at *GR 589975* **(critical point)** south to the Head. Footpath only at the end. (The route by the sea and Seven Sisters is a good walk — NO CYCLING).
- **RECONNOITRED:** 1994, RNH

AREA WN

Wales
Wales, North (Clwyd and Gwynedd)

WN1

- **From COAST to COAST across LLEYN PENINSULA**
- **COUNTY:** GWYNEDD
- **QUIETNESS:** *
- **MILEAGE:** 30
- **DIRECTION:** south west to north east
- **TRAIN STATIONS and TIMETABLES:** PWLLHELI *GR SH3735*, BANGOR *GR SH5771*, 65, 75, 76, 83
- **MAP(S):** OS 123, 115
- **WEATHER FORECAST:** 0891-500415
- **TOURIST INFORMATION OFFICE:** PWLLHELI 01758613000, BANGOR 01248-352786
- **PUBLICATIONS:** Tourist Information PORTMADOC 01766-512981
- **ACCOMMODATION:** YH Bangor or consult Tourist Information
- **PLACES OF INTEREST:** CAERNARVON Castle and many others
- **ROUTE:** track

PWLLHELI *GR 3735*. The road A499 is quiet out of season to CAERNARVON. Avoid A487(T) to BANGOR. Leave time to divert into Snowdonia.
- **RELATED ROUTES:** WN3
- **RECONNOITRED:** November 1982, RNH

WN2

- **CONWAY and FFESTINIOG VALLEYS at their Autumn best**
- **COUNTY:** GWYNEDD
- **QUIETNESS:** **
- **MILEAGE:** 10
- **DIRECTION:** north east to south west
- **TRAIN STATIONS and TIMETABLES:** BLAENAU FFESTINIOG *GR SH6946*, PENRHYNDEUDRAETH *GR SH6138*, 76, 85

- **MAP(S):** OS 115 (pt), 124
- **WEATHER FORECAST:** 0891-500415
- **TOURIST INFORMATION OFFICE:** At Planning Office of National Park authority *GR 612388* near station
- **PUBLICATIONS:**
- **ACCOMMODATION:** YH at FFESTINIOG
- **PLACES OF INTEREST or NOTE:** Narrow gauge railway, slate quarries
- **ROUTE:** road. **Not suitable for young families.**
  BLAENAU station: go north west then south west on new A496 (old B4414); steep. Junction *GR 6187415* west (not signposted) over river; back road to rejoin A496 at TAN Y BWLCH. Visit SNOWDONIA National Park Study Centre (courses include Walking Snowdonia for over 50s) on to PENRHYNDEURAETH. In dry weather leave A487 at *GR 641399* **(critical point)** and walk along flood bank path to join delightful minor road at *GR 634398* leading to station.
- **RELATED ROUTES:** WN5
- **RECONNOITRED:** November 1985, RNH

WN3

- **THE LLOYD GEORGE TRAILWAY and return through SNOWDONIA to CONWAY station**
- **COUNTY:** GWYNEDD
- **QUIETNESS:** *** for Lloyd George Way, remainder *
- **MILEAGE:** CAERNARVON 20, LLANDUDNO 60, 2-3 days
- **DIRECTION:** south to north
- **TRAIN STATIONS and TIMETABLES:** CRICCIETH *GR SH4938*, BETWS Y COED *GR SH5956* or LLANDUDNO JUNCTION *GR SH7977*, 76, 83, 85. Llandudno Junction (tables 83 and 85) has most

trains, the approach roads are very busy in summer.
- **MAP(S):** OS 123, 115
- **WEATHER FORECAST:** 0891-500415
- **TOURIST INFORMATION OFFICE:** PORTHMADOC 01766-512981, LLANDUDNO 01492-76413
- **PUBLICATIONS:** Leaflet Tourist Information and County Council. Also Walks in Glynllifon *GR 4555*.
- **ACCOMMODATION:** YH at LLANBERIS *GR 5759*, PEN Y PASS *GR 6455* and CAPEL CURIG *GR 7257*; also ROWEN *GR 747721* April to September only, if time to explore this fine Roman Road. Also consult Tourist Information.
- **PLACES OF INTEREST:** Abundant - see Tourist Information
- **ROUTE:** track. **Hilly, unsuitable for very young families**.

From CRICCIETH station *GR SH4938*. B and B for overnight stay at BRON RHIW *GR 499385* (OS 123). Avoid A497 and make for minor road *GR 495386*. West to LLANSTUMDWY. Lloyd George (1864-1945) Museum and Memorial, simple and in delightful setting (try walk by river). Then careful map reading north west to crossroads at *GR 454396*. North east to BETTWS BACH *GR 4741* and LLECHEIDDIOR *GR 4743* to BRYNCIR *GR 4744* start of TRAILWAY proper. Then plain cycling north to CAERNARVON. Generous specification for the way including laybys for parking cars due to intended use by disabled drivers. Very few gates, but one muddy crossing about midway. (Divert at PENYGROES *GR 4653* for GLYNLLIFON Country Park with Tower, Fort and Mausoleum). CAERNARVON plenty of interest. From CAERNARVON east on A4086 to LLANRUG *GR 5363* and A4086 to LLANBERIS *GR 5760* acceptable in winter; push up the LLANBERIS PASS to PEN Y PASS YH GR 647556, superb hostel with a climbing history and best drying room seen. After push up, mostly downhill A4086 CAPEL CURIG *GR 7557*. YH on to UGLY House (TY GHYLL) - Telford bridge and Snowdonia National Park Society Centre *GR 756575*. BETWS Y COED station north on B5106 through TREFRIW *GR 7863* to CONWAY SUSPENSION BRIDGE *GR 785775* another Telford work (National Trust) on to LLANDUDNO JUNCTION station.

- **RELATED ROUTES:** WN1, 2, 4, 5.
- **RECONNOITRED:** November 1989, RNH

WN4

- **BLAENAU FFESTINIOG-DOLGELLY-BARMOUTH**
- **COUNTY:** GWYNEDD
- **QUIETNESS:** **
- **MILEAGE:** 35
- **DIRECTION:** north east to south west, unusual direction but may be cycled in reverse
- **TRAIN STATIONS and TIMETABLES:** BLAENAU FFESTINIOG *GR SH6946*, BARMOUTH *GR SH6115*, 75, 76, 85
- **MAP(S):** OS 115, 124.
- **WEATHER FORECAST:** 0891-500415
- **TOURIST INFORMATION OFFICE:** PORTHMADOG 01766-512981
- **ACCOMMODATION:** YH at Kings (Dolgelly) LLEDR VALLEY (Betws y Coed) near PONT Y PANT station and FFESTINIOG near Blaenau Ffestiniog. Both these stations are on table 85. Ask Tourist Information for other accommodation.
- **PLACES OF INTEREST:** Snowdonia scenery; also slate mines, power stations and steam railways.
- **ROUTE:** road. **Hilly, not suitable for very young families**.

Overnight stay at LLEDR VALLEY YH *GR 749534* close to PONT Y PANT station. The last 'train' from LLANDUDNO JUNCTION is a bus (folded cycle accepted). Train to BLAENAU FFESTINIOG. Thence no very quiet route A470(T) or A496 and A487 to north of LAKE TRANSFYNYDD. Power station and Nature Trail at *GR6938*. Please divert through village itself to cross dramatic footbridge at *GR 7035* built by Electricity Company before 1939. On rejoining A470 go north just to take the old minor road at road junction *GR 711348*: this rises to 325 metres but worth it. Note carved slate milestone at farm entrance *GR 7133* 'DOLGELLY 11 miles' (Ancient or modern?); follow gated, cattle-gridded road south east to PONT ABERGEIRW *GR 7629* (remote phone box by former chapel). Go south west, eventually following the south east side of river to tricky road junction at *GR 743226*. Here ignore signpost to DOLGELLY and find the road which keeps south east of the river below PRECIPICE WALK south on to bridge **GR 7118** west of DOLGELLY (YH at KINGS four miles at **GR 683161**). After seeing the town return to bridge for start of TRAILWAY (PENMAENPOOL -MORFA MAWDDACH WALK) along edge of estuary (a few gates to lift over) nine miles of perfection to station at **GR 6214**, then wooden Toll Bridge to BARMOUTH, the site of the National Trust's first acquisition (cafes and B and B).

- **RELATED ROUTES:** WN5
- **RECONNOITRED:** November 1989, RNH

WN5

- **BARMOUTH NORTHWARDS by MOUNTAIN ROADS**
- **COUNTY:** GWYEDD
- **QUIETNESS:** **
- **MILEAGE:** 20. **Hilly not suitable for young families.**
- **DIRECTION:** south to north
- **TRAIN STATIONS and TIMETABLES:** BARMOUTH **GR SH6015**, PENRHYNDEURAETH **GR SH 6139**, 75.
- **MAP:** OS 124
- **WEATHER FORECAST:** 0891-500415
- **TOURIST INFORMATION OFFICE:** PORTHMADOG 01766-512981
- **PUBLICATIONS:** General guides from Tourist Information
- **ACCOMMODATION:** YH at LLANBEDR **GR 585267**
- **PLACES OF INTEREST:**
- **ROUTE:** road

From BARMOUTH north on A496 through LLANABER, TALYBONT to COED Y STUMGWERN **GR 5823** minor, gated road north east to viewpoint near GELLI-BANT **GR 6125**. At next road junction **GR 626258** resist temptation to go to road end at NANTCOL **GR 6427**. Instead descend north west through magical country over two rivers and north east to PEN Y BONT **GR 6028**. Further on at **GR 608284** go uphill two miles to crossroads (chapel and phone box) at **GR 590304**. (B and B at TYDDYN Y GWNT **GR 601302**). From this crossroads go north east (FONLIEF HIR on 1:25,000 Leisure

sheet) to top at about 100ft then descend EISINGRUG **GR 6134**. Keep north east to CILFOR 6237 alongside railway to PENRYN-DEUDRAETH station.

- **RELATED ROUTES:** WN4
- **RECONNOITRED:** November 1989, RNH

WN6

- THE WALES TRAIL, CARDIFF to HOLYHEAD, Northern part. See route WS3. [road]

AREA WM

Wales
Mid Wales (Dyfed and Powys)

WM1

- THE WALES TRAIL, CARDIFF to
  HOLYHEAD, middle part. See route
  WS3. [road]

Various border routes (such as E5) take you
into central Wales.

AREA WS

Wales South
Gwent and the Glamorgans

WS1

- **THE WYE VALLEY: HEREFORD to MONMOUTH and CHEPSTOW**
- **COUNTY:** GLOUCESTER, HEREFORD, GWENT
- **QUIETNESS:** **
- **MILEAGE:** 20 to MONMOUTH, 30 to CHEPSTOW
- **DIRECTION:** north to south
- **TRAIN STATIONS and TIMETABLES:** HEREFORD *GR SO5140*, CHEPSTOW *GR ST5393*, 56, 126
- **MAP(S):** OS 149, 162
- **WEATHER FORECAST:** 0891-500400
- **TOURIST INFORMATION OFFICE:** HEREFORD 01432-268430, ROSS-ON- WYE 01989-62768, Chepstow 01291 623772
- **PUBLICATIONS:** SUSTRANS Project Report
- **ACCOMMODATION:** YH MONMOUTH *GR 505013*, open March to October but not winter, YH ST BRIAVELS CASTLE *GR558045*, the nearest to Chepstow
- **PLACES OF INTEREST:** TINTERN and many others
- **ROUTE:** track

HEREFORD station Victoria Bridge B4399 to *GR 552355*; BALLINGHAM *GR 5731*; HOARWITHY; over river WYE to re-cross by SELLACK BOAT bridge *GR 565280*. HAYSHAM; ROSS B4228 WALFORD. Cross WYE at 581192 (Kerne Bridge) and 567182 then road and riverside Forest Trail to outskirts MONMOUTH. Not yet reconnoitred, but reliable SUSTRANS Project. Route hugs river WYE and old railway from WYESHAM *GR 524117*; to right bank at REDBROOK *GR 535097*. To left bank at BIGSWEIR *GR 5305*. To right bank at BROCKWICK for TINTERN; return left bank by Wireworks bridge at *GR 530004*. South then east to B4228 PARSONS ALLOTMENT *GR 554984*. South west to CHEPSTOW station.

- **RELATED ROUTES:** WS2 for continuation over SEVERN BRIDGE
- **RECONNOITRED:** North part, RNH

WS2

- **THE SEVERN BRIDGE**
- **COUNTY:** GWENT, AVON
- **QUIETNESS:** **
- **MILEAGE:** 10 minimum
- **DIRECTION:** north west to south east
- **TRAIN STATIONS and TIMETABLES:** CHEPSTOW *GR ST5393*, SEVERN BEACH *GR ST540847*, 127, 131, 133
- **MAP(S):** OS 172
- **WEATHER FORECAST:** 0891-500405
- **TOURIST INFORMATION OFFICE:** CHEPSTOW 01291-623772
- **ACCOMMODATION:** YH — nearest now ST BRIAVELS Castle (King John's Hunting Lodge, dungeons) 11 miles
- **PLACES OF INTEREST:** Several, but the most interesting is the Youth Hostel!
- **ROUTE:** road

Station at CHEPSTOW *GR 5393*. Find way south on estate roads and public path (parallel with railway) to end of BULWARK ROAD at *GR 538916*. Cycle path on upstream side of the bridges; beware of servicing vehicles. Wind little problem as cycleway below level of roadway. From service station on Avon side use footbridge above toll barriers and follow side road B4055 to SEVERN BEACH station *GR 540846*. Avoid busy A403. If time permits, leave the train at Avonmouth and try whole or part of the river Avon-Bristol-Bath route.

- **RELATED ROUTES:** E11
- **RECONNOITRED:** November 1986

WS3 (WM1)(WN6)

- **THE WALES TRAIL — CARDIFF to BANGOR and HOLYHEAD.** Reconnoitred by Dave and Alistair of New Zealand May 1992. Allow at least six days. WARNING: a superb route but long and hilly.
- **COUNTY:** MID GLAMORGAN, POWYS, GWYNEDD
- **QUIETNESS:** **
- **MILEAGE:** 245 miles
- **DIRECTION:** south to north
- **TRAIN STATIONS and TIMETABLES:** CARDIFF OS 171 *GR 1875*, CAERPHILLY *GR 864872*, BUILTH ROAD OS 147 *GR 0253*, MACHYNLLETH OS 135 *GR 7401*, BLAENAU FESTINIOG OS 115 *GR 6945*, BANGOR OS 114,115 *GR 5771*, HOLYHEAD OS 114 *GR 2489* with the Rhymney lines in South Wales and with five intermediate stations on ANGLESEY. Cardiff 56, 123, 125, 129, 132. Bangor and Holyhead 83.
- **MAP(S):** OS 171, (160), 161, (148), 147, 136, (135), 124, 115, 114 (maps in brackets cover less than half sheet)
- **WEATHER FORECAST:** 0891-500409 (south west), 0891-500414, 415 (central and north west)
- **TOURIST INFORMATION OFFICE:** CARDIFF 01222-227281, CAERPHILLY 01222-851378, MERTHYR TYDFIL 01685-79884, BRECON 01874-622485, BUILTH WELLS 01982-553307, RHAYADER 01597-810591, MACHYNLLETH 01654-702401, CORRIS 01654-761244 (closed during winter), DOLGELLAU 01341-422888, BANGOR 01248-352786, HOLYHEAD 01407-762622
- **PUBLICATIONS:** *Three Castles cycle route* from Tourist Information
- **ACCOMMODATION:** YH CARDIFF *GR 185788*, LLWYN-Y-CELYN (BRECON) *GR 973225*, KINGS (DOLGELAU) *GR 683161*, BRYN GWYNANT *GR 641513*, PEN Y PASS *GR 649556*, BANGOR *GR 590722* and B and B list from Tourist Information. There are at present no Youth Hostels on Anglesey.
- **PLACES OF INTEREST:** Consult Tourist Information. Magnificent mountain scenery should suffice.
- **ROUTE:** mostly road

Part 1: Cardiff to Brecon, OS 171, (160), 161 OS 171 (50 miles)
CARDIFF station *GR 183758*, YH at *GR 185788* two miles north of station. Castle is half a mile north north west of station and start of Three Castles Cycle Route (leaflet) go north on east bank of river TAFF 'great though could be muddy in Winter'. Ends CASTELL COCH at TONGWYNLAIS *GR 1382*, go to minor road north east BWLCH CWM and to road junction *GR 151853* **(critical point)**; go to minor road to B4600 and north east through CAERPHILLY to crossroads *GR 170885* **(critical point)** north west and north on minor road on east side of RHYMNEY Valley, YSTRAD MYNACH *GR 1594*, north on B4252 (quiet) road junction PENGAM *GR 1597*, go to BARGOED and west over A469 **(very busy)** at *GR 153976*. North on minor road through BARGOED, north west and west on minor road — 'Ridgeway Footpath' — to road junction *GR 122988* **(critical point)**; go north north west by minor road, now OS 160, and down past rubbish tip to MERTHYR TYDFIL by way of road junction *GR 063061*; go to minor roads north over A4060, A4102 and A465 to GARTH *GR 0609* (Brecon Mountain Railway), go to PONTSTICILL *GR 0511* and minor road on west and beyond the two Reservoirs turning south east and east at *GR 055175* **(critical point)**, now OS161. North north east, passing TALYBONT Reservoir to join B4558 at CROSS OAK *GR 1023*, go north west to PENCELLI *GR 1025* (OS 160 again) and minor road to LLANFRYNACH, north to meet river and canal at *GR 0727*. For accommodation in BRECON follow the towpath west; for YH go north to *GR 073288*.

Part 2: Brecon to Rhayader, OS (160), 161, 147, (148) (48 miles)
Resuming route at road junction GROESFFORDD *GR 076278*, go east (back to OS 161) through LLANFIHANGEL and road junction *GR 115284* **(critical point)**. Minor road north north east following river AFON LLYNFI to TALGARTH *GR 1533*, go north east on A4078 for one mile (wide verges), go to road junction *GR 1635* **(critical point)** and minor road VELINDRE *GR 1836*, go north by minor road over river GLASBURY *GR 1739*, go west north west on B4350 to minor road at *GR 167396* **(critical point)**, CWMBACH through FFYNON GYNYDD *GR 1641*, north for two and a half miles, now OS 148 — three

mile overlap, go to PAINSCASTLE **GR 1646** and west on B4594 (quiet) detour to minor road south of the B road at **GR 121451** **(critical point)**. This avoids going over a superfluous hill; go to B4594 west, now OS 147. Steep drop down (hairpins) to WYE VALLEY and north west on A470 for a mile: **busy**, no footpaths. At road junction **GR 077442** **(critical point)** take minor road north go to HENDY **GR 0646**. **Very steep (for very fit only)** to BUILTH WELLS **GR 0450**. For the less fit B4567 has been reported quiet (May 1992). Follow both routes by minor road to PARK WELLS **GR 0252**, over railway north west and north to join B4358 **GR 9957** **(critical point)**, go north east to NEWBRIDGE on WYE **GR 0158** and on A470 (not too busy — no footways). RHAYADER **GR 9768** (B and B WYE Lodge: 'Best in UK' — Dave).

Part 3: Rhayader to Machynlleth or Aberdyfi, OS 136, 147, (135), 124) (38 miles)
Leave RHAYADER on minor road west of river WYE 14 miles — 'totally delightful' — gates deter cars; cream teas at LLANGURIG **GR 9079**. (Now OS 136 nine mile overlap). Minor road **steep** start north east alongside AFON BROCHAN to road junction. MOUNT SEVERN **GR 9484** and west by SEVERN Valley and through HAFREN FOREST: good picnic spot **GR 856869** go generally north east STAYLITTLE **GR 8892** to B4518, road junction **GR 8893**, minor road **(busy)** DYLIFE **GR 8694**: over top and **steep** eight miles, now OS 135, overlap of more than six miles, down to MACHYNLLETH **GR 7400**.

Part 4: Machynlleth (Aberdyfi) to Pen y Pass, OS 124, 115 (53 miles)
Leave Machynlleth go to A487 over river Dovey at **GR 751023 (critical point)**, north on east bank — another delightful road past Centre for Alternative Technical College, **hilly** but well worth a visit, avoid traffic by turning off main road and walking up minor signposted road, now OS 124. Through CORRIS **GR 7508** join A487 **(busy road, take care)** CORRIS U CHAFF **GR 744089**, seven miles to CROSS FOXES GR 7616, turn onto minor road north west near TABOR to DOLGELLAU (**GR 7317** (YH at KINGS west south west **GR 683161**). From town cross river at **GR 728180** and minor road winding to PANDY BACH **GR 7319**, west and north east below PRECIPICE WALK **GR 7320** to enter forest at **GR 737227** **(critical point)**. Route finding is difficult

through COED Y BREMIN Forest as many trails are dead ends. If you are deterred by what follows, divert onto tarmac route WN4 of this book in reverse and take minor road north east to PONT ABER GEIRN at **GR 7620**, north west mostly unfenced to A470 south of TRAWSFYNYDD. For Forest route at **GR 728244** bridge over river; sealed road on east bank becomes gravel; signed both No Entry and Mountain Bike Trail Sign, cross river at **GR 735251** on footbridge with Mountain Bike sign; keep to east side of river go north to road junction **GR 735285**, north east of GWYN FYNDD (careful map reading needed). Then fast down (mostly) to TRAWSFYNYDD; divert over A470 to enjoy long wooden footbridge at **GR 7035**. The fit and tough can reconnoitre the west side of LLYN, lesser mortals keep to A470 and A487 to MAENTWROG **GR 6640**. From TRANSFYNYDD go north and north west to road junction **GR 687397**, GELLILYDAN **GR 6839**, MAENTRWROG, cross river at **GR 665407**; take B4440 north of SNOWDONIA Study Centre to RHYD and GARREG, go north on A4085 to crossroads **GR 607446**. **(Critical point)**, follow minor road, lonely, **mountainous** to NANT GWYNANT (YH at BRYN GWYNANT **GR 641513**). Go to A498 to minor road at **GR 650522** go to PEN Y GWRYD (famous climbing hotel) go to **steep** up to PEN Y PASS YH **GR 649556** where you should stay (easiest access to SNOWDON summit on foot). Easier (longer) route from PEN Y GWRYD **GR 6555** to BANGOR. Take A4086 east north east downhill to cross roads at CAPEL CURIG **GR 7258**; then OLD road over river and keep south of A5 west north west LLYN OGWEN **GR 6660**. One mile of A5 to YH (IDWAL Cott — 3 decker beds in the past) and gated road **GR 649604 (critical point)**; regret take A5 at **GR 6364** to B4409 and Railway Path BETHSEDA to BANGOR station and YH about one and a quarter miles apart.

Part 5: Pen y Pass to Bangor, OS 115 (16 miles)
Leaving Pen y Pass YH make early start down LLANBERIS PASS **GR 6256** before traffic builds up **(critical point)**. Avoid much of A4086 by going east of LLYN PERIS at **GR 600587** push up zig zag quarry road (gates) to View Point at **GR 592605** Padarn Country Park DINORWIG quarry and power station; go to minor road DEINIOLEN **GR 5863** B4547 north north west for just over a mile to

(critical point) crossroads *GR 562660* then trace line of minor roads crossing B4366 and A5 to MINFFORDD *GR 5770* and BANGOR station and YH.

Part 6: Bangor to Holyhead by minor roads, OS 114, 115 (37 miles)
From BANGOR station OS 114 *GR SH575716* by minor roads to A5122 for MENAI station and PONT BRITANNIA *GR 5471* to minor road north of Llanfairpwll, in full it is the longest named station *GR 526716*, go under A5 to cross roads **(critical point)** *GR 514723*, then south west under A5 and over railway all way to north west on B4419, go to **(critical point)** *GR 453671* over B4421 at LLANGAFF *GR 4468*, under railway and over and alongside dyke north west to BETHEL *GR 3970*, north west twisting across railway to BRYN DU *GR 3472*: make for minor road at **(critical point)** *GR 342737*. North to crossroads *GR 345770*, south west of BRYNGWRAN go north west and south west through LLANFIHANGEL YN north HOWYN *GR 3277* round north edge of VALLEY AIRFIELD (Mountain Rescue) south west of railway to VALLEY station *GR 2979*, swing round south of the Bay to TREARDOUR *GR 2579*: go as far north west as time allows by minor road including SOUTH STACK Lighthouse *GR 2082* before returning by minor roads to HOLYHEAD station *GR SH248822*: No longer a YH, used to be in ship-wrecked Mariners' hostel.
- **RELATED ROUTES:** WN1, 2, 4
- **RECONNOITRED:** Map work RNH, legwork Dr DK (New Zealand and Cambridge) May 1992. Help from Arnold Robinson (Sheffield), SUSTRANS (Bristol) and CTC.

Note: This route is divided into six stages as ridden by Dave using B and B accommodation spending half a day at the Alternative Technology Centre at Machynlleth and also going up Snowdon. Other cyclists will vary the stages to stay at some of the six Youth Hostels named (plenty more in Snowdonia) and according to their special interests.

The Taff Trail from Cardiff to Brecon via the Taff Valley:
Since this route was reconnoitred in May 1992 there has come to hand the *Taff Trail for Walkers and Cyclists. A provisional route linking Cardiff and Brecon*, 30p from Fedw Hir LLwydcoed, ABERDARE CF44 ODX.

Following as it does the Taff Valley (as opposed to the Rhymney Valley) this provides an alternative to the middle part of Part 1 of this route, i.e. from TONGWYNLAIS *GR SO1382* to VAYNOR *GR SO0510* and thus avoids the unattractive approach to Merthyr *GR 0705* in this route.

WS4

- **OFFA'S DYKE — HEPSTOW TO PRESTATYN** — A Touring Cyclist's version, close to the Official National Trail (footpath).
The quiet route which follows is intended to provide a good cycling version of the popular National Trail known as the Offa's Dyke which is a footpath route promoted by the Countryside Commission. The idea has the approval of the Commission who are working on a cycling version of the Pennine Way from Hexham to Matlock.
Already in the *Quiet Cycle Routes* book are cycling versions of two National Trails: the North Downs (Pilgrims) Way; the Peddars Way and one Regional Trail: the Three Shires Way (Milton Keynes to Cambridge) via Grafham Water.
From Bristol Channel to Irish Sea (Dee Estuary) a cycling version of the Offa's Dyke Path — National Trail (footpath) 225 miles of quiet beautiful country on the Welsh border; strenuous at times.
- **COUNTIES:** GWENT, GLOUCESTERSHIRE, POWYS, SHROPSHIRE, CLWYD
- **QUIETNESS:** ** minor roads which can be enjoyed in all seasons
- **MILEAGE:** 225 approximately
- **DIRECTION:** south to north
- **TRAIN STATIONS AND TIMETABLES:** CHEPSTOW OS 162 *GR ST5393*, ABERGAVENNY OS 161 *GR SO 3013*, KNIGHTON OS 148 *GR SO 2972*, WELSHPOOL OS 126 *GR SJ2207*, GOBOWEN OS 126 *GR SJ3033*, CHIRK OS 126 *GR SJ2837*, PRESTATYN OS 116 *GR SJ0683*, 74, 83, 87, 105, 129, 131.
- **MAP(S):** OS 116, (117), 137, (148), 161, 162, 172 (brackets indicated small area only).
- **WEATHER FORECAST:** 0891-550 409 (south) 414 (mid), 413 (north)

Wales South WS4

- **TOURIST INFORMATION OFFICES:**
  CHEPSTOW 0291-623772, MONMOUTH
  0600-713899, HEREFORD 0432-268430,
  KNIGHTON 0547-528753, WELSHPOOL
  0938-552043, OSWESTRY 0691-662488,
  LLANGOLLEN 0978-960828, RUTHIN
  0824-703993, PRESTATYN 0745-854365.
- **PUBLICATIONS:** National Trail Guide
  Offa's Dyke Path, 2 vols. HMSO (1992)
  £7.95 each. *Offa's Dyke Path, Where to
  Stay*, 1994 edition £1.70 (including P&P)
  from O D Association, West Street,
  Knighton, Powys LD7 1EW for youth hos-
  tels and over 200 bed and breakfasts.
- **ACCOMMODATION:** Youth hostels at ST
  BRIAVELS, MONMOUTH, CHAPEL Y
  FFYN, (GLASCWN) CLUN MILL
  (BRIDGES) LLANGOLLEN, MAESHAFN.
  Brackets indicate the youth hostels some
  miles from route.
- **PLACES OF INTEREST:** Offa's Dyke Path
  — official route
- **ROUTE:**

**Part 1: Bristol Channel (Sedbury Cliffs)
Chepstow to St Briavels YH and Monmouth
YH, OS 612 (31 miles)**
From CHEPSTOW station OS 162 *GR 5393*
go north over bridge over river Wye *GR 5394*.
South east by Offa Dyke Path (signed) to
official start SEDBURY CLIFFS *GR 5592*
(viewpoint). Access to cliffs on foot only but
worth it for dramatic start. Retrace through
SEDBURY *GR 5493* then north over railway to
WOODCROFT *GR 5495* north on minor road
on west of river Wye to REDBROOKE
GR 5310 to A466 three miles to MONMOUTH
GR 5012. YH in old school. Note: A466
REDBROOK to MONMOUTH could be busy;
the energetic could go via WHITEBROOK
GR 5306 to HOOP *GR 5107* to Meend farm
GR 5009 to MITCHELL TROY *GR 4910*
further west.
**Part 2: Monmouth YH *GR 5012* to Capel y
Ffyn YH *GR 2532*, OS 162, 161 (35 miles)**
Leave Monmouth by Model farm *GR 4912*
south west, now OS 161, to WONASTOW
GR 4810. North west to WORTHY BROOK
GR 4711 to Hendre farm *GR 4512* to
LLANVIHANGEL *GR 4313* then on minor road
to LLANTILIO CROSSENNY *GR 3914* (church
and moat). Offa's Dyke Path to TREADAM
GR 3815 to CAGGLE STREET *GR 3717* to
LLANGATTOCK LINGOED (pretty pontis) to

PENBIDWAL *GR 3322* (divert through
LLANVIHANGEL CRUCORNEY *GR 3220* for
last shops before the mountain road). Resume
the route under the railway three times to
STANTON *GR 3121* go north west to CWMYOY
GR 2923 (amazingly distorted church). Minor
road up the VALE OF EWYAS to LLANTHONY
GR 2827 (Abbey) and CAPEL Y FFYN YH
GR 250328, has mercilessly steep drive,
friendly warden and good drying facilities.
Detour to monastery; briefly the home of
sculptor and print designer Eric Gill (Prospero
and Ariel on BBC headquarters and 'Gill'
family of type faces).
**Part 3: Capel y Ffyn YH *GR 2532* to
Knighton *GR 2872* or Clun YH, OS 161, 148
(35 miles to Knighton, 46 to Clun)**
From the YH continue up minor road to
GOSPEL PASS *GR 2335* (542 metres) then
six mile descent, now OS 148, to HAY ON
WYE *GR 2242* the 'book town' good also for
maps. The Granary tea shop. Go north west
B4351 to CLYRO *GR 2143* home of the Rev
Francis Kilvert (diary) then north on minor road
just over two miles to Tump farm *GR 2146*.
Generally north and north west narrow lanes
with grass centres to point 295 ADO — Above
Ordnance Datum (spot heights) *GR 2248*.
West to CROWTHERS POOL *GR 2148*
(nearest point for diversion to GLASCUM YH
GR 158533 by mountain roads). Go east to
point 285 at *GR 2449* then north to
HUNTINGTON *GR 2553* (pub and views of
HERGEST Ridge) then north east alongside
river Arrow to KINGTON *GR 3056*. Leave by
A44 to road junction *GR 2757* **(critical point)**
then minor road north to B4362 to LOWER
HARPTON *GR 2760* to DITCHYELD BRIDGE
GR 2760. Minor road north west to EVENJOB
GR 2662 and on B4357 north for five miles.
Road junction (TCB) RHOS-Y-MEIRCH
GR 279691 **(critical point)**. Go north west by
north by minor road *GR 2770* to A488 and B
road to KNIGHTON *GR 2972*. Headquarters of
Offa's Dyke Association. Tea shop opposite
clock in square. Station *GR 2972*.
**Part 4: Knighton *GR 2972* or Clun YH *GR
3081* to Welshpool, OS 148, 126 (36 miles)**
KNIGHTON to CLUN — the most magnificent
section of the whole ride. Tiny lanes, no traffic,
stupendous views across Wales and the river
Teme and the Dyke. Walk on the Dyke on
LLANFAIR HILL *GR 2579* said by many to be
the best section. Leave KNIGHTON *GR 2872*

by minor road north west to SKYBORRY GREEN **GR 2674**. Leaving TEME Valley at LLANFAIR WATERDINE **GR 2476** go north and north west, now OS 137, to crossroads **(critical point)**. At SPOAD HILL **GR 2580** divert east to CLUN **GR 3080**. YH, castle and museum; tranquil village, detour well worth extra miles. From CLUN A488 go north west on minor road to BICTON **GR 2982** then west to BRYNDRINOG **GR 2582** by unbelievably quiet lanes and breathtaking countryside and via point 246 **GR 2684**, good views of the Dyke, to crossroads TWO CROSSES **GR 2486** point 424 **GR 2588** at EDENHOPE **GR 2788** to cross from Shropshire to Powys at Dog and Duck **GR 2689**. North west to CWM **GR 2590** and north east over B4385 to CHURCH STOKE **GR 2794**. North west to RHISTON **GR 2695** to GWARTLOW over Offa's Dyke Path to B4385 to MONTGOMERY **GR 2296**. Castle abrupt and imposing (free). Leave MONTGOMERY **GR 2296** on B4388 north, now OS 126. At KINGWOOD **GR 2402** leave Offa's Dyke Path north on B4388 for just over three miles to join B4381 east to WELSHPOOL **GR 2207**. Ample bed and breakfast accommodation in *Where to Stay*. One at KINGSWOOD and another at HOPE **GR 2507** to avoid descent to the valley.

Part 5: Welshpool to Llangollen, OS 137, 126 (117) (36 miles)
From WELSHPOOL **GR 2207** retrace your way east by B4381 and north by B4388 to road junction **GR 248076 (critical point)** steep ascent to LONG MOUNTAIN Road (Roman) **GR 2803**. North east over railway and A458 **GR 3211** to WOLLASTON **GR 3212** then minor road to CREWGREEN **GR 3215**. East on B4393 then minor road north east to MELVERLEY **GR 3316** half-timbered riverside 13th century church. Go north west to cross B4398 at **GR 2820** (divert to LLANYMYNECH **GR 2620**. Half Wales/half England. Pubs with food and good chippy. Back to road junction **GR 287207 (critical point)**, go north to REDWITH **GR 2821** to join B4396 near LLYNCLYS **GR 2824**. West over A483 on A495 and minor road to PORTH Y WAEN **GR 2523** then north to TREFLACH **GR 2625** to CROESAU BACH **GR 2428** and north to B4580 LLANT RHYD Y CROESAU. Minor road at road junction **GR 249309 (critical point)**, go north east over B4579 at SELATTYN **GR 2634**. Attractive village, good for bed and

breakfast. Minor road north east over river Ceiriog into CLWYD at CHIRK **GR 2837**, station. CHIRK castle and park (English Heritage and National Trust). Leave CHIRK over canal tunnel near station **GR 283377**, go north west on minor road to NEW HALL **GR 2738**, now OS 117, to FRON ISAF **GR 2740**. North over PONT CYSYLLTE, aqueduct 127ft high, over 1,000ft long. No railings on the canal side — stomach-churning stuff. To join towpath of Shropshire Union Canal (LLANGOLLEN branch) obstacle free route west to LLANGOLLEN **GR 2142**. YH at TYNDWR HALL **GR 232413** top quality drying room, inadequate members' kitchen.

Part 6: Llangollen to Ruthin, OS (117), 116 (23 miles)
(Alternative is Maeshafn YH add seven miles)
From LLANGOLLEN retrace east along towpath to TREVOR UCHAF **(critical point) GR 2442**. Minor road north west and north (official Offa's Dyke Path) round edge of EGLWYSEG Mountain **GR 2246** well worth it. Craggy mountains feeling like edge of Snowdonia, leave Offa's Dyke Path at **GR 2349** to MINERA **GR 2651**. North west and west to join A525 at **GR 2252** then west, now OS 116, to PEN Y STRYT **GR 1951**. North west on minor road to LLANDEGLA **GR 1952** to PANT MYHARAN viewpoint **GR 1754** to join B5429 **GR 1456 *** and north west to RUTHIN **GR 1258** attractive old town perched on hill with fine views; all services.
* Note: Out to MAESHAFN YH omitting RUTHIN. At crossroads LLANPHYDD Mill keep on B5429 north to join the A494(T) go north east to LLANBEDR DYFFRYN CLWYD at **GR 145595 (critical point**. Go east of church and take the minor road and another minor road, steep and cattle grids, to Halfway House **GR 1559**. North east to viewpoint **GR 1660** then north east on Forest Trail to road junction. Point 267 **GR 176613 (critical point)** east on minor road over A494(T) to MAESHAFN YH beyond the village at **GR 208606**. Timber building; architect Clough Williams Ellis of PORTMEIRION fame.]
Part 7: Ruthin to Prestatyn, OS 116 (21 miles)
(Alternative Maeshafn YH add seven miles *)
Leave RUTHIN by minor road to cross B5429 **GR 1360** then north east to HIRWAEN **GR 1361**. North north west on minor road to LLANGYNHAFEL **GR 1263** to LLANGWYFAN

GR 1266 to best view of Northern section. Road junction edge of woodland GR 117682 looking north to MOEL Y PARC also glimpses of the sea up here; magic. Go round and down to B5429 at GR 1068 then north west and on A541 briefly to resume B5429 to BODFARI GR 0970. Go north west on minor road at PISTYLL GR 0970 to SODOM GR 0971 Fron Haul bed and breakfast GR 099717 (highly recommended) on minor road (official Offa's Dyke Path) through PANTGLAS GR 0973. Go north and west by minor roads to RHAULLT GR 0775 then minor road north north west to crossroads at TAN Y BRYN GR 064768 (critical point). North east to MARIAN CWM GR 0777 then north east to TRELANNYD GR 0979 over A5151 on minor road to crossroads GR 094803 (critical point). Go north west round to GWAENYSGOR GR 0781. Viewpoint at GR 074816 and through PRESTATYN GR 0782 one way streets. Northbound goes via bus and rail station to the sea (Irish Sea). Offa's Dyke Centre on sea front opened in 1992 record your route and time taken — then get blown along the prom.
* **Note**: From MAESHAFN YH to PRESTATYN. A choice at start (1) Retrace route back to RUTHIN (2) Strenuous mountain route. Retrace only as far as A494 at cross-roads GR 1861 (critical point). Follow A494 north for a mile to road junction GR 188617 (critical point). Minor road north to CILCAIN GR 1765 then winding roads following contours to MOEL ARTHUR GR 1643 to further winding roads above RHIWBEBYLL GR 1265 to join our main route at viewpoint near woodland GR 117682 (critical point).
- **RELATED ROUTES:** WS1 an alternative partly off-road route CHEPSTOW-MON-MOUTH
- **RECONNOITRED:** AM Spring 1993

WS5

- **WELSH CASTLES and VALLEYS — KIDWELLY to SHREWSBURY with a stopping train in attendance**
- **COUNTIES:** DYFED, POWYS, SHROPSHIRE
- **QUIETNESS:** ** mainly minor roads
- **MILEAGE:** 140 approximately with variations
- **DIRECTION:** south west to north east

- **TRAIN STATIONS AND TIMETABLES:** (selected) KIDWELLY OS 159 GR SN4006, LLANDEILO OS 159 GR SN6322, LLANDOVERY OS 160 GR SN 7634, BUILTH ROAD OS 147 GR SO0253, KNIGHTON OS 137 GR SN2972, CHURCH STRETTON OS 137 GR SO4593, SHREWSBURY OS 126 GR SJ4912, 74, 128, 129, 131
- **MAP(S):** 159(1985), 160(1991), 148(1992), 137(1985), 126(1991)
- **WEATHER FORECAST:** 0891-500 4, south west 14, north east 10
- **TOURIST INFORMATION OFFICES:** (selected) CARMARTHEN 01267-231557, LLANDOVERY 01550-20693, BUILTH WELLS 01982-55330, LLANDRINDOD WELLS 01597-822600, KNIGHTON 01547-528753, CHURCH STRETTON 01694-723133, SHREWSBURY 01743-50761
- **PUBLICATIONS:** Consult Tourist Information
- **ACCOMMODATION:** Youth hostels (further details in text) LLANDDEUSANT, BRYN POETH UCHAF, GLASCWM, CLUN MILL, BRIDGES and SHREWSBURY. For other accommodation consult Tourist Information.
- **PLACES OF INTEREST and NOTES:** Castles galore especially KIDWELLY, Nelson's Tower (National Trust) GR 5419, LONG MYND GR 4193 and SHREWSBURY town
- **ROUTE:**

Part 1: Kidwelly to (A) Llanddeusant YH, GR 7724 (29 miles) or (B) Llandeilo OS 159, 160 (20 miles)
From Kidwelly station GR SN4006 (Don't omit the castle remarkably complete and well presented) go north east crossing A484 by minor road north east to LLANGADOG GR 4207. North east to FOUR ROADS to crossroads GR 4510 (critical point) then east north east to MEINCIAU GR 4510 crossing B4309. Go north east by winding minor road to B4306 then south east to BANCFFOSFELEN. North east by winding minor roads to RHYD OLAU GR 5012 then north east and north to road junction GR 516146 (critical point).
Choice (A): to LLANDDEUSANT YH. From road junction GR 516146 go east on minor road crossing A48 by minor road to HEOLDDU GR 5315. North east and east north east to

B4297 to MAESYBONT *GR 5616*, go south east on B4297 to road junction *GR 577158* (critical point). East by minor road crossing A476 to GARN *GR 5915* then winding minor road to join A483 to PENTRE GWENLAIS *GR 6116*. South to LLANDYBIE *GR 1615* then minor road north east (station) and all way to BLAENGWECHE *GR 6417* to TRAPP *GR 6518* to CARREG CENNEN castle (Welsh Heritage) — a must — *GR 6619* — dramatic situation. East to FERDRE and north east to CEFN-FEDW *GR 6820*, now OS 160, winding minor roads north east to NEUADD *GR 6921*. North and north east to CAPEL GWYNFE *GR 7222*, north east crossing A4069 to PONT NEWYDD *GR 7323* to minor road crossing AFON SAWDDE. North east to TWYNLLANAN *GR 7524* (critical point), east to YH at LLANDDEUSANT *GR 776245* (former Inn in truly Welsh area).

Choice (B): for overnight stop LLANDEILO. From road junction *GR 516146* go north to PORTHYRHYD *GR 5215* crossing A48. Go north B4310 to road junction *GR 523167* (critical point). Minor road to PENALL *GR 5318* then east north east to Nelson's Tower (National Trust) *GR 5419* magnificent view. East and south east on minor roads crossing B4297 then east to road junction *GR 589190* (critical point). Go north to GOLDEN GROVE and road junction at *GR 590196*, east through Agriculture College (daylight hours) to GELLIAUR Country Park B4300 and A476 to LLANDEILO *GR 6322*.

Part 2: Choice (A) From Llanddeusant YH to Glascwm (31 miles) with Choice (B) From Llandeilo to Glascwm YH, (46 miles) (with option to visit remote mountain hut type of YH at Gryn Poeth Uchaf *GR 7943*) Youth hostel is 16 miles from Llanddeusant YH and 21 miles from Llandeilo, OS 159, 160, 148

Choice (A): LLANDDEUSANT to GLASCWM. Leave YH on minor road north to TALSARN *GR 7725*, go north on winding roads to MYDDFAI *GR 7730*. North on minor road (boundary of Brecon Beacons National Park) to LLANDOVERY * *GR 7634*. Tourist Information and station. Leave by A483 north east. If traffic bad divert at road junction *GR 793372* (critical point) for hilly winding minor road to CYNGHORDY *GR 8039* (* If strong in wind and limb consider diversion to

remote mountain YH at BRYN POETH UCHAF *GR 796439* (gas lit). Approach either (a) from LLANDOVERY by minor road north to AFON TWYI valley to DINAS BACH to RHANDIRMWYN *GR 7843*, or (b) from CYNGHORDY go north west under railway to DINAS BACH *GR 7740* as for (a). RESUMING MAIN ROUTE. Road junction at CYNGHORDY *GR 808396* (critical point) to minor road north east and east all way to TIRABAD *GR 8741*. North and north east on minor road, now OS 147, to CEFNGORWYDD *GR 9045* to LLANGAMMARCH WELLS *GR 9347*, station. Minor roads south of river Irfon all the way to BUILTH WELLS *GR 0351*. Tourist Information and station near. Leave town by A481 north east, soon OS 148, A481 crossroads *GR 110542* (critical point, care). South east of HUNDRED HOUSE go south east on minor road 'Hungry Green', south east and north east to GLASCWM YH *GR 158533*.

Choice (B): LLANDEILO to GLASCWM TH OS 159, 160, (46 miles)

Leave LLANDEILO *GR 6322* south by A476/483 crossing AFON TWYI to *GR 627215* (critical point) go north east under railway keeping near river Tywi to PONTBREN ARAETH *GR 6623*, now OS 160. Minor road north east A4069 to LLANGADOG *GR 7028* then minor road east north east and north east to CILGWYN *GR 7429*. Rejoin A4069 to LLANDOVERY *GR 7634*. Tourist Information and station. Leave town by A483 to GLASCWM by Choice (A) route above.

Part 3: Glascwm YH to Clun Mill YH, OS 148, 137 (25 miles)

Leave YH by minor road east to COLVA *GR 2053* to GLADESTRY *GR 2355*. Go north east on B4594 to BURLINGJOBB *GR 2558* to OLD RADNOR *GR 2559*. Crossing A44 by B4357 to EVENJOB *GR 2662* go north crossing river Lugg to WHITTON *GR 2767* then B4357 north to B4355 to KNIGHTON *GR 2872*. Tourist Information, Offa's Dyke Centre, station. No YH 1994. Leave KNIGHTON north east by A488 briefly on minor road north west opposite station *GR 291724* (critical point) go to SKYBORY GREEN *GR 2674*. Go north to SELLEY HALL to UPPER TREVERWARD *GR 2778*, now OS 137 overlap of nearly twelve and a half miles, to CLUN. Castle ruins, church. YH at MILL *GR 304813*.

Wales South WS5

Part 4: Clun Mill YH *GR 3081* **to Bridges YH** *GR 3996* **via the Long Mynd, OS 137 (six miles) plus exploration of the Long Mynd**
Leave CLUN YH *GR 3081* east to B4368 to CLUNTON to PURSLOW *GR 3681*. North on minor road to KEMPTON *GR 3683 to B4386 to minor road to Red House farm GR 3686* **(critical point).** For shop divert west to LYDBURY NORTH *GR 3586* minor road north east to EYTON crossing river Onny and join A489 south east to PLOWDEN *GR 3887* go to road junction *GR 383874* **(critical point).** Minor road north east to ASTERTON *GR 3991* then east and north east (25% hill) to LONG MYND *GR 4193*. The 'Portway' — fascinating area worth exploring. Choice of two ways to BRIDGES YH *GR 394965*. Either via MEDLICOTT *GR 4094* from south south east or to RATLINGHOPE *GR 4096* from north east.

Part 5: Bridges YH *GR 3996* **to Shrewsbury YH, OS 137, 126 (13 miles)**
From BRIDGES YH follow minor road north north east to New Leasowes farm *GR 4099*, now OS 126. Go north east to PULVERBATCH *GR 4202* then north east to LONGDEN COMMON to LONGDEN *GR 4406*. North east over railway to NOBOLD *GR 4710* then on minor road crossing A5 to SHREWSBURY *GR 4912*. Fine county town. YH near Shire Hall GR 505120 in Victorian iron master's house.

- **RELATED ROUTES:** WS3 The Wales Trail, WS4 Offa's Dyke Cycling version
- **RECONNOTIRED:** September 1994, Herman Ludwig of Munich. Map work RNH.

124

AREA SN

Scotland North
North of the Great Glen — Inverness-Kyle

SN1

If touring in Scotland, note the address of the Scottish Youth Hostels Association, 7 Glebe Crescent, Stirling.

- **JOHN O'GROATS AREA with two Scottish fishing ports**
- **COUNTY:** CAITHNESS
- **QUIETNESS:** *
- **MILEAGE:** 40
- **DIRECTION:** west to east and north to south
- **TRAIN STATIONS and TIMETABLES:** THURSO **GR ND1167**, WICK **GR ND3650**, 51, 231, 239, 245
- **MAP:** OS 12
- **WEATHER FORECAST:** 0891-500426
- **TOURIST INFORMATION OFFICE:** WICK 01955-2596, THURSO 01847-62371
- **ACCOMMODATION:** HUNA **GR 3573** and YH at JOHN O'GROATS
- **PLACES OF INTEREST:** CASTLE OF MEY **GR 2973** (Queen Mother, open a few days). CAITHNESS can be quite mild in November. From the train, forests are looking their best and deer visible.
- **ROUTE:** road

THURSO station. Road A836 to JOHN O'GROATS is quiet off-season, alternatives are hillier; return by A9 to WICK station (no alternative, pleasant coastal route).
- **RELATED ROUTES:** SN2
- **RECONNOITRED:** November 1984

SN2

- **ORKNEY**
- **COUNTY:** ORKNEY ISLANDS AREA MAINLAND
- **QUIETNESS:** **
- **MILEAGE:** 28 (with bus back from St Margaret's Hope)
- **DIRECTION:** north to south and reverse
- **To get there:** fly LOGANAIR from WICK **GR ND3650** to KIRKWALL, train station, WICK, 50, 239.
- **MAP:** OS 7
- **WEATHER FORECAST:** 0891-500426
- **TOURIST INFORMATION OFFICE:** KIRKWALL 01856-2856
- **ACCOMMODATION:** 20 St Catherine's Place 01856-4243, YH KIRKWALL (Summer)
- **PLACES OF INTEREST:** Magnificent sunset over SCAPAFLOW, but watch the limited daylight as cycling by night is not recommended
- **ROUTE:** road

One of many cycle routes in these fascinating Islands. From KIRKWALL AIRPORT south east by A960 and south west by B9052 to join A961, south over CHURCHILL BARRIERS. ITALIAN CHAPEL at **GR 4800** and over three more islands to BURWICK **GR 4483**. No ferry service in Winter but local bus service in ST MARGARET'S HOPE **GR 4493** will take you and your cycle (unfolded) back to KIRKWALL.
- **RELATED ROUTES:** SN1
- **RECONNOITRED:** November 1987

SN3

- **A sample of the KYLE OF LOCHALSH to INVERNESS route**
- **COUNTY:** SCOTLAND HIGHLAND REGION, ROSS and CROMARTY
- **QUIETNESS:** **
- **MILEAGE:** 29
- **DIRECTION:** west to east
- **TRAIN STATIONS and TIMETABLES:** ACHNASHEEN **GR 1658**, DINGWALL **GR 5459**, 26, 65 for England; 231, 239 for Scotland

- **MAP(S):** OS 25, 20, 26 (24, 33)
- **WEATHER FORECAST:** 0891-500425
- **TOURIST INFORMATION OFFICE:** INVERNESS 01463-234353
- **PUBLICATIONS:** Publications about Scotrail
- **ACCOMMODATION:** YH at INVERNESS and KYLEAKIN. Other B and B through Tourist Information.
- **PLACES OF INTEREST:** Refer to Tourist Information
- **ROUTE:** road

KYLE OF LOCHALSH *GR NG7627*. Overnight stay at B and B (YH Now at KYLEAKIN on SKYE (ferry 5 minutes) *GR 752264*. Preferably catch early train, alighting at ACHNASHEEN *GR 1658*, hotel and other facilities. Follow A832 east, single track road follows railway closely to south end of LOCHGARVE *GR 4159*. Keep on A832 to road junction CONTIN *GR 4555*, then A834 STRATHPEFFER, or A832 MARYBURGH, both to DINGWALL *GR 5459*. INVERNESS if time permits (as alternative to coach trip to LOCHNESS MONSTER — all year) consider cycle trip to impressive CULLODEN MUIR MEMORIAL OS 27 *GR NH7344* (names of the Clans are inscribed) B9006 is quiet in winter. For quiet route for station and town centre ask for ST STEPHENS ST, MID MILLS ROAD, DIRIEBOGHT south to CULCABOCK Road and east to PERTH Road, 11 miles round trip.

- **RELATED ROUTES:** SN4, SN5
- **RECONNOITRED:** November 1989, RNH

SN4

- **FORT WILLIAM to INVERNESS**
- **COUNTY:** HIGHLAND REGION
- **QUIETNESS:** *** and **
- **MILEAGE:** 63
- **DIRECTION:** south west to north east
- **TRAIN STATIONS and TIMETABLES:** FORT WILLIAM *GR NN1074*, SPEAN BRIDGE, INVERNESS *GR NH6645*. From LONDON 26, 65, 404; in SCOTLAND 227, 231
- **MAP(S):** OS 41, 34, 26
- **WEATHER FORECAST:** 0891-500425
- **TOURIST INFORMATION OFFICE:** FORT WILLIAM 01397-703781, INVERNESS 01463-234353

- **PUBLICATIONS:** many guide books
- **ACCOMMODATION:** YHs GLEN NEVIS *GR 1271*, INVERNESS and LOCH LOCHY *GR 2997* (LOCH NESS YH is on opposite side)
- **PLACES OF INTEREST and NOTES:** The route is along the Caledonian canal, an extraordinary series of ship canals linking large lochs
- **ROUTE:** track

Part 1: Fort William to Gairlochy *GR 1784* for Spean Bridge station
From FORT WILLIAM station (Tourist Information nearby) go east and north east over playing field to cross river Nevis close to its junction with river Lochy at *GR 106746* — then over river near railway bridge at *GR 1175* and B8006. Follow shore line for quarter mile to CORPACH BASIN and start of the Caledonian canal — large working canal with sea-going ships and a wide, firm towpath. Note the hand operated bridge at MOY, *GR 1682*. At GAIRLOCHY *GR 1784* we sadly had to take a short cut and take the B8004 past the COMMANDO MEMORIAL at *GR 2082* to SPEAN BRIDGE station *GR 2281*.

Part 2: Gairlochy, *GR 1784* to Inverness
The rest of the route has not yet been personally ridden, but guidance is derived from SUSTRANS *Guide to routes in the making II*, 1985 page 9. From GAIRLOCHY B8005 north east to CLUNES *GR 2088*, go to Forest Road through CLUNES and SOUTH LAGGAN Forests to LAGGAN LOCKS *GR 2896* go to towpath to the NORTH LAGGAN swing bridge *GR 3098* by lochside path (old railway, rough road); on south east of LOCH OICH go to ABERCHALDER *GR 3403*. Towpath on north west bank to FORT AUGUSTUS *GR 3809*. Then B862, General Wade's hilly Military Road to WHITEBRIDGE *GR 4915*. B852 at *GR 4917* near ATHERRICK to lochside road rejoining B862 at DORES *GR 5934*, go north west to INVERNESS (not found possible to use the towpath on this section).

- **RELATED ROUTES:** SN3, SC5
- **RECONNOITRED:** July 1990, RNH

SN5

- **MALLAIG and SKYE**
- **COUNTY:** HIGHLAND REGION — ISLE OF SKYE
- **QUIETNESS:** *
- **MILEAGE:** 24
- **DIRECTION:** south west to north east
- **TRAIN STATIONS and TIMETABLES:** MALLAIG *GR NM6797*, KYLE OF LOCH ALSH *GR NG7627*, 65, 227, 239, 247
- **MAP(S):** OS 32, 33, 40
- **WEATHER FORECAST:** 0891-500425
- **TOURIST INFORMATION OFFICE:** KYLE 01599-4276 (summer)
- **PUBLICATIONS:** Scotrail and Tourist Information issue a fine glossy brochure on *Great Railway Explorations of the Scottish Highlands*
- **ACCOMMODATION:** YH at KYLEAKIN BROADFORD and ARMADALE
- **ROUTE:** rad

EUSTON station to GLASGOW and MALLAIG *GR 6797*. Ferry (30 mins) to ARMADALE *GR 6403* (Skye). 24 miles cycle by A851 and A850 to KYLEAKIN, spend longer in SKYE if time permits. Ferry (5 minutes) to KYLE OF LOCHALSH.
- **RELATED ROUTES:** SN3
- **RECONNOITRED:** November 1984, north east to south west, RNH

- **MAP(S):** OS 21, 17
- **WEATHER FORECAST:** 0891-500425
- **TOURIST INFORMATION OFFICE:** All year — INVERNESS 01463-234353, part year — BONAR BRIDGE 018632-333, HELMSDALE 014312-640
- **ACCOMMODATION:** Carbisdale Castle YH *GR 574954* and HELMSDALE *GR 028155*. Both close 30 September. Also consult Tourist Information.
- **PLACES OF INTEREST:** If starting from CULRAIN or INVERSHIN station (half a mile apart) try approach to route via BALBLAIR and MAIKLE WOODS *GR 5994* and *GR 6094* (not reconnoitred)
- **ROUTE:** road

From ARDGAY station *GR 6090* north east with **care** on A9 to BONAR BRIDGE *GR 6191*, east to road junction *GR 626922*, then north north east on minor road up to moors to go east by LOCH BUIDHE and largely unfenced road by STRATH CARNAIG to join A9 at the causeway bridge (THE MOUND) at *GR 7798* go east on A9 GOLSPIE station *GR 8299*, now OS 17, and further seven miles on A9 to HELMSDALE station and YH.
- **RELATED ROUTES:** SN1
- **RECONNOITRED:** September 1990, RNH

SN6

- **ARDGAY TO GOLSPIE and BRORA and HELMSDALE. Note that much of this route is over exposed Scottish moors; cold weather gear needed at all seasons, but north east Scotland can be mild and pleasant even in November. Not suitable for young families.**
- **COUNTY:** HIGHLAND REGION, SUTHERLAND COUNTY
- **QUIETNESS:** **
- **MILEAGE:** 18 to GOLSPIE, 25 to BRORA, 37 to HELMSDALE
- **DIRECTION:** south west to north east
- **TRAIN STATIONS and TIMETABLES:** ARDGAG *GR NH6090*, BRORA *GR NC9004*, 239 (very few trains)

AREA SC

Scotland Central
Between the Great Glen and the Forth Clyde Line

SC1

- **LOCHS RANNOCH, TUMMEL and FASKALLY**
- **COUNTY:** TAYSIDE
- **QUIETNESS:** *
- **MILEAGE:** 40
- **DIRECTION:** west to east
- **TRAIN STATIONS and TIMETABLES:** RANNOCH *GR NN4257*, PITLOCHRY *GR NN9358*, 227, 231, 403, 404
- **MAP(S):** OS 42, 52, 43 (small part)
- **WEATHER FORECAST:** 0891-500423
- **TOURIST INFORMATION OFFICE:** PITLOCHRY, 22 Atholl Road Tayside 01796-2215
- **ACCOMMODATION:** YH PITLOCHRY
- **PLACES OF INTEREST:** See text and consult Tourist Information
- **ROUTE:** road. **Hilly**.

From RANNOCH station keep south of LOCH RANNOCH, make for BRIDGE OF GAUR *GR 5056* (post office and general store) take B846 east. For easier gradients make for KINLOCH RANNOCH *GR 6657* and follow B846 north of DUNALASTAIR Water to TUMMEL bridge *GR 7659* where make sure you go south of LOCH TUMMEL by taking minor road at *GR 779574* continuing to keep loch on your left. LOCH FASKALLY to PITLOCHRY station (Fish Ladder, Festival Theatre and YH).
For quieter but steeper route omit KINLOCH RANNOCH follow minor road south of DUNALASTAIR WATER south south east over ridge to the B846 where go left and join original route at *GR 779574*.
- **RECONNOITRED:** November 1987, RNH

SC2

- **In the HEART of the SCOTTISH MOUNTAINS (AVIEMORE)**
- **COUNTY:** HIGHLAND REGION, INVERNESS
- **QUIETNESS:** *
- **MILEAGE:** From NEWTONMORE 30, from AVIEMORE 40
- **DIRECTION:** north east to south west
- **TRAIN STATIONS and TIMETABLES:** AVIEMORE *GR 8912*, NEWTONMORE *GR NN7198*, TULLOCH *GR NN3680*, 227, 231, 403
- **MAP(S):** OS 35, 36, 42
- **WEATHER FORECAST:** 0891-500423
- **TOURIST INFORMATION OFFICE:** AVIEMORE 01479-810363
- **ACCOMMODATION:** Normally either AVIEMORE YH or LOCH MORLICK YH
- **PLACES OF INTEREST and NOTES:** No refreshments between NEWTONMORE and TULLOCH (30 miles).
- **ROUTE:** road. **Hilly**.

AVIEMORE station *GR 8912* (overnight from EUSTON: beds and seats). South west by B9152 KINCRAIG, KINGUSSIE A86, NEWTONMORE station LOCH LAGGAN, TULLOCH station *GR 3680*. Return on MALLAIG-GLASGOW line to GLASGOW and the south.
- **RELATED ROUTES:** SC5
- **RECONNOITRED:** November 1982, RNH

SC3

- **GLASGOW to LOCH LOMOND (an ingenious Trailway by Sustrans)**
- **COUNTY:** STRATHCLYDE REGION
- **QUIETNESS:** ***
- **MILEAGE:** 23
- **DIRECTION:** south east to north west

- **TRAIN STATIONS and TIMETABLES:**
  GLASGOW (Central or Queen St)
  GR NS5865 and 5965, BALLOCH
  GR NS3881, 51, 65, 226
- **MAP(S):** OS 64, (56), 63
- **WEATHER FORECAST:** 0891-500421
- **TOURIST INFORMATION OFFICE:**
  GLASGOW 0141-2044400
- **PUBLICATIONS:** A leaflet from the Tourist
  Information or SUSTRANS is essential for
  enjoyment of this route; take the OS for the
  wider picture
- **ACCOMMODATION:** GLASGOW YH
  GR 575662 0141-332304 is a good base
  with its own nearby access to KELVIN
  PARK. Cycle hire.
- **PLACES OF INTEREST:** Return by train
  from BALLOCH or any intermediate station
  as time, the weather and your energy
  dictates. The route even goes through a
  modern shopping complex at Clydebank.
- **ROUTE:** road

This excellent route was designed and super-
vised by SUSTRANS (Bristol and Glasgow) for
completion in time for the Glasgow Garden
Festival of 1988; a most ingenious route using
old railway and river or canal paths to full
advantage. Old railway section starts at
GR 555604 to WHITEINCH, SCOTSTOUN,
CLYDEBANK below ERSKINE Bridge A898,
DUMBARTON, river LEVEN to BALLOCH
GR 3881.

- **RELATED ROUTES:** SS2, SC2, SC3
- **RECONNOITRED:** November 1987, RNH

SC4

- **LOCH LOMOND to the
  TROSSACHS, KILLIN and CRIANLARICH
  WITH EXTENSION to PITLOCHRY.**

Introduction
This route is taken, with grateful acknowledge-
ment, from the *Glasgow-Loch Lomond-Killin
Cycleway — New Route* published 1990
(Stirling Tourist Information), a Sustrans
Railway Path Route and the 'Jewel in the
Crown' in Scotland. **Note**: This route has not
yet been fully ridden by any member of the
Editorial Team but it is too good a route to
leave out. The Editors are grateful to Sustrans

Scotland for informally vetting this description.
Nonetheless, this description is provisional
and careful map reading is called for in parts
in the absence of signs. Feedback on this
route would be especially welcome. The route
is 'dry land', but mention is made of 'steamer'
alternatives: On LOCH LOMOND from
BALLOCH Pier *GR NN 4010* to INVERSNAID
GR NN3308 and on LOCH KATRINE from
STRONACHLACHER *GR NN4010* to
TROSSACHS Pier *GR NN4907*. The future of
some steamer services is uncertain — check
with Tourist Information.

- **COUNTY:** STRATHCLYDE and CENTRAL
- **QUIETNESS:** **
- **MILEAGE:** To ABERFOYLE 19; circuit of
  LOCH KATRINE (including INVERSNAID)
  to TROSSACHS 35; TROSSACHS to
  CALLANDER and KILLIN 36; KILLIN to
  CRIANLARICH 15; Total 105; with
  extension to PITLOCHRY add 37.
- **DIRECTION:** south west to north east
- **TRAIN STATIONS and TIMETABLES:**
  ALEXANDRIA *GR NS3979*, CRIANLARICH
  GR 3825, 226, 227, 404
- **MAP(S):** OS (63), (64), 57, 51 (+56 for
  LOCH KATRINE)
- **WEATHER FORECAST:** 0891-500421/3
- **TOURIST INFORMATION OFFICE:**
  STIRLING 01786-75019
- **PUBLICATIONS:** *Glasgow, Loch Lomond,
  Killin Cycleway* from Tourist Information
  Stirling. The section from LOCH LOMOND
  to KILLIN first published 1990. Also LOCH
  ACHRAY FOREST DRIVE Tourist
  Information.
- **ACCOMMODATION:** YHs (1990) LOCH
  LOMOND *GR 368834*, LOCH ARD
  GR 467022, KILLIN *GR 569338*,
  CRIANLARICH *GR 368250*. Also consult
  Tourist Information STIRLING.
- **PLACES OF INTEREST:** See publications
- **ROUTE:** road. **Hilly.**

Note: This description assumes that you
have cycled the Glasgow-Loch Lomond
Cycleway, included as route SC3 in this book.
Hence this route starts at ALEXANDRIA
station *GR NS3979*, but with an alternative at
BALLOCH especially if you stay overnight at
LOCH LOMOND YH at *GR NS368834*.

Scotland Central SC4

Part 1: Alexandria (with Balloch as an alternative) to Aberfoyle, OS 63 for one and a quarter miles only (19 miles)

From ALEXANDRIA station *GR NS3979* east over river LEVEN to A813 and estate roads, north and north east to WOODSIDE *GR 402808*, now OS 64 for three miles only, go to AUCHENCARROCH *GR 4182* to crossroads, west of 'The Merkins' *GR 439832*, north and north west past BALQUHAIN *GR 4484*, now OS 57 — two mile overlap, MAVIEMILL *GR 4584*. Minor road close to old railway line to CROFTAMIE *GR 4786*. North on A809 to DRYMEN *GR 4788*. Minor road north and north east for eight miles via GARADHBAN FOREST *GR 4890*, strong climbs and descent, via GARTMORE *GR 5297* and A81 to ABERFOYLE *GR 5200* — QUEEN ELIZABETH FOREST PARK VISITOR CENTRE (including cycle trails), to *GR 5101* and DAVID MARSHALL LODGE *GR 520014*, (Carnegie Benefaction). There are now a number of options for you to consider (LOCH LOMOND steamer for as long as it continues).

Part 2: Detour to Lochs Ard, Chon and the circuit of Loch Katrine (with extension to Inversnaid for the steamer). If not doing the detour, go direct to Part 3.

(Full Route including LOCHS ARD, CHON and KATRINE, OS 57 (35 miles)). From ABERFOYLE west on B829 go north of LOCH ARD and to KINLOCHARD *GR 4502*, north west, now OS 56, on B829 past LOCH CHON *GR 4205* to road junction *GR 3909*. Here you have a further choice, either: from road junction *GR 3909* go west by minor road past CORRIE ARKLET *GR 3709*, GARRISON, to hotel and pier at INVERSNAID *GR 3308*. Nearby hotel by Royal Society for the Protection of Birds reserve and nature trail. Then (in season) steamer to TARBET station *GR 3204*, or BALLOCH PIER station *GR 3882*. Or: from road junction *GR 3909* resume LOCH KATRINE route north east to STRONACHLACHAR *GR 4010* (SS 'Sir Walter Scott' services check Tourist Information). North west alongside LOCH KATRINE to head near GLENGYLE *GR 3813* then back south east on north east side of Loch, now OS 57 again, to LOCH KATRINE Visitor Centre *GR 4907* in heart of THE TROSSACHS go to BRIG O' TURK *GR 5306* by A831 north of LOCH RAY on quieter track south of LOCH.

Part 3: If not doing circle of the Lochs Aberfoyle to Brig o' Turk and Callander, 7 miles

(Cuts out 28 miles of the Loch Katrine circuit.) From ABERFOYLE take the signposted **very steep** track north west for three miles to LOCH DRUNKIE *GR 5404* and track to west end of Loch *GR 530043*. Then north to junction of tracks between LOCHS ACHRAY and VENACHAR *GR 5206*. Hairpin left (sign) to forest road at 'Loch' side heading east Marshes — bird reserve, if you reach a cattle grid you've missed it, go to to BRIG O' TURK on A821 *GR 3301*. Turn in BRIG O' TURK by Byre Restaurant and cross Black Water (Oioge dubh). Follow track to ACHRAY farm and turn left (against flow of traffic) and keep to lowest road possible *GR 536054*. Leave Forest Drive and go round barrier by signpost. Follow route by Lochside to CALLANDER.

Part 4: Callander to Killin, OS 57, 51 (25 miles)

TRAILWAY 'CALLANDER and STRATHYRE CYCLEWAY' north west through PASS OF LENY *GR 5908*. Keep to west shore of LOCH LUBNAIG to STRATHYRE *GR 5617*, leave railway north and north west to BALQUHIDDER *GR 5320*, ROB ROY'S grave, minor road east to A84 and north east, now OS 51 — one and quarter mile overlap. LOCHEARNHEAD *GR 5923*, go north west by GLEN OGLE TRAIL *GR 5726* to A827 at LIXTOLL (telephone call box) *GR 5430* and north east to KILLIN *GR 5732* YH.

The old railway (mentioned above) is the GLEN OGLE TRAIL. Although it has steep descents and deer stiles, it can be walked and cycled extensively. The section to Killin Junction is dramatically beautiful.

Part 5: Killin to Crianlarich (the nearest railhead), 11 miles

KILLIN south west take minor road north of A85 at *GR 573326* for just over six miles to rejoin A85 at LEDCHARRIE *GR 5028*. Then A85 again (unless you try the old railway) to CRIANLARICH *GR 3825* station. Good YH at *GR 386250* — not on OS 87.

Part 6: An alternative route from Killin to Pitlochry, 37 miles

Valuable if you wish to maintain a following wind. OS 51/52. From KILLIN *GR 5732* keep on south and south east side of LOCH TAY by minor road to ARDEONAIG *GR 6635*, minor road to ARDTALNAIG, ACHARN, KENMORE

GR 7745. A827 for half a mile to minor road at **GR 769458**, to COMRIE CASTLE **GR 7848** and east on B846 to WEEM, now OS 52, **GR 8448**. North east on minor road to **(critical point)** road junction near PITNACREE **GR 9253** to join A827. West on A827 for short distance, then south east on B898 to BALNAMUR **GR 9651**. Cross river TAY on track, briefly west on A827 for hilly minor road via TOMACHOILLE **GR 9555** to PITLOCHRY. (Fish ladder, Festival Theatre, YH and other attractions). Station **GR 937582**.

- **RELATED ROUTES:** SC1, SC3
- **RECONNOITRED:** 1991, RNH

SC5

- **AVIEMORE to ELGIN (The WHISKY TRAILWAY)**
- **COUNTY:** HIGHLAND and GRAMPIAN REGIONS of SCOTLAND
- **QUIETNESS:** **
- **MILEAGE:** AVIEMORE TO ROTHES 42; AVIEMORE TO ELGIN 52
- **DIRECTION:** south west to north east
- **TRAIN STATIONS and TIMETABLES:** AVIEMORE **GR NN896125**, ELGIN **GR NJ2162**. To Scotland 26, 65, 403, in Scotland 231, 240
- **MAP(S):** OS 36, 28
- **WEATHER FORECAST:** 0891-500424
- **TOURIST INFORMATION OFFICE:** INVERNESS 01463-234353
- **PUBLICATIONS:** GRAMPIAN (MORAY DISTRICT) four leaflets
- **ACCOMMODATION:** YH AVIEMORE, LOCH MORLICH (one always open)
- **PLACES OF INTEREST:** Numerous - consult Tourist Information
- **ROUTE:** track

From AVIEMORE station **GR 895125**. Overnight stay at AVIEMORE YH, half a mile south south west of station or B and B. Take B road across railway to COYLUMBRIDGE **GR 9110**, then north on B970 to NETHY BRIDGE **GR 0020**. Continue B970 to SPEYBRIDGE **GR 0326**, old bridge at **GR 039264**, do not omit next five miles of SPEYSIDE WAY for fear of getting lost. Pinpoint the start of very minor road at **GR 039265**, east and north east, gated at

times; your distance from river SPEY is a guide; a magic stretch through CRAIGROY **GR 0527** to bridge near 'MAINS OF CROMDALE' **GR 0628** and through woods (not riverside path) to join B9102 at **GR 074306**. CRAG VARREN **GR 1134** to cross river SPEY at **GR 120354**. ADVIE **GR 1234** go west a few yards to get access to railway track, north east bad path **GR 1536** but worth it. CRAGGANMORE **GR 1636** (distillery closed winter). Long distance path proper easily followed CARRON **GR 2241**, CHARLESTOWN OF ABERLOR **GR 2642**, CRAIGELLACHIE **GR 2844**, near old Telford bridge **GR 285453** follow A941 to ROTHES **GR 2749**. B and B at Station Hotel (CTC 'Winged Wheel' sign close by). A941 to ELGIN (OK in winter). **Note**: Speyside Way long distance path ROTHES to the sea at SPEY BAY **GR 3565** needs check for cycling.

- **RELATED ROUTES:** SC2
- **RECONNOITRED:** November 1989, RNH

Scotland South
South of the Forth-Clyde Line

SS1

- The **FORTH ROAD BRIDGE**
- **COUNTY:** FIFE and LOTHIAN
- **QUIETNESS:** ** **Young families beware**
- **MILEAGE:** 7 minimum
- **DIRECTION:** south to north
- **TRAIN STATIONS and TIMETABLES:** DALMENY **GR NT1377**, NORTH QUEENSFERRY **GR NT1380**, 26, 65, 242
- **MAP:** OS 65
- **WEATHER FORECAST:** 0891-500422
- **TOURIST INFORMATION OFFICE:** EDINBURGH 0131-5571700
- **ACCOMMODATION:** EDINBURGH YH — one of the two usually open
- **PLACES OF INTEREST and NOTES:** Try to make time to explore EDINBURGH by cycle, excellent cycle routes being made
- **ROUTE:** road

DALMENY station **GR 1377**. Go west to track 'Cyclists only' below bridge at **GR 124783**, near toll barrier. Separate wide cycle and footpaths on both sides; wonderful view of FORTH BRIDGE (rail) to which no access on foot is now permitted. Access from QUEENSFERRY station, by steps at **GR 125807** or by cycle track further north.
- **RECONNOITRED:** November 1986, RNH

SS2

- **KILWINNING to PAISLEY TRAILWAY (for GLASGOW)**
- **COUNTY:** STRATHCLYDE REGION, AYR, RENFREW, LANARK
- **QUIETNESS:** ***
- **MILEAGE:** 22
- **DIRECTION:** south west to north east
- **TRAIN STATIONS and TIMETABLES:** KILWINNING **GR NS2543**, PAISLEY **GR NS4864**, 65, 218, 221

- **MAP(S):** OS 63, (64)
- **WEATHER FORECAST:** 0891-500421
- **TOURIST INFORMATION OFFICE:** PAISLEY 0141-8890711, GLASGOW 0141-2044400
- **PUBLICATIONS:** three new leaflets 1991 Local Authority, Tourist Information
- **ACCOMMODATION:** Scarce in KILWINNING in Winter. If so, try IRVINE (next station), several including Mrs Angus, 29 West Road **GR NS318391**.
- **PLACES OF INTEREST:** Consult Tourist Information. Burrell Collection. POLLOCK PARK **GR 5562**. In 1991, there were two good SUSTRANS extensions to the Coast at ARDROSSAN and IRVINE **GR 3139**.
- **ROUTE:** track

Route should be signposted all the way to PAISLEY, but expect some signs missing. KILWINNING station past school at **GR 330435** go east to pick up old railway but in less than a mile **GR 307446** road to north and under railway **GR 3046** to HIGHFIELD **GR 3050**, west to pick up track proper **GR 304500** to GLENGARNOCK/KILBIRNIE **GR 3153** (slight diversion through town) stretches north west of LOCHS. KILBIRNIE, BARR and CASTLE SEMPLE (with Country Park); spectacular rocky cuttings. On through built up area to JOHNSTONE **GR 4463** diversion of one mile on A737 (take a walk), resume at **GR 458634** and trail ends PAISLEY **GR 483635**. Station due north. Route being steadily extended to GLASGOW using RIVER WHITE CART **GR 4963** and the parks at ROSS HALL **GR 5063** and BELLAHOUSTON **GR 5463**.
- **RELATED ROUTES:** SC4
- **RECONNOITRED:** November 1989, RNH

SS3

- **SCOTTISH BORDER CYCLEWAY, STRANRAER to BERWICK.** This route is derived, with kind permission of the Author, from the handiest and most informative guide to a long cycle route found in sixty years of adult cycling. This is *Scottish Border Cycle Way* by Phil Horsley of 'New Riders of the Open Road' Laurieston Hall, Castle Douglas, Kirkcudbrightshire DG7 2NB. A two-colour, 16 page A5 booklet, showing Tourist Information, shops, cafes and no less than 16 cycle shops (unevenly distributed). The Booklet also includes two interesting diversions: The Machars (51 miles) and The Smugglers Coast (48 miles), which are not described in this route. The Booklet covers notes on history and topography as well as gradient diagrams
- **COUNTY:** DUMFRIES and GALLOWAY, BORDERS
- **QUIETNESS:** **
- **MILEAGE:** Total coast to coast approx 210. (1) PORTPATRICK to CASTLE DOUGLAS, 68 (2) CASTLE DOUGLAS to GRETNA GREEN, 52 (3) GRETNA GREEN to JEDBURGH, 48 (4) JEDBURGH to BERWICK, 40.
- **DIRECTION:** south west to north east
- **TRAIN STATIONS and TIMETABLES:** STRANRAER *GR NX0601*, DUMFRIES *GR NX9776*, CARLISLE *GR NY4055*, BERWICK ON TWEED *GR NT9953*, 26, 65, 218
- **MAP(S):** OS 74, (75), (77), 79, 82, 83, (77), 85
- **WEATHER FORECAST:** 0891-500419 and 500418
- **TOURIST INFORMATION OFFICE:** STRANRAER 01776-2595, NEWTON STEWART 01671-2431, CASTLE DOUGLAS 01556-2611, DUMFRIES 01387-53862, GRETNA GREEN 01461-37834, HAWICK 01450-72547, JEDBURGH 01835-63435, COLDSTREAM 01890-2607, BERWICK 01289-330733
- **PUBLICATIONS:** *Scottish Border Cycleway*, see note above
- **ACCOMMODATION:** YH at MINNIGAFF OS 83 *GR 4163*, KIRK YETHOLM OS 74

GR 8228 mentioned in text, CARLISLE YH near route, SNOOT six miles west of HAWICK OS 79 *GR432135*
- **PLACES OF INTEREST and NOTES:** See Booklet mentioned above
- **ROUTE:**

Part 1: Portpatrick to Stranraer to Castle Douglas, OS 82, 77, 83 (68 miles)
PORT PATRICK OS 82 *GR NW0054* by A77 to crossroads west of PINMINNOCH *GR 0154* (critical point), go north east on minor road KNOCKGLASS *GR 0358*, go to STRANRAER station *GR 0560*, leave by A75 less than one mile at *GR 077607* (critical point), go south east to Old Military Road and push along long distance path to cross A75 at *GR 109598*, go to minor road north east leaving CASTLE KENNEDY on north west over hills to cross railway and river to NEW LUCE *GR 1764*, go north east to road junction *GR 197652* (critical point), and east to TARF BRIDGE *GR 2564*, (now OS 83), south east on B7027. CHALLOCH *GR 3867* to NEWTON STEWART *GR 4065*. Keep east of river PENKILN BUR, north east to MINNIGAFF (YH at *GR 411663*) and GLENHOUSE to join A712 to TALNOTRY on OS 77, MURRAY'S MONT *GR 4871* go to bridge over river DEE *GR 546752* (critical point), and south east to FOREST DRIVE (RAIDERS Road) on north east (turn left) of river bearing north east after STROAN LOCH *GR 6470* to join A762 at *GR 6572*, go south east on A762, now OS 83 again, to road junction north of LAURIESTON at *GR 681657* and north east on minor road turning south east at *GR 7068* on south west side of LOCH KEN to GLEN LOCHAR *GR 7364* over B795 by minor road south to BRIDGE OF DEE *GR 7360* over A75 and right by minor road RHONEHOUSE *GR 7459*, north east past THREAVE Gardens (NTS) to CASTLE DOUGLAS (Tourist Information).

Part 2: Castle Douglas to Dumfries to Gretna Green, OS 84 (52 miles)
Leave CASTLE DOUGLAS *GR 7662*, pick up minor road at *GR 767629* (critical point) under new A75 north CLAREBRAND go to OLD BRIDGE OF URR *GR 7767*, to KIRKPATRICK DURHAM *GR 7870* and north east over A712 to road junction south of GLENKILN reservoir *GR 851772* (critical point) south east SHAWHEAD go east north east and south east to TERREGLES *GR 9377*

south east to DUMFRIES **GR 9776**. Leave by B725 close to River NITH, go to GLENCAPLE **GR 9968**, circle round with B725 to BANKEND **GR 0268** south east still on B725, now OS 85; leave B725 at road junction **GR 089675 (critical point)**, go to RUTHWELL and swing round to CUMMERTREES **GR 1366** join B724 east to ANNAN **GR 1966** (station), east on present B721 (old A75) through DORNOCH and EASTRIGGS **GR 2466** to minor road at junction **GR 289666** for quiet entry to GRETNA: by minor roads to OLD SMITHY at **GR 3268**.

Part 3: Gretna Green to Newcastleton to Hawick to Jedburgh, OS 85, 79, 80, 74 (48 miles)

Leave GRETNA by minor road over railway at **GR 327688**, north east above river SARK to SARKHALL **GR 3471** north north west to join B6357 at **GR 3375**, east north east to EVERTOWN, to CANNONBIE **GR 3976**, over A7 still on B6357 to ROWANBURN **GR 4077**, north east on B6357 over B6318 at **GR 4278**, north east, now OS 79, north east to NEWCASTLETON **GR 4887**, road junction **GR 4989**, go north north west on B6399 to HERMITAGE Castle **GR 5096**, above WHITROPE TUNNEL **GR 5200** to B6399 past STOBS Castle (private, GR 5008), north alongside river to HAWICK **GR 5014**. Leave by minor road north east after crossing river TEVIOT **GR 505152**, **(critical point)** for just over 3 miles. KNOWETOWNHEAD **GR 5418** south east, now OS 80 for two and a half miles and then OS 74, to minor road north east FATLIPS Castle **GR 5820**, above river TEVIOT ANCRUM **GR 6224** to crossroads A68 at **GR 635245**, **(critical point) ***. For JEDBURGH go south east by A68 over river TEVIOT for 4 miles of A road **(great care)**.

Part 4: Jedburgh to Coldstream to Berwick, OS 74, 75 (40 miles)

* To continue ride without visit to JEDBURGH, resume on B6400 north east to NISBET **GR 6725**, go to ROXBURGH **GR 6930** to join A699 north east to KELSO **GR 7233**. Leave by B6352 south east to road junction **GR 7431 (critical point)**. Here note that KIRK YETHOLM YH lies six miles to south east at **GR 826282**, north end of PENNINE WAY — a drink given by Wainwright was available at the local pub to Pennine Way Walkers from Edale. Resuming from junction of B6352 and B6396 north east to WARK COMMON **GR 8136** go to EAST

LEARMOUTH **GR 8637**: the battleground of FLODDEN FIELD (1513) lies a little short of two miles to the east, north on minor road to COLDSTREAM **GR 8439**. First home of *New Cyclist* magazine, The Lees Stable — fastest growing cycle magazine of the 1980s, also cycle repairs. Nearby The Hirsel — home of Sir Alex Douglas Home, 14th Earl and Prime Minister 1963. Leave COLDSTREAM by minor road **GR 844399** north west to road junction **GR 834411, (critical point)** north east to join B6437, to road junction **GR 871460**, by minor road north east and north to join B6470, east over river TWEED to NORHAM, leave by minor road **GR 9248** north east and north west to HORNCLIFFE **GR 9349** (pub), minor road east north east to join A698 at **GR 959506** near MIDDLE ORD, now OS 75 — just over four miles overlap, north east to A1 round-about at **GR 9751**; trace minor road and B roads to TWEEDMOUTH — old Bridge and BERWICK ON TWEED Pier and Lighthouse **GR NU0052**.

• **RECONNOITRED:** RNH, July 1992